From Himalaya

To

South Pacific

Arne Fronsdal

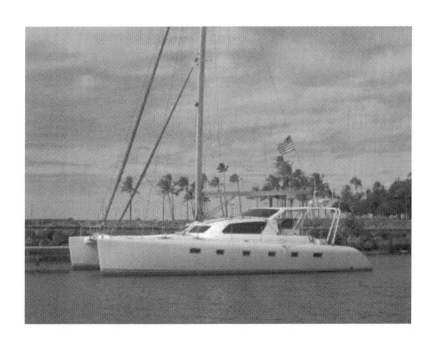

Copyright © 2022

All Rights Reserved

Contents

THE DEMISE OF IRIS 4

THE IRIS The Demise of "Iris" 7

AUTHOR'S NOTE 34

EDITOR'S NOTE 35

Over Khyber Pass to the Caspian Sea 37

PROLOGUE 38

CHAPTER I: OVER THE KHYBER 43

CHAPTER II: JALALABAD 51

CHAPTER III: KABUL 57

CHAPTER IV: THE ROAD TO GHAZNI 64

CHAPTER V: RAMZAN EVENING 75

CHAPTER VI: KANDAHAR 85

CHAPTER VII: DOWN TO THE HELMAND 96

CHAPTER VIII: GIRISHK HOTEL 104

CHAPTER IX: GIRISHK-FARRAD 110

CHAPTER X: LAST STAGE TO HERAT 117

CHAPTER XI: HERAT 123

CHAPTER XII: AN ENGINEER'S TROUBLES 131

FROM HIMALAYA TO SOUTH PACIFIC

CHAPTER XIII: INTO IRAN 137

CHAPTER XIV: MESHED AND THE RUSSIANS 143

CHAPTER XV: NISHAPUR AND OMAR KHAYYAM 150

CHAPTER XVI: END OF THE ROAD 160

CHAPTER XVII: TEHERAN TRAIN 167

CHAPTER XVIII: OVER THE HILLS TO THE CASPIAN 176

CHAPTER XIX: BABOLSAR 184

CHAPTER XX: CASPIAN LUXURY 191

CHAPTER XXI: IRAN'S CAPITAL 202

CHAPTER XXII: THE PEACOCK THRONE 208

CHAPTER XXIII: OIL CITY 217

CHAPTER XXIV: TANKER PASSAGE 222

CHAPTER XXV: LIABLE TO BE TORPEDOED 228

EPILOGUE 234

Traveling the 243

Annapurna Circuit 243

Traveling the Annapurna Circuit: 1998 244

To Kashmir 258

FROM HIMALAYA TO SOUTH PACIFIC

A Norwegian Tale 270

KJEAASEN, HARDANGER 270

PRE-HISTORY 272

Norwegian Literature 281

The Norwegian Women 284

The 14th Century - Bergen 288

Eidsfjord 309

The 17th Century - Denmark 324

The 20th Century 361

THE SOURCE OF THE GANGES 384

THE SOURCE OF THE GANGES 385

DOWN THE OMO RIVER, ETHIOPIA 394

The Valley Where Man was Born 395

Our Journey Down the Omo River 400

THE DEMISE OF IRIS

I extend all gratitude to my better half, Lise, for her gift of the Magellan CSC100, an Orbcomm Satcom GPS-powered data transceiver with a built-in GPS. I am also extremely grateful to my stepson Jorgen for receiving and acting up on our Mayday call and for quickly contacting his mother.

As our VHF antenna hit the pole and we had no EPIRB, we sent out a distress message via our GSC100M via Jorgen/Lise, which quickly reached the Maritime Rescue Coordination Center in Canberra, Australia. Every time this framework was used for transfer problems, it worked admirably.

The public rescue dispatched two planes and a fishing vessel; the latter helped us get off the sinking boat.

The 1998 Sydney to Hobart Yacht Race staged the 54th annual 'blue water classic' Hobart yacht race to Sydney. It was facilitated by the Cruising Yacht Club of Australia, located in Sydney, New South Wales. During the race, five yachts and six people got lost. It was the most harrowing experience, however, later, 55 sailors were saved in the greatest peacetime search and rescue effort Australia has ever seen. We could have benefited from the redesign of the

FROM HIMALAYA TO SOUTH PACIFIC

Canberra Rescue Center after this event; We will be eternally grateful for your incredible life-saving stewardship.

FROM HIMALAYA TO SOUTH PACIFIC

THE IRIS

The Demise of "Iris"

At a very early age, Christian fell for the sea. He was in his teens when he made two kayaks, which took him to the fjords of Bergen. It was the place we grew up in; once, he and his companion needed to be rescued as the boat got stuck in the rolling sea.

He was focused and determined and had an incredible personality – wise and considerate. He moved toward any problem with the intention of arriving at a logical result. If time did not permit, he continued the subject with an open the door to reach a closure rapidly. He stayed at the course and was wary of all questions. He had real sympathy for the sea and all that surrounded it, the humidity, the roughness, and the tumult. After 30-40 years of collective navigation, crossing seas and rivers, fixing, stopping, reviewing, a constant course of 1,000,000 things, repairing water, overturned hatches, repairing automatic rudders, sewing sails, water, and diesel. Engine, electrical panel contacts, fix units, change breeze propeller, ports, customs; eliminated all inconveniences.

He was a professor of mathematics and physics. After a

long time at the Nils Bohr Institute in Copenhagen and Zern in Geneva, he was in the residence at UCLA in California. Throughout the years, he explored the most puzzling and indifferent problems of physical science.

For more than 30 years, he and his scientific peer explored together to determine the angle of the matter when a light beam hit it. His other projects have been defining the origin of stars.

Currently, he is working on a large book on the subject of Thermodynamics. Here is an extract from his internet website: *"This work has some controversial elements and deviates from conventional perspectives and techniques in many ways. For example, an action principle dominates the whole theory. This is a very strong constraint that greatly improves its predictive power since, for a given system, one Lagrangian density has to be effective in all contexts. The New Action Principle covers adiabatic thermodynamics, not just equilibria; it is a complete dynamical theory that embraces the classical theory of equilibria but also dynamical problems such as sound propagation and planetary dynamics. I propose an improvement of Landau's two-fluid theory of superfluids, and I take a controversial approach to (mixed) atmospheres."*

In reference to the above, I was not shocked when one

day, while we were sailing in the South Atlantic Ocean and having our midday tea, Chris casually mentioned that he had established his theory of relativity of 'Einstein in 1958 but did not open up to the world about his review. The following year, 1959, Robert Pound and Glen Rebka planned, fabricated, and performed an examination that allowed them to quantify the redshift of light. It traveled a few floors in Jefferson University's laboratory from Harvard.

CHRISTIAN

Chris' most memorable first boat, "Kontina", was a triple-framed wooden trimaran that he built himself in Italy and crossed the Atlantic several times until it broke on its way from Brazil to Gibraltar. Lucky for him, he was picked up by a Russian fishing boat while the ship was abandoned.

He learned Russian by playing chess with his new mates while returning to Europe. Later, he had several sailboats work in a shipyard in Belgium according to the plan of the famous French multi-structure designer Eric Le Rouge.

Since his first Mediterranean crossing in 1974, I have been sailing with my brother Christian, especially throughout his mid-year semesters. We have been sailing around the planet for the last 44 years if we add this year too.

We have crossed the North and South Atlantic oceans, including Norway, Spitsbergen, Greenland, Iceland, and Ireland. We have crossed the South Pacific Ocean 5 times, crossing the Atlantic several times to the Caribbean. I cruised through Panama twice and around the Cape of Good Hope once. It was fun and exhilarating, and the best part is, the adventure is still on.

The following story is about our journey from Vanuatu to Australia.

Melanesian individuals first occupied Vanuatu. Vanuatu is an archipelago of volcanic origin, located 1,750 km in Northern Australia, around the east of New Caledonia.

The Portuguese and Spanish governments were united under Spanish rule in *1580*. The Spanish campaign was led by the Portuguese guide, *Fernandes de Queirós*. The

FROM HIMALAYA TO SOUTH PACIFIC

Europeans visited the islands and reached the larger island in *1606*. Following the opportunity of the high Portuguese position, which lasted till *1640*, the Portuguese government was restored. In the *1880s*, the United Kingdom and France guaranteed parts of the archipelago.

In the year 1906, they agreed to mutually manage the archipelago, as the New Hebrides. (The primary school dialects are English and French. The use of English or French as their language is divided along political lines.) Development of autonomy emerged during the 1970s, and the Republic of Vanuatu was created in 1980.

While in Vanuatu, we visited Tanna Island and were close enough to the volcano. The liquid magma source from Mount Yasur Vanuatu, formed by the rocks from the ejecta, came close to us.

We partook in the paradisiacal sea shores of Vanuatu and its wide range of local products and flavors. It included banana, garlic, cabbage, peanuts, pineapple, sugarcane, taro, sweet potatoes, watermelon, leaf flavors, carrots, radishes, brinjal, vanilla (both green and embossed), bell pepper, cucumber, and many more. (Still, the Vanuatu burger is considered to be probably the most amazing on the planet, which is a great decision. Vanuatu steers are raised in Espiritu).

Moreover, Santo Island and farming standards are exceptionally high and strictly controlled with cows grazing on grass and wild tropical plants year-round. The Japanese are known for purchasing a large portion of the Vanuatu burger. It is the key as they are informed of food sources such as fish and meat.

After half a month, we loaded our boat with food and various tents and headed for our next stop: Brisbane, Australia. We continued our watch schedule at the helm alternating with 3 hours on 3 hours off. Some days we would stop for an hour to take a dip around the boat and enjoy the warm water. One day, when I was in the water I felt a strong sting on my thigh, I hurried aboard, and quickly realized that I had swum into the tentacles of a Portuguese man of war. It hurt a lot.

My brother directly looked in our clinical book and followed its advice:

Bourbon Wash: Mix boiling soda with salt water and place on the bitten area; after about 10-20 minutes, remove it, wash with boiling water and let dry, then scrape off the remnants with a blade not to sharp. If you see any hint of thin threads, remove them immediately.

We found that a serious burn could affect your lungs and

breathing. Then we took Aloe Vera, and the feeling of consumption decreased. The torment gradually wears off, putting you on guard for your next dive.

Later, I left the rudder and hit the sack. The weather began to change. I became hopeless with the expands stirring things up around town cockpit between the bodies so hard that I thought we had hit a reef. It went on during that time with abrupt, huge bangs. The sailboat had its cockpit around 2-1/2 feet above water between its structures. The waves between the two frames constantly hit the cockpit floor with intense power. The extraordinary water developments with the loud bangs practically sounded like the structure was prepared to surrender.

Sooner or later, it could cause you nausea. You might not be able to peruse or do anything constructive, be it resting or perusing. The banging went on as the night progressed, and the following day was most unpleasant. One wave had the option to lose the auto steerage, so I took the actual guiding for a few hours while Chris was fixing the helm. It was freezing and dim, so we could scarcely see and were stressed overnight traffic around us.

We finally came to the Chesterfield Islands, having logged 572 miles from Loganville. We had a long way to go for our objective Gladstone, Australia, with a course set at

220 degrees. We moored here for the evening yet were excessively far on a mission to wander shoreward with the dinghy.

We were playing Haendel's Violin Sonatas, and Chris had his espresso. I was composing and wondered whether Lise had accepted my email sent on our Magellan gadget.

Once more, we were moving, and I was cold and tired of watching the aversion of the boat's development in the heavy water at midnight. The breeze was around 15 bunches, and the waves estimated a few 5-6 meters. Most of the water made a lot of bangs and clamor, and the boat was shaking and moving brutally; maybe the weather conditions were acting aggressively.

A Passage from Sailing Magazine January 2000 issue:

The accompanying record of their dismasting and salvage gives a few significant experiences into what's in store. In August 1999, Arne and Christian Fronsdal lost the pole of their sailboat Iris because of gear disappointment. They wound up in some hot water, many miles from the closest land. It was a miserable circumstance. It helped us discover what one should and shouldn't do when your boat is in a difficult situation. The story likewise fills in as a demonstration of the ability and commitment of salvage administrations and expert sailors all over the planet.

It was soon after 12 pm, and we were going from Vanuatu to Australia with around 350 miles to go. We had around 15 bunches of wind and were cruising with just a little foresail, averaging 6 bunches in a few huge enlarges. Everything appeared all good. I had recently wrapped up reading one more section in my book. I went out to locate any boats not too far off and awakened my companion Chris for the next watch.

After four hours, I woke to a lot of commotion at hand. The pole was quickly moving to and fro. Leaping out of my bunk, I saw Chris during the time spent folding the foresail, so we were down to exposed posts. I asked him what was happening, and he pointed above where the stay was available.

As time went on, the unpropitious sounds from above developed so awful that we looked for shelter in the lodge. Since we were apprehensive, the pole would break. After around 15 minutes, as we watched out the window, it did exactly that; it tumbled down between the two frames of our 40 feet sailboat, absent a lot of exhibition.

FROM HIMALAYA TO SOUTH PACIFIC

Log of Events – Onboarding of MN "Iris" 18th, 1999, prompting dissertation of a vessel.

At 4:00 am, I awakened as I heard a lot of commotion from the fundamental deck. As I get out, I see Chris during the time spent moving up the foresail. We had 15 bunches of wind and had been cruising on a little foresail just, averaging around 6/7 bunches. We were down to the gear and the actual structure to get the breeze behind the shaft port side. We were on our way from Vanuatu to Australia with an expected four additional days or nearly 350 miles to our last objective Gladstone. We saw that the stays were slack, and the pole was returning and forward. The reason for this was impractical to decide since the highest point of the pole was out of view due to obscurity. A couple of moments later, we chose to look for shelter in the lodge since unpropitious sounds were exuding from the highest point of the pole. We had the feeling that falling over the stern was about. After 15 minutes, as we looked through the window, we saw the pole had descended between the two hulls aft without ballyhoo. It gave the idea that the sea had padded its fall. Thus, we had not seen any restlessness from the rooftop. Our most memorable contemplations were to attempt to get the pole at hand. However, we immediately found that in the 5 meters waves, it was hard to get a leg.

FROM HIMALAYA TO SOUTH PACIFIC

At 4:30 am, we sent our first message via our Magellan GSCI00:

MAYDAY MAYDAY! MAST LOST. NEED IMMEDIATE ASSISTANCE. PLEASE NOTIFY MARITIME RESCUE COORDINATION CENTRE CANBERRA AUSTRALIA phone 06278871 fax 06252036. SUGGEST JORGEN LIEN SAN DIEGO MAKES CONTACTS. WE ARE WELL END

The message was sent to the following family members:

- JORGEN@BLUESKY.COM
- H.WEDON@OSLO.ONLINE.NO

The GSCIOO only allows 229 characters per message. While typing the above message, I realized I had run out of characters. Rather than correcting the message, I sent it. I sent the following immediately to follow up with our vital coordinates:

JORGEN 20.47 SOUTH, 156.53EAST, OFT, WGS84, 04:39:42AM, 18AUG99

(The GSCI00 has a function that automatically allows the coordinates, altitude, datum time, and date to be included in any message).

We then realized that the GPS position was not up to

date. However, we had sent the coordinates possibly as long as 1 hour or more ago. It was a result of not having updated the GPS when we turned it on to send the message.

We sent the following message 10 minutes later:

LATEST POSITION 20.47.72S, 156.48.57E, 324FT, WGS84, 04:52:42PM, 18AUG99

At 06:00 am, we came back out and decided that the flagpole was in the process of chafing up the sib hull and agreed that we had to cut it loose as soon as possible. We proceeded with pliers and knives, cutting off the stays and ropes.

First, we went off the mast, heaved it over the railing, and dropped it into the ocean. It was still fast, and we had to undo various lines aft and scrap the boom, which would impede our flotation at this juncture. Examining the hull, we observed a larger hole on the inside portion of the sib hull. Our immediate hope was that the integrity of the bulkhead between this section and the cabin was intact.

Water was already a foot in the bilge, and we realized we needed to act immediately. We had reached a deadlock; the hull could have further damage, and it might eventually sink. We were about 350 miles from Gladstone, the nearest harbor. The speed attained with a submerged damaged hull may have been as little as 1 knot under present conditions, requiring 300 hours and 600 liters of fuel. Towing was out of the question. But most important, remaining on board would have put us in danger. The big seas were thrashing over the port side with great force, and if we had remained afloat for a while, we had no assurance of being able to keep the boat off the reefs in the area.

We sent out an additional message:

JORGEN SHIP TAKING IN WATER AND CREW REQUEST TO BE TAKEN OFF. ARNE & CHRIS

I stood in the cabin and filled a bucket. I passed it on to Chris, who emptied it through the door. We then activated the three pumps on board; two spares hooked up directly to the 12v battery. But this was not enough to stem the flow, so we commenced bailing.

We kept the water at bay for about 30 minutes. We then realized that we could not keep this up at such a pace, and we switched to a position of observation to see what would happen without bailing. We perhaps had hoped, without expressing it, that the water filled to about five feet, to an approximately equal height to the outside water level, and then stabilized.

The port side cabin was free of water, and the center

cockpit on the "bridge" between the two hulls was also dry. The water in the sib cabin would occasionally halfway up the inclining floor of the cockpit. We took a short pause. While we had been bailing, we had also been unloading the debris in the cabin, including books, bookshelves, paper, maps, clothing, and paint buckets. Some of the paint had come out of their bucket, and it started to smell. The water was discolored. Chris then discovered his wallet with his credit cards, green card, and passport was missing. For the next hour, he submerged, diving into the greenish paint water, then standing up to his shoulders, searching with his feet for objects stranded on the floor. As he brought these up, I would pass them out through the door. Just as he was about to give up, he found them at the very reachable section of his cabin, and he was quite relieved.

We examined the rig in an attempt to understand what had happened. All stays were intact at their lower ends. The starboard remained on board so we could examine its upper end. It was intact, with its 16mm shackle still attached. Therefore, it was certain that the point of attachment to the mast, common to all three storyboards, failed. This point was a stainless steel rod of approx. 18 mm diameter shaped like a U. We could not inspect it since it was underwater. A photograph of the upper end of the starboard stay was taken with its shackle attached.

09:30 am:

We received the first response to our messages:

NEAREST SHIP 13 HRSAWY. SENDING AIRCRAFT, NO ETA. PLS ADV YR SITUATION & SAFETY EQUIPMENT ASAP. SET WATCH VHFC H16 Fr Sar Ctr Aus

This message was from the Savings and Rescue Center in Canberra. We did not realize who it was from, although we assumed this message was from Australia. Obviously, our message had been relayed and acted upon.

We felt a tremendous sense of relief at this juncture. We never received another message from Australia. We assumed the vessel was 3 hrs. away and was en route to us. We did not have it confirmed. We then proceeded to pack our essentials based on two possible scenarios:

(1) Pick up by helicopter - only able to carry a daypack

(2) Pick up by vessel- backpack + daypack. We found out later that the maximum reach of any Australian-based helicopter was 400 miles - roundtrip.

FROM HIMALAYA TO SOUTH PACIFIC

10:30 am:

We heard the roar of an aircraft flying very low - right above our cabin top. We discovered a package 200ft off the port side stern when we left the cabin. As we contemplated what it could have been, it inflated into a larger raft with a pitched roof. Then we discovered an orange rope across our cabin top and found it tied to the raft. We soon pulled in alongside after investigation.

We remained on the catamaran, which was luckily more comfortable than the raft. Still, we felt extraordinarily fortunate to have received the first acknowledgment that our coordinates were known. We learned later that Canberra's Marine Coordinating Centre had enlisted the French government to support their rescue operations. The French military immediately dispatched a large Guardian aircraft from their Noumea base in New Caledonia. They had circled our area for about 1 hour before finding us and had complained to Canberra that we did not send up smoke flares as soon as we heard them. However, we never heard their engine before they were right over us and made the drop. The remarkable precision of this large aircraft reminded me of the Israeli planes which, with pinpoint accuracy, bombed Kadaffi's villa in Tripoli about ten years ago.

FROM HIMALAYA TO SOUTH PACIFIC

12:00 am:

It was the approximate time, and the other times are also sometimes approximate. The times are all Vanuatu time which was 1 hour ahead of Canberra, Australia.

Another aircraft flew very low over our deck. They dropped a package that dissolved into smoke and left a dye that colored the ocean light green over an area several hundred feet long and a few feet wide. Shortly afterward, the plane came back and appeared to observe the smoke's direction, and then a third time, they dropped a package some 300 feet off the port side near the vessel. It left us in a quandary. There was no rope attached this time. We had the dinghy. We felt our chances of a successful pick-up were slim since the size of the waves at the time would most probably fill up the dinghy within a few minutes. The only alternative was to swim out with a line attached around the waist. However, we felt this was not a very inviting option.

Chris was not keen, and I had recently had a very severe burn on my left arm from a Portuguese man of war, and its after-effects were still with me. We were aware of the sharks off the Australian coast, but our debate did not discuss that threat. But what could ever be in the package that would improve our lot at this point? Evidently, only a freighter or similar vessel would now be able to assist us, and we hoped that such a vessel was en route to our position. Even if we had this information confirmed with hours of ETA, it would not intrinsically improve our position. We did not have to know the details as long as they arrived. Only when the package was out of sight a thought came up that it could have been a message that a helicopter was on its way with exact instructions for us to be prepared. We learned later that this was not the case and that the package contained a two-way radio. The aircraft was a Hercules from the Australian Air Force.

06:00 pm:

We suddenly witnessed a powerful beacon outside our window and hurried out. The raft appeared equipped with two lights, one with a continuous low beam and one very strong strobe light that switched continuously as a floating lighthouse. We were relieved.

07:30 pm:

We had our last meal on board; still no sight of any vessel. We reckoned that if the vessel had proceeded at 09:30 am with 13 hours steaming, it should be here around 10:30 pm. But we had not received any further news that that vessel had been dispatched to our rescue.

FROM HIMALAYA TO SOUTH PACIFIC

08:00 pm:

We went to bed for a rest; I was in my cabin in the port side hull, and Chris was upstairs in the cockpit on the sofa. Amazingly, we heard the plane circling us, from sometimes late for the better of 4 hours. The last plane that arrived stayed with us, circling above us in large circles, in and out of audible reach. It was a private aircraft owned by a company in Queensland chartered by RCC for rescue operations. It was incredibly reassuring since it could only mean they were waiting for a ship to be guided to our position.

09:45 pm:

I was checking the GSCIOO for further news, then suddenly, floodlights came through my vent, and there was a lot of commotion. Our rescue vessel had arrived. I shouted to Chris in excitement. We were greeted by a large-sized passenger-type vessel of about 70 feet in length, with a complement of many crew members standing on deck shouting at us. We dropped whatever we had in our hands, including my GPS, into our respective packs and carried this outside.

After some hard-to-hear exchanges, we finally understood that they wanted us to transfer via the raft.

According to the captain's assessment, he felt that even if he came alongside the catamaran on its windward side. Thus, he calmed the water on our side. His drift which was considerably faster than ours, together with the fairly high speed, could have him bear down on us with an undesirable force. We pulled in the raft alongside, threw our packs into its 2 feet water-filled floor, and followed. At this point, the GSCI00 stopped functioning; it was not water-tight. Although I had packed it into a water-tight zip lock bag, I did not zip it completely in my excitement after the arrival of the rescue vessel at our doorstep. No matter, it had done its incredible service - it had saved our lives.

As we were pulled up onto the cruise (fishing vessel *"Capricorn Star"),* we saw a crew of 16 trained rescuers. In fact, there were 12 passengers and 4 crew. Still, due to the ability and respect commanded by the master, they had all been drilled to this maneuver before their arrival. Everything worked like clockwork as we were hauled aboard.

Christian and Arne aboard the "*Capricorn Star*" are in good hands.

The following was the log aboard the fishing Vessel: "Capricorn Star"

Fishing and diving

75' Loa, 2' 97.69 draft

Australian flag, built Brisbane 1974, commissioned 1975 international survey for survey work, charter work, cargo, 3,000 miles' reach. Specialized in fishing and diving in the Coral Sea. 12 passengers, 4 crew.

2 VHF Radios, Satellite Phone, 2 MFIHF Master; Robert Benn - 28-year-old

Descendant of great-great-grandfather and original Master Laurence Janson, both father and grandfathers, operated fishing vessels. His father named many reefs.

06:04 am:

Australian time received a mayday radio message over Townsville radio to the effect that "Iris" was dismasted with her position and that any vessel within 12 hours' steam should report. After this message, Capricorn said it was the closest vessel. The master was asked to proceed towards "Iris" for rescue purposes.

06:10 am:

The vessel lifted anchor and started steaming towards "Iris." Fortunately, the master, most competent and cautious in all respect, had loaded the dories on deck the previous night rather than hanging these from the stern. Therefore, he was able to proceed with utmost dispatch. He gave 14 hours ETA.

Weather: 25 knots wind, ground level 3 meters, sea 2 meters. These messages were received via Townsville radio. However, he continued his dialogue directly with MRCC over satellite Phone.

09:40 am:

They were told that aircraft were overhead "Iris" and thought the vessel would stay afloat for another two hours.

10:40 am:

I Was informed draft was dropped.

11:40am:

We were informed that "Iris" had received the raft and its coordinates: **20.48S 156.49.5East**

05:40 pm:

We tried to make contact with the aircraft named "Rescue 161" over the VHP. However, the message was distorted and switched to Townsville Radio. Received "Iris" position **20.48S 156.48East**

We appeared to have a speed adrift of 1/1.5 knots in a South Westerly direction.

06:40 pm:

Air force Sydney patched together ship and plane via satellite phone.

The plane started to drop flares. It dropped 4 flares in all.

08:30 pm:

About 7/8 miles before arrival, we spotted the probe light from the raft that lit up the horizon.

08:45 pm:

Saw "Iris" in their spotlight; had 4 crew members on the back deck and 2 people on the landing platform. (The master had previously determined who amongst the passengers was most appropriate and fit to assist).

The mood onboard the "Capricorn Star" had been exhilarated and anticipatory. However, at this point, with no apparent life aboard the "Iris," they were depressed. Panic was setting in over speculation as to whether the men were still aboard, were they to haul out emaciated bodies - alive? Then they saw two men coming out of the cabin and the mate who had prepared ahead and cast the line over to "Iris."

Letter from the G130 Hercules aircraft pilot came to our rescue from Sydney, Australia.

FROM HIMALAYA TO SOUTH PACIFIC

1.18.2000

Greetings from Australia,

I meant to reply to your thank-you letter earlier, but it always seemed busy!

I was the captain of the G130 Hercules aircraft, which held over Arne and Christian's catamaran.

It always feels good to do tasks such as this one. We arrived at work that morning expecting to do a practice Air Sea Rescue Kit drop in Sydney. We were informed of the situation with Arne & Christian, the airplane was topped up with fuel, and we took off around 10 am. When we arrived overhead the catamaran, we could see they were both fine but could not raise them on the radio.

The ETA of the rescue ship was about 10 hours later, so to conserve fuel, we shut down one of the engines and flew as slow as was safe. Because of the cloud, we had to hold at 3000 feet. We did not drop a life-raft as the catamaran was still floating. After dropping a raft, people got into trouble on previous rescues by abandoning their boats. ·

I have a few questions for Arne & Christian - how did they feel knowing we were orbiting but not having dropped a life-raft? Also, we dropped a radio to them but never heard anything - how close to the boat did it land? Did they retrieve it and try to use it? Sorry about the questions, but it would be good to know how people in distress feel about what we do as standard procedures.

During the afternoon, we had a lead on our portable GPS that received a short out and filled the cockpit with smoke. It put us in an emergency ourselves. The crew went on oxygen, and we thought we had a fire in the cockpit until we isolated the cause. None of the crew reported any problem with smoke inhalation, so we elected to stay on station until the rescue ship arrived. We recovered to the Air Force base near Brisbane around midnight when it did. My partner and I would love to visit Norway, we have heard how beautiful it is, and both love cross-country skiing. Perhaps next year we may have time. Thank you for your letter.

Darryl Ferguson,

49 Snailham Crescents Windsor NSW Australia 2756

The sinking of Iris 8.18.199

The Voyage from Loganville, Vanuatu, to Gladstone, Australia, with the motor yacht "Iris." The mast came down on August 18, 1999, resulting in the abandonment of the Vessel on August 18, 1999, 2200 hours are 20.47.72 South 156.48.57 East." Iris" described as Azuli catamaran

Built-in France in 1979

FROM HIMALAYA TO SOUTH PACIFIC

Builders" Chantier Naval de Soubise, Village Soubise (near Rochefort) Designer : Erik Le Rouge

Fiberglass construction.

Captain: Christian Fronsdal, Professor in Physics UCLA Sailing since 1974 worldwide.

Mate: Arne Fronsdal. Retired shipowner. Sailing since 1974 worldwide.

AUTHOR'S NOTE

Do not expect to derive any political knowledge from what you are about to read. I know nothing of politics and care less. I am quite unqualified to give you a book about "Inside Anywhere." Do not expect to improve your knowledge of countries, their historical and cultural backgrounds, their geographical peculiarities, or the difficulties of their economic system. While traveling across a country, it is sufficient to establish that I am in the country I intend to go to. After that, my interest lies in the people I meet, their reactions to meeting me, the immediate effect of my surroundings on me, and whatever companions I have. Above all, my interest lies in the day-to-day difficulties of making a journey in countries where communications are bad and hotels worse.

It is something in the record of a journey from India, done in wartime by my husband and myself. The countries we visited were Afghanistan and Persia. You may be able to determine the route we took from the following narrative.

EDITOR'S NOTE

I met Ruth in Paris in the early sixties and rented a flat from her. She was then an accomplished artist, awarded a Grand Prix for her African natural paintings. She was a strong naturalistic painter with Norwegian fjords and African mothers and children. She was a warm human being with many interests. She was married twice. Her first husband was a Norwegian Consulate in Bombay, and they lived here from 1930 to the end of World War II. She devoted herself to painting, traveling, tennis, golf, and diplomacy during this time.

She participated in both the Indian Golf Open and Indian Tennis Open and was a devout Yogini. On her arrival in India, she had frequent colds and migraine headaches. She was then advised to take up Yoga with a Guru in Bombay. Later, she gained complete health and never again had any type of illness. She was over 60 when I met her, and she looked like a woman of 30. Tor and Ruth took an extended trip from India through Kashmir, Afghanistan, and Iran. They returned by a Norwegian tank ship from Iran through the perilous Persian Gulf. Where the Germans frequently attacked and sank numerous ships carrying vital, strategic oil from Iran and Iraq to the West. Her book was considered the best travel book for these countries during her lifetime, describing the warmth and strength of the people of Afghanistan and Iran. I am grateful to her for conveying the daily routine of Hatha Yoga and meditation.

Her book was originally published in Bombay in 1944; I recently came across it by accident.

Ruth Adam, Author

Arne Fronsdal, Friend and Editor

Over Khyber Pass to the Caspian Sea

PROLOGUE

Tor and I made up our minds to go sightseeing together in Delhi. We intended to be very thorough, so we bought a guidebook and studied it. Next, we buttonholed an old guide at the Cecil Hotel, persuaded him to come with us, and booked a taxi for the trip without difficulty. The guide gave us his card there was written '*THE ONLY GUIDE IN DELHI*' - **S. N. BILLE**. We laughed and said that was a pretty big claim to make. He answered: "They call me Uncle Bille, and I am sixty-two. Now you put away the guide book for I will tell you much better of all the things that are written in it."

We drove through the dusty streets of Delhi, passing innumerable bullocks and camel carts, which many times blocked our path. We could see that the old guide was very excited and anxious to start his job. He wanted to show us what he could do because we had laughed over his card. We passed through the old Delhi Gate and took the road to the Fort.

Here Uncle Bille embarked immediately on a summary of the main events in the history of the Fort. He gave a very good imitation of an actor playing his part on the stage. At the end of his lecture, he said: " Now do you believe I am a good guide? "

"We will proceed," he said in a peremptory tone, and we walked into the Fort as if we were proceeding to a coronation.

When we came to some cut marble windows, he claimed: "Look through here. Do you know who used to sit here staring through those windows?" I peeped through and said: "I am sure it was the poor women in the Fort who were not allowed to participate in any glamourous life," but guide Bille responded: "Shah Jahan often came here to see his women." Then he added: "Of course, the fact that he promised his wife on her death bed that he would never marry again did not prevent him from having something like 100 women in his harem." "I suppose he had to have someone to admire him in his kingly state," I said. "Yes," he went on. "Here the women sat looking at the King on the Peacock Throne." I said: "What throne?" It flashed through my mind that it had been given this name because the king had been pompous and proud. "I will show you," Uncle Bille said, walking along to the Durbar Hall. The hall looked magnificent.

The old guide said with a gleam in his eyes: "Have a look round and guess what is old and what has been restored in this hall." I looked around and saw that the frescoes on the walls and pillars were fresh and brightly colored, while the wooden ceiling looked old and moth-eaten, so I guessed quickly that the ceiling was old. He laughed and said: "That is the only thing in the hall which is new. The Mahrattas looted the ceiling in 1760 and melted it down." It was amazing how fresh the frescoes looked. In the olden days, with gems inlaid, pillars, walls, and ceilings covered in gold and silver, the hall must surely have been one of the world's wonders.

Then the guide went on: "Here was placed the Peacock Throne." He marked off a square in the middle of the hall. "It was built by Shah Jahan and was the pride of the Moghal Empire." Then, as guides do, he added: "It took seven years to complete," he extended his arms to full length as if to touch the bygone days with his fingers," at the cost of six and a half million pounds sterling. There were eighty lakhs of rupees in precious stones alone; one single stone was worth one lakh of rupees." ·

"The name of the Throne," he went on, "came from the fact that two peacocks, inlaid with gold and precious stones, were placed at the back of the throne."

The old guide was thrilled as he told us more about the history of Shah Jahan, whom he thought to be a great man. At the same time, he almost burst into tears when he came to tell us of his cruel son, who had thrown him into prison and kept him there.

In 1739 Nadir Shah invaded India, looted Delhi, and carried off the Peacock Throne on seven elephants." By now, there was quite a crowd around us listening to the guide's story. He was at the very peak of his dramatic performance. One of the onlookers said: "Surely, the throne could have been carried away on one elephant. It was not so big as all that."

It was six feet long and four feet wide," the guide flung at him furiously, "but do you think Nadir Shah, who came all the way from Persia, would only take the throne when he saw walls inlaid with jewels and big cushions embroidered with gems and pearls? He made a big platform covering seven elephants and placed the throne and all the rest of his loot on these."

Uncle Bille was furious at having been interrupted in his histrionics. He had lost his temper by this time and had to contemplate on his favorite Shah Jahan to regain his composure. So now he said: "Here sat Shah Jahan in all his glory," and we could picture him sitting there in the world's most beautiful room, certainly the most valuable room. We could see him enjoying the lovely view over the Jumna River, which in his day flowed just beneath the walls of the

Fort.

No wonder there is an inscription on the wall:

"If paradise be on earth, it is here; it is here, it is here."

Fascinated by guide Bille's story, I told Tor: " If anyone is going to see that throne, it is me, it is me, it is me." Tor laughed and said: "Where is it now?" The guide answered: " It was taken over the Khyber Pass to Kabul, and eventually, it ended up in Teheran." In astonishment, Tor said, "I have been to Teheran, and I never knew it was there."

CHAPTER I:
OVER THE KHYBER

We arrived at Peshawar by train, drove through the broad streets of the town, and went to Dean's Hotel. After paying off our coolies, I sat on the edge of the bed and forgot time and the unopened luggage which lay around me in wild disorder. My thoughts went back to the very warm day in Delhi when we had seen the deserted site of the Peacock Throne. I was on the same road as the throne, on the way over the Khyber Pass.

I was brought back to the present again when my husband came into the room and saw me still sitting on the bed, surrounded by unopened luggage. "It is late," he said, "you must hurry up and dress for dinner. We must get up early tomorrow, for we have several things to do, and by lunchtime, we will be off over the Khyber Pass."

"Where the throne went," I said and went into my bathroom. I think he thought I was a bit mad.

Three o'clock in the afternoon, the following day saw, we settled in a motor car, ready to start on our journey. Our first stopping place was not far from the hotel, however. It was the Peshawar Post Office. It was, in a way, fortunate that we had to stop there. For a while, we were impatiently waiting. We suddenly remembered that we had forgotten to change our money into Afghan currency. My husband went off to the Post Office again to do the changing.

KHYBER PASS

While he was inside, a car drove up alongside ours. Inside the car sat a big man, some north-country Indian, with eyes as big as prunes lying in water overnight. He asked me why we had come back again, and I explained that we had not even started because of the money problem. He seemed intensely interested in the matter. When my husband returned and handed me a big fat envelope bursting with money, his eyes became twice as big. We traveled in a legation car with diplomatic passes and crossed the border into the Khyber without difficulty.

Jamrud fort looked like a battleship and was a grand opening to the Khyber Pass. It was like driving on holy ground, going up the Khyber Pass. I found everything I had been led to expect. Those brown-colored mountains created an atmosphere of historical romance and fantastic adventure. The little watch tower on the hills conjured up scenes of olden times, colorful scenes full of glory and honor. I could see the plumed horses of the cavalry. I felt terrifically thrilled going over the border, so much so that I got out of the car and walked across to have the feeling that I had really made a physical effort.

As we crossed the border, we found that Afghan time was two hours behind Indian time. I found that I got an impression of entering France, for the uniform of the Afghan soldier is rather like that of his French counterpart, and the flat cap is almost identical.

We had to have our passes examined. The soldier who stopped us was unqualified to let us pass, for he went to fetch another soldier who again had to fetch the third one. The latter seemed determined to fill himself with water from a well where he was drinking before he attended us. Having finished drinking, he disappeared m.to a house, and I felt certain we would never see him again.

Meanwhile, I chatted with our driver. He was concerned

about the rain falling at the wrong time of year. I pointed with some dismay to the bad state of the road in front of us. It didn't look very promising. He laughed and said with pride: "I am an Indian," then with scorn in his voice, "This is Afghanistan. What do you expect?"

At last, the soldier emerged from the house, accompanied by another man. Together, and with some aid from our driver, they had another long scrutiny of our passes. Our driver learned that we were not Ministers of State, as he had previously thought, and after that, treated us with scant respect. We were, however, allowed to pass, and on we went into Afghanistan.

The road was terrible. But because stones marked it out, you could not have told where the road was supposed to be. It was like driving in the middle of a desert. The sky in front of us threatened heavy rain. It changed from dark blue into the most beautiful violet hue and was intermittently streaked with fierce zigzags of lightning. It looked magnificent against the golden-colored mountains. We passed a lonely tree by the road, and it became conspicuous as many small rags were on it. From the motor driver, I learned that there was a shrine nearby. Superstitious people had each put a rag on the tree after visiting the holy grave.

I asked the driver why people had visited the shrine. He

gave a fascinating account of the many shrines nearby. There were many similar shrines roundabout in the hills, he said. I was told that there were shrines for curing lame horses and suffering cattle. People went there to secure relief from sickness. Some, for instance, visited Shrine " A " for cures for boils or Shrine "B" for rashes and skin diseases. What surprised me the most was that there were "specialists" among the shrines as among medical practitioners. It was natural in a country where no proper treatment was available to resort to such means of getting a cure. I could not help feeling sorry when the driver told me about the shrine frequented by childless couples. The story was pathetic.

When you visit the shrine, you pass a small *charpai* nearby with a stone on it, and you pray to the dead saint to use his good offices so the woman can have a child soon. "*Charpai* "-is a simple and portable local cot (lit: *charpai* =four legs.)

All the way along, the road was crossed by little streams of water, through which the driver shepherded the car with great care. He was beginning to impress on us the importance of having a good driver. Suddenly he stopped, and I saw in front of us something more than a stream; it was quite a river this time. I thought at first he had stopped to make himself more important. Still, when I asked him whether we could cross or not, he shook his head. He thoroughly enjoyed his position of being the custodian of our precious lives.

The bridge had gone, and I realized that it had gone many years before. I felt sure our Indian driver told every newcomer that it was difficult to pass because the bridge had just gone. I tried to appear very impressed with the difficulties of the situation. Still, I said: "Surely nothing can stop an experienced driver like you."

Meanwhile, my husband had found a shallow spot higher up the river where we could cross. Vile drove up to this place, followed by a lorry that had just arrived behind us. Our driver, joined by the one from the lorry, tested the river bed to ensure it would not shift or give way when weight was put into it. We crossed safely in the end but had not gone far when another badly swollen river barred our progress. It was growing late in the evening by now. We did not relish the idea of perhaps having to spend the night in the car,' stuck by the roadside, especially in a well-known vicinity for organized dacoity. However, there was nothing else to do but wait until the flood water had subsided a little. The sun had already gone down and had left a lovely orange glow over the mountains. The effect was to make the thunderous sky look still more threatening. The new moon looked so tiny and shy compared to the boldness and power of the other heavenly gods.

The driver and his companion, an older man with red hair who always put such an air of importance around everything he did, went on to the roof of the car. At the same time, we made ourselves as comfortable as possible inside.

Outside the car, a guard walked up and down, but I was never quite certain whether the idea was that he should protect us or that he would rob us while we were sleeping. Consequently, I would wake up and watch him every time he passed my head.

These guards who keep watch on the roads all the way through the Khyber and the mountains to Jalalabad are usually local people paid by the government. I wondered if this spot was where the cycling incident happened. A man made up his mind to cycle from Peshawar to Kabul. He got safely over the Khyber Pass and cycled happily towards Jalalabad when he saw a guard behaving very strangely. On the other hand, the guard had never seen a cycle before. He apparently thought the devil himself was after him, and they both fought for their lives.

But eventually, I must have fallen sound asleep, for I do not remember anything more until our driver awakened me.

He opened the car door to tell us that the water had gone down and that he thought we would be on our way.

Of course, this did not prevent him from becoming important again by walking into the middle of the river to test the bed once more, and his sense of importance was gratified. We solicitously asked him if he did not feel very, very cold sitting with wet trousers. It was still dark, and it wasn't easy by this time to find the road in places where the rain had washed it away. Huge boulders had been carried onto the road by the flood water to make matters worse. We were lucky not to have the axle of the car broken. But it was tedious, and now and again, I fell off to sleep. I was frightened that the driver would do the same, for he must have been very tired by this time.

CHAPTER II:
JALALABAD

At last, we arrived at civilization, and I awoke in time to find we were driving through the gates of a house. The road led us through a garden, and we stopped in front of a big bungalow. It was the British Consulate's bungalow in Jalalabad, where we had been expected to arrive in time for dinner the previous evening. We had, of course, arrived somewhat late for dinner. It was, in fact, early morning but still dark, and I lay down flat on the cold stone of the verandah floor. It was pleasant to lie down anywhere after being bunched up for so long in the car. It was so lovely that I think it went to my head, for I suddenly found everything going round and round in the most disconnected manner. We had been shown two rooms with beds, and I expressed my delight to my husband.

JALALABAD PHOTOS

After a while, servants arrived, and we relished the preferred food we ate on the lawn by the light of hurricane lamps. I was famished, except for a little fruit; I had eaten nothing all day. When we finished eating, our driver announced his intention to get started. But we insisted on having one hour's sleep. Had I realized at the time that he was again only playing his part of importance, I would have slept very much more. An hour later, we were having coffee on the lawn in bright sunshine. Around us in the garden were fruit trees of all kinds, orange, apricot, grape vines, and a lot more. The Consulate's Secretary stood talking to us. I had time to look around. I saw a magnificent range of mountains in the distance, some of the peaks covered with snow. I told the Secretary how lovely the snow was on the mountain peaks. His reply took me aback, for he said we could not see snow-covered mountains from where we were. I was afraid to pursue the matter as I suddenly thought my giddiness of a little while before must have arisen from some complaint of the eyes which I had developed. I was later relieved when a person in Kabul to whom I related the little episode convinced me that I had been right and had seen the snow-capped peaks of the Hindu Kush range.

Jalalabad had a green loveliness, with a rich fertile look about it. There were many tempting-looking walled vineyards. It seemed absurd to leave this haven of fertility behind us and deliberately enter the country. We now found ourselves in the country, displayed nothing but a sea of brown stone and mud before our eyes. Only occasionally was the monotony broken by a black tent, the humble dwelling of those tribes which make seasonal migrations from one valley to another, always through the same mountain passes. They mainly survived by keeping camels and chickens, with occasional dacoity thrown in. I heard later that they were expert camel breeders and made quite a good trade from them. I thought I saw cactus growing near the summits of the hills. Still, on closer inspection, I found they were very simple graveyards, consisting of a variation of long vertical and horizontal stones.

The long vertical stones are the men's graves- the bigger and higher the stone, the greater the man's personality. The flat horizontal ones are the women's. The body is always buried with the face towards Mecca.

The road turned gradually into a hill road; the car worked its way higher and higher up the barren mountainside. From a height of 7,500 feet, the mountains seemed to lose their plainness and acquired a quality of beauty. One could see an ethereal blue mist haunting the valley through the clouds. I could not help being impressed by the hardness of the countryside; I thought with admiration of the gunners of old campaigns, who had to carry their guns across these forbidding mountains.

I saw the oceans of barrenness aroused my sympathy for the tribes who had to wrest a living from this countryside. Small wonder that they occasionally took to robbing and pillaging and did not count it any sin. It was indeed problematical whether anything at all could be grown amongst the desert of stones. Soon we were going downhill towards a valley; it started to rain, and we put up a sheet of raincoats around the open car. Temporarily the rain stopped, only to start again with a real fury this time. It was a mixture of rain and hailstones as big as hazel nuts. We were forced to stop, and in a few minutes, the mild little stream down in the valley ahead had changed into a torrent of water.

Then from the bare hillside, water began to gush down; just in front of us, we watched the very foundations of the road being washed away. It seemed rather illogical to stop and watch these powerful forces gradually surround us on all sides and perhaps trap us. We shared our concerns with our driver. But he was in a very stubborn mood and refused to drive ahead.

Gradually the rainstorm lessened, and we had only gone a little ahead when we realized how wise our driver had been. Around the first bend, we saw that the rain had washed the hillside onto the road. It would not have been pleasant to have had a landslide on top of us. We cleaned the loose mud from off the top of the road; the remaining few feet of stones and boulders we went over with difficulty. There was a sheer drop of hundreds of feet down the valley from the road. The river still rushed at a terrific speed, overfilled with water. As we went along, it was an unpleasant thought that the road might give way at any moment. It delayed us for about a day; that did not matter in the least to any of us, but the driver seemed very upset. We were still descending into the valley. Now we could see the hills above Kabul; Kabul itself was hidden away securely out of sight.

At last, we reached the bottom of the valley, only to find our progress barred by another river. There was a heaven-sent opportunity for the driver to get a grip on our lives again, and he set about doing so in his usual way. Unfortunately for him, just before he reached the river, a car came from the opposite direction and went through the river without difficulty. However, our driver was determined not to be robbed of his opportunity and continued walking right through. I told him again that I was sure he would catch pneumonia, which pleased him. He purred with pride at the thought of the difficulties he had brought us through, and I am sure he hoped that we would mention his sterling qualities to his employer. We came to a village where we used the telephone to inform our hosts in Kabul to expect us shortly. The driver said we needed more petrol. Very soon, a car arrived, and our tank was replenished. We embarked on the last lap of our journey into Kabul.

CHAPTER III:
KABUL

To drive into Kabul was like a dream. The stress and strain of the journey had drained out of us, and we were able to relax. Kabul must always be a joy as there was a lot of struggle to get there. The old town was surrounded by an air of mystery, with its high walls and burqa-clad women. After the cold of the barren mountains, I felt it hot in the town. Still, the Kabul residents did not seem to think so. They walked around dressed up in big Astrakhan caps and overcoats, sometimes European-style coats but more often in something which resembled a double-padded Chinese dressing gown. At night, the latter serves as a sleeping bag so that they can sleep using them on the street or on the hillside. It did not seem to matter.

We found the Legation, where we were staying, outside the town and on a hillside commanding a fine view over the surrounding countryside.

The Legation boasted tennis courts, a bowling green, and a magnificent park-like garden. Living there was like being in paradise. Our hosts were among the most charming people I have ever met. Our days were filled with engagements.

FROM HIMALAYA TO SOUTH PACIFIC

With an officer who knew Kabul well, we explored the old bazaars of the town. Here one saw an amazing mixture of races. The west and the east seemed to meet and fuse in the bazaars of Kabul. Most of them were attractive, alive, and vivid-looking people. Strangest to my eyes were the Turkoman types; I was intrigued with their slanting eyes, beards, and Russian caps they invariably wore. One of these offered me an old coin, and I regret not accepting it. Afterward, I felt sure Alexander the Great had probably used it as current coinage. I was all eyes as I walked through the big streets. I did not know who stared most. It could be either me at the merchants or them at me without a *burqa* or *purdah* (a veil to cover my face as they were unused to seeing an unveiled woman in the streets).

I saw good pieces of very blue lapis lazuli, one piece was very big, and I was dying to ask the price. But I dare not talk to the men when I had no purdah on. Also, Tor was convinced that the stone was not real. I was determined it was real. However, I had been told that it was to be found for the picking in the surrounding mountains. My assertion was proved correct the next day when we saw some people digging in the hillside for the stone while walking out.

Kabul has one of the best climates in the world. It stands at about five thousand feet and has a dry and cold winter for skiing. While we were enjoying the refreshing walk over the hills, I asked our officer friend the origin of the name Kabul. He laughed and said: **"Believe it or not, here is the story:**

Old Noah had two sons, Kakul and Habul. When they built a city, they pondered over its name. At last, they came to a happy compromise to combine the names Kakul and Habul to make it Kabul."

The officer warned us to take steps while walking across a graveyard carefully. There are many outside Kabul because the mud might give way. I asked if they were hollow. Our friend replied: "They dig the graves with sufficient space for the corpse to sit up at ease." The dead have to answer questions put to them by angels who are supposed to find out all their good and bad deeds in their past lives.

From the top of a hill, we could see over two valleys. In one lay the old town with its population of about eighty thousand, and in the other lay an abortive new town built by King Amanullah. He had chosen what certainly seemed the more fertile of the two valleys. Right across the valley on the hillside opposite us stood the unfinished palace in ghostly splendor. We could see the six miles long approach avenue. He had even laid tram tracks to provide easy conveyance to his new Secretariat. But it was a short-lived dream, for his people disliked the idea of modernizing the country intensely. His queen had moved about freely, not in purdah, to the dismay of the orthodox priests.

They disliked his new education system too. I was sure they feared spreading education would rob them of their tremendous power because the priests were big landowners. The tramways were forcibly removed and broken to pieces, and no one ever occupied the beautiful palace and Secretariat. Now, these buildings have acquired a tradition of ill luck.

Strangely enough, the only building which is used is the museum, a fine building. It was worthwhile going there if only to see an old Persian black granite bowl. It was about four inches thick and about a half-foot in diameter. It stood at least four feet high and reminded me of the sort of bow. I had often seen it in the pictures of Persian courts. I tapped it with my fingernail, and it tinkled like porcelain. It rested on a base of stone carved lotus leaves and was covered with beautiful writing.

It was a most attractive piece, but when my friend said: "It always reminds me of the plate I had as a little boy. It was written around the edge, *Eat your porridge, and you will grow into a big boy,*" my aesthetic feeling for the bowl was dissolved in fits of laughter. The beauty of Persian plates with inscriptions was spoiled for me after that. I discovered it was known as Ali's begging bowl or the priests' collecting bowl. Judging from the size, the priests expected a lot.

When I was in Herat, I met an engineer who took me to a museum, saying: "You must come and see some old Persian writing. Don't you think it looks like musical poetry? You can almost see from the delicacy of the handwriting exactly what the scribe wants to express." I saw a poem framed and hanging on the wall, and at first glance, I thought it was a painting. The handwriting of another seemed to express anger, for it looked like a thunderstorm. In another, one could sense love in every stroke. It was so soft, appealing, and sensitive.

One of the great historical attractions of Kabul is the tomb of Baber, the founder of the Mughal Empire. It is in a picturesque spot with a beautiful garden. He had asked to be buried there.

He was in Delhi when he died. After having fallen down the steps in the palace, his son Humayun was ill. Baber prayed to God, saying he was willing to suffer his son's illness, thus sparing Humayun. "I am old," said Baber, "Does it matter if I die?" He was only fifty years of age at the time. Humans recovered soon after this, while Baber got ill and died shortly afterward.

It was surprising to find a temple of a Hindu goddess in Kabul. I was told it is the guardian deity of the Afghan capital. Mothers with their newly born babies visit the temple, which is known as Aasmai.

A big stone and a crude oil lamp kept burning inside the temple.

Going into a shop and having the perfect *Karakul fur* was a real treat. One could dream of the most beautiful warm coats in either black or grey lamb. Of course, one could not help thinking of the poor mother sheep who must die with the three or four months old lamb in her womb.

We saw thousands of broad-tail sheep (they are called *"Dumba,"* and the lambs are called *"Burra"* around the country). Their tails were so broad that it looked like half of their bodies were moving when they ran about. The sheep were shorn twice a year, and they gave excellent wool.

One of the Afghan delicacies is a well-cooked *"Dumba."* It is the privilege of the guest to kill it, and the feast takes place with a big ceremony.

People thought us rather crazy when we told them that we intended to go to Kandahar by bus. Still, we explained that we thought this would be the best way to meet the country's people as we wished to do so.

We went to the bus office and booked our seats three days in advance. To confirm the seats, we went down again after a day or two when we were told that we would have to wait three more days because all the buses were fully booked. This seemed most unlikely to us, but our hosts told us that there was a possibility that we would have to wait another month before we could get seats. Actually, we did not mind very much as it was very enjoyable staying where we were.

* Karakul =Persian lamb.

CHAPTER IV:
THE ROAD TO GHAZNI

Eventually, it was the day for our departure. When we saw the bus, we were supposed to travel in. It seemed impossible to take any more people, for it was already full. The Legation car which took us to the bus waited to ensure that the bus had not already left. As in this country, that could easily have happened.

I was delighted to get the front seat for which I had asked. I felt very well as I relaxed with the added comfort of my big pillow and a small cushion behind my head. The number of people the bus could take seemed to be countless. By now, there were about twice as many as when we arrived. Our luggage was piled on the roof, which was the end of our precious bottles of fruit juice.

At last, after endless delays, we were off. As one does on these occasions, I looked attentively at the streets and wondered when I would see Kabul again. My last-minute sentimental came to a pause as the bus had only gone a short distance when it stopped. The driver, of course, looked inside the engine, and I felt sure we would have a slow journey with a capricious engine. I was relieved when I heard that we were waiting for the mail.

Here, I thought, was an opportunity to get friendly with the burqa women sitting behind me. One had a small baby, and I gave it my perfume bottle to play with. I opened the bottle so the baby could smell the perfume, but his mother immediately snatched it out of his hands and put the scent on her blouse under her burqa. Another woman did the same with the scent bottle; I could see both got a great thrill out of it. I guessed they were not supposed to put on any scent during Ramzan. When I offered them the scent a second time, this time after the arrival of their husbands, the men shook their heads in censorious disapproval, and the women dared not take any. But after that, the ice was broken, and we understood each other. The Afghans usually purchase their wives. The man is about twenty years old when he marries while the girl is about sixteen. The richer people marry earlier or as soon as they can afford to keep a family.

The girls are usually chosen, and matches are made through elderly female relatives. But the contract of marriage that is created must be agreed to by the woman and the man. The man, of course, has no opportunity to see his wife-to-be before he marries her.

A husband can divorce his wife without assigning any reason whatsoever. If the husband dies before the wife, the husband's brother has a preferential claim on the widow. Anyone who wants to marry her must have his consent. But the widow can refuse to marry if she does not want to.

Polygamy is allowed by Mohammadan law but to the extent of four wives only.

It is said that no census has yet been attempted in the country. It is considered bad manners to ask the names or the number of women in the house.

At last, the driver returned with the mail bag but still no sign of getting started. An old man with a long white beard came along and looked at the bus. To me, it looked full, but when the old man saw that the toolbox beside the driver was empty, he laid his bundle there, and there was no doubt in his mind that he would get that seat. The seat belonged to the bus cleaner, so I was surprised that the driver said nothing when the old man stepped into the bus and sat down with a proprietary air.

Now we were off. It seemed for good this time. Everyone was settled, and the bus packed to the last inch. Imagine how surprised I was when we stopped again immediately outside the town to pick up more passengers. However, they all went on the roof, and I thought they gave some extra profit to the driver.

In the country between Kandahar and Kabul lived the tribes whose chief occupation was breeding camels. We saw many herds of camels on the way. The road lay through a green and fertile valley. We met donkeys loaded with fruit, and dignified camels carried their colorful camel bags. The baby camels became very frightened when they saw us and ran off the road in wild gallops. The mothers looked furious over the misbehaviour of their children.

We made a terrible noise going along. It was a very old bus, and everything in it rattled. I felt that after two hundred miles of driving on those bumpy roads, we would find ourselves with only the chassis left. I opened the little side window beside me to get some fresh air, but after a mile or two, it shut back again at the same old place. I got quite annoyed in the beginning, but after a while, I became used to opening it to be able to breathe in the heat.

The old bus shook its way along the valley. A hen got very alarmed when she heard us coming into a field. I would not blame her. She thought she had better run for it, but apparently, she could not tell where the noise was coming from. She ran for her life right before the bus just as if she wanted to commit suicide. I thought: "Please, God, look after the innocent but make no excuses for the stupid."

Eventually, we came to the end of the valley. We found

ourselves in the desert country where the only signs of fertility were small green patches around the villages. The village people enjoyed it when the bus arrived. They crowded around to sell us melons, grapes, and other fruits. Big Pathans ran tea shops in the village. An added attraction was when they staged cock fights. There were massive cocks ready for a fight strutting across the round platform outside the tea houses. The cocks were just as proud of their physical strength as the people. Their legs were very long and thick. Their bodies were strong, but some with very few feathers looked much worse.

Another attraction was the egg game. The idea was to put the points of the eggs towards each other and press very hard. If a person was disliked, sometimes a bad egg was used.

When we stopped at these villages, it was usual for the men to get out of the bus, and women remained inside. So I was able to talk to them alone. The woman with the baby uncovered her face and smiled at me. She looked very beautiful; her skin was as fresh and rosy as a Nordic woman and just as fair. She had red lips, expressive blue eyes, and brown hair and looked like a lovely painting. Her mother, who sat next to her, was also the most charming to talk to, but I never got a chance to see her face. I thought the less attractive women must love purdah, for they can hide their plainness. My new friends signified that it was very hot beneath their veils, and they obviously envied my uncovered state.

The woman's husband with the child returned with some nice riped apples; they offered me. They, poor things, could not eat anything until the sun had set because of Ramzan. I pointed to my watch and told them there were not many hours left before they could eat and drink. I accepted the apples, and they all laughed again and seemed to enjoy my pleasure in eating them.

Ramzan is the ninth month in the Mohammadan year. Mohammad used to devote this month to a cave for meditation and prayer. The Quran was, at this time, revealed to him. That is why it has become a season of great sanctity.

During this month, the Mohammadans are supposed to recite the Quran and strictly a fast between sunrise and sunset. The fast is understood in many ways. The Prophet's idea was that people should think of the poor and give them one or two meals a day instead of eating themselves.

One thing I was positive about was that the Prophet did not mean them to fill themselves with food as soon as the sun sets and keep getting up in the night to feed again and again as some do.

They are allowed to eat after night prayers. The poor people were very badly struck because they kept strictly to the day fasting and could not afford to feed at night. The country's people were very sincere. They did not take a drop of water or even swallow the moisture in their mouth. The young people suffered intensely in the heat. Others again exclude themselves from all worldly conversation and read the Quran.

After a while, I could see we were approaching a big town which turned out to be the historic city of Ghazni. It was exactly like a town from medieval times. The old town was perched on top of a hill and surrounded by a high wall. The entrance to the town was through a magnificent gateway thronged with people, camels, and donkeys. It was the right background for burqa-clad women and toga-clad men.

Ghazni has a bracing climate on a plateau, about seven thousand feet high. The snow lay on the ground from about November to the middle of March. The land around Ghazni is of remarkable fertility where tobacco and cotton are grown as well as vegetables and fruit.

It was from this place that Mahmud of Ghazni invaded India twenty-six times. Every time he looted rich capitals and temples and brought the treasures back with him. There were still two towers from his time in exquisite brickwork near the town. Below the towers was a popular place to go looking for precious stones. One could sometimes find some remains from olden times jewellery bazaars, which were present around the two *minars*.

On his deathbed, Mahmud ordered all his jewelry to be brought and displayed before him. He gazed at it with painful eyes and ordered the whole lot to be locked up without having the heart to give anything away to his people. The bus had stopped, and I was so engrossed in the beauty of the old town that I did not notice till Tor nudged me that I had quite a large audience. I looked around and found twenty-five Pathans on one side of the bus, and about ten on the other, all of them stood staring at me. I looked at one of them straight in the eyes, but he did not look away. That made me feel very uncovered, so I put on my goggles and coat, despite the hot weather. I was embarrassed by all the attention, so I took out some sandwiches to have something to do. It was a good idea as I was very hungry. Sitting there, pouring out tea from my thermos, and eating sandwiches, I felt like a caged monkey. The man with the persistent stare frightened me, for he came right into the bus, and I knew he was not a passenger. I realized why the people became so alarmed when the King ordered the abolishment of the purdah system. I had a last look at the historical little town before we set off again.

After about ten minutes, we stopped in front of a little mosque outside the town. An aged priest *(Mulla)* with a white beard was kneeling in prayer on a carpet in the mosque garden. I felt something very beautiful in the undisturbed nature of the Mohammadan worship. The priest in the garden and the old man sitting on the toolbox in the bus were so alike that I had to look twice to see if perhaps the latter had somehow got in front of us. But the old man on the toolbox was still there. Presently he roused himself from sleep but still looked as if his mind was very far away and I blamed the two thick winter coats he wore, one on top of the other. It was rather fortunate that he wore a very thick turban, as, during his sleep, he kept falling forward with his head on the wooden dashboard of the bus.

Eventually this old man rose and, with great dignity, left the bus. The driver *salaamed* him most respectfully, and as there was dead silence in the bus, I got the impression that he was a *Mulla*. He asked the driver how much it was for the day's trip, but the driver just waved his hand as if to say, *"nothing at all - it was a pleasure."*

The young car assistant now became very busy. He took off the boiling hot radiator cap with his bare hands. I would have burnt myself if I had done it, but he wanted to show off.

Then he brought an attractively shaped earthenware vase filled with water. After pouring water into the radiator, he threw the vase with the exuberance of youth into a garden, where it broke into pieces. The driver spoke to him sharply but the youth, determined to establish his personality, answered him rudely. He laughed heartily, and so did all the other youths on the bus while the older people remained completely silent.

After this, we went off again, and the driver drove much faster. The other people on the bus also became talkative and had a pleasant atmosphere all around.

Suddenly there was a bang like a pistol shot. I noticed that some women ducked and held their hands in front of their faces. I was sure that it was a holdup. Fortunately, it was an ordinary puncture which was serious enough, for tires were extremely difficult to find in Afghanistan. We all had to crow outside.

A cool, clear stream that looked like spring water ran by the roadside, and we all rushed for it. I felt very hot and dusty, so I sat down and washed my face and neck, which was a natural thing to do. I had forgotten that I was a woman in Afghanistan and one young boy who sat near me said in a very quiet voice: "Don't be frightened." Whether I was supposed to be frightened of the water or him, I do not know, but his voice sounded very sweet.

I washed the grapes we had brought with us and poured diluted potassium permanganate over them. With Afghan bread, they made a glorious meal. Mending the tire was a long job, so we had the leisure to contemplate the country around us. My impression of the country from the bus had been of a desert. When I looked at it again, I saw people ploughing the fields and stacking the corn already harvested. The vivid color of the corn stacks broke up the monotony of the desert.

An officer of the Afghan army, who gave us the impression that he had been deputed to watch us, spread out his carpet to pray. After removing his shoes, the man in the *Astrakhan* cap joined him. They all seemed to enjoy having a turn of pumping the old fashioned pump which was being used to blow up the tire and this gave the witty heads a chance to crack jokes over the clumsiness of some of them. It was so entertaining watching them all that I did not notice the length of time it took to mend the tire. Why would time matter anyhow?

CHAPTER V: RAMZAN EVENING

While passing through another small village, we met more tribes with camels. They gushed through the street, and I saw small boys running fast to collect the providential bounty dropped by the camels. It must have been of great value because the small boys risked being kicked to death when they crept right underneath the camels. Maybe it was the same everywhere else in the world, like a matter of sport amongst the boys?

One little boy was very sweet. He was so busy looking at us that he forgot what his basket contained and planted himself right in the middle of it to sit and stare.

Next, we stopped for petrol at an old pump. I was asked to get up as the petrol tank was situated right underneath me. The woman with the baby went over to a stream to wash the child. I followed her. We played with the baby in the water, which he loved. He cried heart rendingly when we took him away.

Back on the bus, I showed the women cosmetics in my bag as I thought it was a good way of entertaining them. I, in turn, was interested in one of their beauty preparations. It was everlasting nail polish, and their husbands explained that it was a preparation made from juice extracted from tree bark and was usually put on at weddings. I remarked it would be a marvelous innovation in wartime, but they did not seem to catch the point. Of course, the world war meant nothing at all to them.

I showed them photographs of my children and the women were very thrilled by them. The husband tried hard to find the right English words to express himself but could not do so at that moment. My daughter's hair color is that of corn. I tried hard to explain, but it was difficult because there was no corn in the fields nearby.

The bus had speeded up because they wanted to reach a certain village immediately after sunset so that they could eat as soon as Ramzan permitted. Suddenly, I felt someone tapping me on the shoulder. I turned as the husband leaned over to me and said in pure English with a deep Afghan voice: "Your daughter is beautiful, and she has golden hair." It sounded like a piece of poetry, and I was very touched. We had established a mutual understanding between us.

I glanced behind me into the bus, and they were all sitting watching the setting sun, eager to have their evening meal. I could easily understand why people say: "You must be careful with an Afghani during Ramzan. They are very easily upset." I would be the same if I were to eat nothing all day. At this point, a great argument arose; the driver seemed to be in acute disagreement with the others. There was a great deal of back-chat, and eventually, the driver stopped the bus.

Apparently, the argument had arisen over the desire of the passengers to pray before the sun had set too low. The Afghan Army officer led the way again, but I noticed many young boys didn't move out of the bus. I sat down by the roadside and enjoyed another apple and thanked my lucky star that I had not been born in a country where Ramzan was observed. Seeing these powerfully built tribesmen kneeling in prayer towards the setting sun was a magnificent sight; it certainly was a good exercise for them, especially for the fat ones. The officer's cap looked very drab beside the galaxy of colors the turbans made, and I thought how honest and innocent they looked.

We all went back onto the bus because now we had very little time to reach the village, just as the last golden rays from the sun were leaving the last cloud in the sky. They said they could not eat before that.

The bus shook along as fast as it could, and soon some houses became visible in the distance. We had barely reached a standstill before all the men and I crowded out of the bus to buy tea, bread, and melons.

Our sandwiches and coffee tasted better when we knew all the others could enjoy their food too. I went to the ladies again who sat inside the bus eating some kind of pancake bread, and one of them offered me a piece to eat, which I accepted. It tasted very good, but I was frightened to death if I would get typhoid or smallpox. I noticed that the baby in her arms looked like it had not quite recovered from smallpox. I noticed, too, that the mother had fresh marks on her arms.

The sweet and cultured Afghan women have very little education. They have superstitions against women learning to read and write, thanks to one *Malik's* daughter. She was famed for her beauty and knowledge and was in love with her father's enemy, a great conqueror, who laid siege to *Malik's fort*. The princess wrote letters that she sent through arrows and shot from the fort's tower to the enemy. In one of them, she disclosed the source of the *Carez*. The Malik was forced to surrender when the water was stopped. The conqueror then married Malik's daughter. *Carez* means an ancient underground canal that supplies water all year round.

But the conqueror got frightened. He thought his wife would betray him as she had betrayed her father. He, therefore, ordered her execution. She is always presented as a bad example and the prejudice against girls' education remains strong.

The men sat in large circles around food bowls, and I felt greatly tempted to go and see what sort of food they were eating. It would have been bad manners to have intruded on their privacy. Even their backs conveyed an unmistakable impression of hearty release, which alone were visible.

After this feasting, the atmosphere in the bus was more settled and contented, and the chat was soft and nerves relaxed. Meanwhile, darkness had fallen, and the moon had risen. I was too tired to ponder over the beauties of the moonlit landscape, and I sat back and fell asleep. The Pathan beside Tor fell forward, and his magnificent turban bumped hard against my head. He was very confused when he got up and realized what had happened. After that, Tor and I erected a barricade of cushions around us, and we were able to sleep well. Now and again, I awoke to see whether the driver looked like falling asleep, but I might have spared myself the trouble, for he looked as if he could stay wide awake for a long time.

About midnight, I was awakened by a great deal of chatter on the bus. Our arrival in a small village had caused excitement, and as we passed along the main street, I felt as if one of Hans Andersen's fairy tales had come to life. Tea shop after tea shop lined the little street, all of them lit up by lamps containing samovars so enormous that they seemed to have been especially fashioned to match the men's size. The flickering light from the fireplace, where delicious bread was being baked, gave a marvelous stage effect of shadow and dancing color. I had to pinch myself to ensure this was real and not a dream. In front of the shops stood trees with benches and long tables underneath them. They brought us carpets to sit on. We had seated ourselves comfortably when Tor dropped his stick and started searching underneath the bench. We discovered we were seated on the very edge of a big ditch full of water. I was alarmed. I could picture ourselves being the victims of some unhappy plot and imagined the bench being tilted up by some sinister mechanism and all of us landing in the water. It was not until the stick was retrieved and I saw that there were ditches for drawing water all over the village that I settled down peacefully again.

The driver ordered tea for us, and while we were waiting for it, a magnificent Pathan offered us a melon. A melon is delicious when you are thirsty; this one was very juicy. The driver brought us some bread and placed it on the carpet. He asked me if I preferred it roasted, and I said I did. I secretly hoped it would come back to me touched by as few hands as possible. The bread turned out to be very good, and along with it, I ate some sweet bread the driver had also produced. The mixture of the two kinds of bread made a delicious meal. The brew of tea was excellent but to have tea served in such miniature cups by such giant men seemed very inappropriate.

Everyone was friendly and kind. The other occupants of the bus all sat around us, but they no longer stared. They had become used to me by now. One of the local policemen stood staring very steadily at me and seemed to have forgotten all about his police duties. The party of women, as usual, sat inside the bus. This time on the far side, which was in darkness, their food was brought to them. The father looked after the baby while the mother had her food. I noticed three huge tribesmen from the desert drinking tea. They looked very fine dacoits, and I could imagine they were efficient at their job. That type of work has become less attractive since the King passed an order for the right hand of all apprehended robbers to be cut off. There had been a distinct decline in the popularity of this type of occupation.

There was a great trade in bread for people who had been in the desert all day and had eaten nothing because of Ramzan. They came into the villages to gorge in the evening. We took a stroll up and down the street, and every baker seemed to be busy baking a fresh supply of bread against the arrival of the next load of hungry people. When we came to pay for our tea, we were surprised when the driver said: "Oh, not at all, you are my guests." I am afraid we suspected his hospitality and that his real intention was to induce us to give him a bigger tip the next day. He had us there; we did not like to protest.

Off we went again out into the night. I sat watching the driver. He looked tired, but I was pleased to see that he had a spare driver sitting next to him on the box, so I could fall asleep with some peace of mind. I was awakened soon by the slam of the driver's door. The bus had stopped, and the driver had just gone out.

I opened the door beside me to get some fresh air but did not get it because the door was blocked by a huge white-cloaked tribesman who looked like a colossal ghost in the darkness. He must have been huge. His head reached as high as mine, and I was seated on top of a cushion in the front seat of a high bus. He spoke to me, which made me rather suspicious, and I was stupid enough to close the door in his face. At that, he went away to return with another man and then I realized that he only wanted to examine our permits. At every little village, we had this examination of permits. On these occasions, I always wondered whether it was a careful check or done out of curiosity.

I was much too tired to be interested in the villages we were passing through in the beautiful moonlit country. The only thing which kept me awake was the look of extreme tiredness on the driver's face, but he was wise enough to let the spare driver take a spell at the wheel.

I lost confidence in the new driver right at the start because he missed the gear change he had tried to make too late at the first small hill he came to. I was wide awake by this time. I thought that if the foot-brake of the bus were not keeping with the rest of the bus, it would not be very efficient. By this time, we had started to go backward. I immediately seized the handbrake and pulled it on hard. No one else knew of our near catastrophe, for they were all asleep. They soon got up when the driver changed into first gear because this made a terrific noise. I was very pleased to have been able to use that handbrake, for it had been annoying me all night. My legs kept getting entangled in it, and every time I got up, I found one of my legs numb. As the first driver took over again, I fell soundly asleep and did not awake till sunrise.

Soon I realized that we were drawing near to Kandahar. The name Kandahar has always fascinated me. I looked around but could not see anything more interesting on both sides of the valley than the *khaki*-colored mountains. I thought I had not missed much during the night, but I soon saw green trees in the distance and now the Customs House. It was a little bungalow with a small garden and a well.

The Customs Officer rested in the verandah, reclining in glory. At the same time, he ordered his juniors to run around and do his job for him. He stayed comfortably in bed, and I went off to sleep again as soon as we left. First of all, he tried to persuade us to go over to him. Still, when he caught sight of our permits, his curiosity must have been aggravated as getting him out of bed to come over and look at us was sufficient. He made a great deal of fuss and wanted to keep the permits. We did not relish the idea of being without our permits, but the driver assured us that they would be handed back to us later on. We had to handover to him.

CHAPTER VI:
KANDAHAR

We drove through the old city and on into the new part. The towns in Afghanistan usually have a "new town "planned outside the old city walls. We arrived at the marketplace, and again we were the sensation of the morning; I felt like a rare specimen of a monkey arriving at the zoo. It was very sad to say goodbye to the bus and all its occupants. I felt I knew them all so well, and the sufferings of the three hundred and ten miles' journey had cemented our friendship.

It cheered me up, however, when I was told that some of my fellow passengers were going on to Herat on the same bus as ourselves. The market looked interesting, and I was reluctant to leave it. By now, so many people had gathered around us that we were glad to have our luggage put into *tangas* and to head to the British Consulate. We said goodbye to the driver, gave him extra tips, and offered him money for our tea the previous evening, but he refused to take it. We still thought there was some catch, but the hospitality proved genuine. All Afghanis reckon foreigners as their guests. As the driver was responsible for looking after us on the trip, he regarded himself as our host. He had been very helpful indeed. We were glad to have the opportunity a week later in Herat to put in a good word for him to the Director-General for Roads in Afghanistan.

They knew at the Consulate that we were due, but as it was nine o'clock on Ramzan morning, all its occupants were still asleep. It was not long, however, before we had a most necessary bath followed by a lovely breakfast when I first tasted Kandahar grapes. I could not have imagined getting better grapes than those we had tasted in Kabul, but these had been sun-kissed. A special guest house was attached to the Consulate where we were staying. After eating, we went to bed and slept until lunchtime. The Consulate of Indian nationality proved to be the most charming and interesting host who, before his transfer to Afghanistan, had lived in Persia for twelve years. After lunch, he drove us to the old city, which at one time had fallen to the conquering armies of Alexander the Great. You could still see big ruined walls, and it was not difficult to reassemble them in one's imagination in the form of fantastic castles. I saw a princess sitting on the balcony, eagerly expecting her prince. I imagined him galloping at full speed towards the castle, mounted on a magnificent Afghan stallion, richly bejewelled, armed to the teeth-all to impress the sweetest lady in the land. My dream did not last long because the Consulate explained that if we wished to see the view from the top of the mountain. Baber's Mountain, as it was called- we would have to be quick, for the sun was already beginning to set. We drove up the mountainside as far as the road would take us and from there walked to a point where we came to steps hewn out of the rock.

The Consulate told us that this was the spot where in 1505, Baber took refuge with ten of his confederates for two weeks. Later to emerge, he raised his battle standard in the neighboring countryside and conquered the northern part of India. I walked up the steep steps to the top of the mountain and saw the small natural cave in which Baber was hiding. Except to the north, where a barrier of mountains limited one's view, you could see as far as the eye could reach. The view was one of the most inspiring I have ever seen, and I could easily understand how the dream of a Moghal Empire had been conceived on this spot

Now the sun was going down behind the mountains and throwing long shadows across the beautiful, fertile valley of Kandahar, a valley whose fertility made for happiness and contentment amongst its inhabitants.

Small wonder that Baber conjured up dreams of conquest when looking out from his nest across the valley. He saw all those green gardens lush with pomegranates, apricots, peaches, grapes, and well-irrigated fields filled with delicious melons.

From the top of the mountain, it was easy to see into the courtyards of the houses. The houses of the rich were built in an attractive style of architecture with a big courtyard to enable the women of the house to move about. Even at that, I could not help thinking that the poorer women. Most of them worked in the fields as they were much better as they were not compelled to live in purdah and, as a result, looked very strong, sunburnt, and healthy.

I was sorry to leave 'the inspiring surroundings of Baber's cave, and I retraced my steps down the steep broad steps with regret. The car took us through the gardens I had seen from the top of the hill. We reached a spot outside the town where there was a swimming pool surrounded by terraces of flowers and a cascade which flowed into a round pond covered with lotus flowers. It was a scene which Cezanne would have enjoyed.

The gardeners were coming to pray by the side of the lotus pond, and when they knelt, their figures were reflected in the clear water. On the ground beside them, they placed their long-stemmed pipes along with the big green and yellow melons with which they would break their fast as soon ·as they had finished praying. Everything was peaceful, and the efforts of the gardeners, this green valley illuminated by the dying rays of the sun, was for us more beautiful than any man-built church in the world. We slept well that night, for the nights in Kandahar were cool. The next morning after breakfast, we went through the town to the bank to draw some money. The bank was an old building in which most windows were broken. The driver called for someone on the first floor. Still, a policeman in a building across the road shouted to him that it was a holiday. We came to the conclusion that they were celebrating the last Friday of Ramzan. There was nothing we could do about it, for we were now in a country where time as such had no meaning, and what could not be done today could wait until tomorrow.

The Consulate, a Mohammadan, kept us company at every meal, for there are some rather charming rules in the

Mohammadan creed. If you are unwell, you are allowed to eat during the day, and the Consulate told us he felt rather unwell. I suppose you are forgiven so long as an illness does not appear too regularly during Ramzan.

At the bus stand, we were told that the bus would leave at four o'clock in the afternoon, but the Consulate said that the bus occupants would not go before they had broken their fast. It would mean a delay of two or three hours more, so we went for a walk. We had already sent a tanga with our luggage to the bus stand, and as we came to the gate of the Consulate, we met the *tanga* coming back loaded with our luggage.

We were then told that there was no mail as there was a holiday and the bus would not leave until tomorrow. We enjoyed our walk the more after that, for we could look forward to at least one more restful night in a good bed.

When we came in for dinner that evening, two other men were in the drawing room- one the Consul's brother and the other the Consulate's secretary. After a while, I asked them why their wives were not with them and remarked that I liked the women folk of the country very much from what I had seen of them. Their wives were in purdah, and one of them said that his wife, who had experienced more freedom in India, suffered greatly in Afghanistan.

He told me of an occasion when Mohammad walked in the street accompanied by a woman in purdah. During the meeting, one of his disciples said, "Come here, my son," and lifted the woman's veil to show the disciple that it was his wife who accompanied him. Many people in the street noticed the incident, and the disciple recognized Mohammad's wife.

"But how could the disciple have known it was Mohammad's wife if he had not seen her before? "I asked. He laughed and was anxious to see if I had understood the cleverness of Mohammad. Then he added sweetly: "So you see, Mohammad did not object to women showing their faces."

I asked him what he thought of Christianity. He paused for a moment and then said with what I thought was a great deal of truth:

"We recognize Christianity, of course, and it is very akin to our religion, but most Mohammadans think that Christianity tends to be an exclusive religion, partly because it does not seem to recognize many of the tenets of the Mohammadan belief. "Of course," he continued, "Mohammadans do not believe that Christ was crucified. We believe God would never allow a prophet such as Jesus to die the same death as a criminal. We believe someone else was crucified in his place. Jesus' friend asked if he would be allowed to bury him in his garden, and he put a Roman guard there. Naturally, it was all pre-arranged, for I do not believe people were any better in those days. They could easily be bribed. When Mary sat crying beside the grave, Jesus came over to her from the corner of the garden and said,' Do not cry; I am here with you.' Later he left the country, taking his mother with him. They walked all through Persia and Afghanistan and over to Kashmir, a famous seat of philosophical learning at that time." He said that Jesus is believed to have lived there to the age of seventy-two. I listened to the story with great interest. I was surprised to hear the same story in Kandahar that a philosophically minded Hindu in Sonemarg (Kashmir) had told me two months earlier. This Hindu had also told me that Christ's mother is believed to have died at Murree - a hill station not far from Rawalpindi on the way to Kashmir, hence its name. He continued: "I am told there is a tomb in Srinagar where it is said that Jesus was buried."

I told him I had been there two months previously and had seen the tomb. But little did I know then that it seemed a common belief in the East. The grave was on the way out from Srinagar towards Nagin Bagh. The temple, built around the grave, was in a good Kashmir style-architecture, with a wooden roof with grass on top, wooden sides halfway down, and the bottom half built of stone. In the middle of one big room was a wooden coffin inside a tomb that looked like an ordinary Mohammadan grave. Beside the tomb was a stone block on which the imprints of human feet were supposed to be those of Christ.

I noticed that they were the imprints of very big feet and that all the toes seemed to be of almost equal length. On the wooden sarcophagus were some words written in Persian, supposed to be by another prophet who lived at the same time as Christ. I had it translated by a Kashmiri, but I cannot vouch for the accuracy of the translation:

Ziarat Us-Asaf, Khanayari. Khawaja Mohamad Azam Dedamari in his history "Waqaat-iKashmir" Nasirud-din khanyari,

States as follows:

There is a tomb in its vicinity known as the tomb of the Holy Prophet, who had, in ancient times, been to Kashmir; his name was Us-Saf (Us-Asaf.) They were all very interested to hear that I had seen the tomb, and one of them said: "There you have the proof."

So I said: "Well, you are ready to believe this story at once. Why couldn't this story have been made up as so many others have been." He just shook his head and laughed.

I went on to talk about the Afghani's stubborn character and good physique. He told me with some pride of Alexander the Great's difficulties in subduing the Afghanis in Kabul. Alexander's mother wrote, admonishing him that such a great man as he was, did not seem to be able to master the Afghanis. Instead of a letter, he sent his mother three of the biggest Afghanis he could find to show her the type of men he had to handle. The queen called them before her and asked if her son had sent any gift by their hand. They showed her three boxes they had brought, each containing Afghan soil. She was very angry because they had brought nothing of greater value and ordered them from her presence. The Afghanis threw the soil out of the boxes on the floor and proclaimed that they were standing on their soil. "No one can remove us except by killing us," they said. She was very impressed with their attitude and realized what her son had to deal with.

Tor had a walk the next morning. It did not last long, for I soon heard his footsteps outside and the noise of a *tanga* coming to the door. "The bus is leaving in an hour," he shouted, "you must hurry." Very soon, everything was packed, and we rushed through our breakfast. The cook of the house, who also served as the car driver and his normal functions, took Tor and some of the luggage down to the bus.

Meanwhile, I talked to my friend the night before. I did not care whether the bus had left or not. Tor came flying back again to say that the bus had already left, but they had promised to wait for us by a petrol pump outside the town. It seemed that they were not keen on taking us at all, but after a short time, the Consulate took us in his car out to the petrol pump, and we arrived there just in time to show our permits before the bus started.

CHAPTER VII:
DOWN TO THE HELMAND

I sat down on my soft cushion on the front seat again but did not know where to put my legs around me. On the floor were petrol tins, my small suitcase, two thermos flasks, and two large hand grips. Tor was seated beside me on a bedding roll with his back against the bus door, which did not close properly, and with his feet resting uncomfortably amongst the petrol tins. Seeing our acute discomfort, the driver removed the tins, and then we went.

The bus from Kabul seemed to be almost on its last legs, but now I realized it had been comparatively luxurious. This bus was a joke; for now, I felt as if I was seated on some vehicle making its final journey to the scrap heap. It creaked and groaned as it crept along, and I expected the roof to fall any minute. As we went uphill, the roof moved backwards about a foot. It usually returned to its correct place, but not before moving to the left and right. The melons on the roof rolled all over it and the water *chaguls*, hanging outside to keep cool, banged vigorously against the windows. There was a big hole in the roof too, which added to our dismay, so in the end, I thought it would be a wise precaution to put on my topi in case the roof came down.

Tor started to look hurriedly through some papers and realized that we had not had our road permits returned. Without them, we could get nowhere. We asked the driver about it, but he did not look in the least concerned, and I wondered if this was part of the game. But presently, the driver stopped the bus and shouted to a man on the roof who came down, and I realized that the intention was that this man should walk back and get the permits. It seemed a surprising arrangement, for we had already driven quite a distance from Kandahar. Naturally, we wondered how the man would be able to catch us up again.

We went again, rolling along as happily as ever, but soon the bus stopped at a spot. There was a small stream on our left and a vineyard surrounded by a big wall on our right. The driver got out, looked at the tires, and told us we could relax until four o'clock in the afternoon, which was six hours. We had been warned that anything might happen, so we accepted the situation philosophically and searched for the most comfortable spot where we could lie down and rest. I at least ensured that we had some rest so they could have no excuse for leaving us behind. It was pleasant to lie underneath the trees, feeding the fish in the little stream. I was afraid not to give them much of my food because they were better off than we were, having the desert in front of us. I gave them what I thought was a reasonable ratio.

Tor, of course, slept immediately. He lay flat while I sat up and watched the life around us. Some of our fellow passengers seemed very interested in the vineyard and had climbed over the high wall. Others were bathing in the river. On the road, we passed donkeys and camels laden with grapes; among the camels, I saw a pure white one. I had never seen a white camel, so I was very thrilled. It did not have one black spot on its skin and looked more regal than usual as it walked along in the distinguished way that camels have. The blue beads around its neck and the colored headdress added to its distinction, and I am sure the owner felt very proud of it.

Even the donkeys are big in Afghanistan. One passed us carrying a beautifully embroidered saddle, wearing blue beads and bells around its neck. One can easily understand why the inhabitants of such a drab country long for color: Gay turbans, colored clothing, and red shoes are frequently seen.

A *tanga* arrived and in it was the man who had gone back for our permits. He gave them to us, laughed, and seemed to have enjoyed the extra trip. Of course, we paid for the tangas, but there was no question of bakshish. A beggar passed us, but he did not ask for money either. He salaamed us, and as he started to wash in the river rights in front of us, I am sure he thought I was a man for I was wearing slacks and my *topi* was on my head, so he did not see my hair. However, some of our friends from the bus soon told him to go higher up the river.

Our traveling companions came up and talked to us. One young boy told me he was a mechanic from Jalalabad and had been educated in Kabul. He had a Studebaker where he could go from Kandahar to Herat in one day. We calculated that it would take about three or four days at the speed we were making. The Afghan Army officer came over too, and soon we had a crowd around us, all enjoying a friendly talk. Being an officer, shopkeeper, or mechanic did not matter as long as the conversation was interesting. That was another characteristic I liked in the people of Afghanistan.

It was much cooler when we set off at about five in the afternoon; driving out into the desert again was pleasant. The landscape was varied today by the presence of the river, along the banks of which grew green grass, but I felt we were driving through a wasteland. As I was brought up in fertile, cultivated land, barren countryside always depresses me. My depression soon vanished when we arrived at one of these charming little villages. There were nicely shaped houses and picturesque wells inhabited by happy country folk whose main occupation was selling juicy melons to thirsty travelers. At every little place, the men rushed out to have a smoke. Even taking Ramzan into account, I could not understand how they succeeded in not yielding to temptation in the shape of those juicy melons. The chief aim of fasting is to teach self-control leading to a strengthening of character. I suppose it must make the one who fasts reflect now and again on the starving condition of many of his fellow countrymen. Certainly, the praying ceremony kept our companions busy during the trip, especially those on the bus roof, which had to climb down every time. I, too, enjoyed the evening prayer time, for it allowed me to sit quietly and reflect on the beauty of the setting sun and the subtle color of the mountains.

Sometimes the effect of the evening mist in the valleys was to make the mountains look as if they were floating in the air. As I sat there, a caravan passed by in the evening. My thoughts went back to childhood when I used to dream of being in the desert with a caravan. I was now sitting listening to the camel bells, each bell with a different note and all of them combining to make a lovely desert song. A friend of mine once told me that he tried to buy one of the camel bells in a caravan. He offered quite a lot for it too. Still, they said they could not sell it as it would spoil the melody, for the bells played in sequence as the camels moved along, and to take one of them would be like removing a note from the piano. The last camel passed slowly by on its way. The driver called us back to the bus. I was left wondering whether the camels had only existed in my imagination, whether they had been ghost camels or real.

We drove faster now, and the day-long fast was broken at a little village. It was so well timed that it appeared as if the villages had been situated so that the fast could be broken with minimum delay. I was always among the first to break the fast with a juicy melon which I had learnt to suck just as skillfully as any Afghan by now. We searched for tea, and I noticed that our tea cups were given an extra wash in the drain. The drains ran along the street where people washed their faces and other parts of their anatomy. I was glad I had the top of my thermos flask to drink my tea. But tea, bread, and grapes tasted as good as an expensive dinner at any first-class hotel.

The moon was full that night, and we drove without lights. I believe, in any case, that the battery was almost finished, but I was able to have the thrill of driving in the desert by moonlight. We were not disturbed at all by the speed of the bus, for we could have walked beside it. In fact, when we came to a steep hill, many of the roof passengers got down and walked up the hill. They took shortcuts and always reached the top of the hill long before us. I enjoyed that moonlight drive.

At about eight o'clock, I saw something ahead which I could not make out, but when the bus stopped, I got out, saw a big river in front of me, and realized that we had reached the Helmand river. The river was spanned by a bridge that looked gigantic in the moonlight. From what we could see, the bridge appeared very well constructed but was unfinished. Apparently, it would remain so because of the war.

We were told that we would have to ferry across the river, but it wasn't easy to do so as the intention was that we should go across that night or sometime the next day. There was supposed to be a good hotel somewhere on the far side where we could stay for the night. We asked again when the bus would leave and were told it would leave sometime about four o'clock the next afternoon. It sounded highly probable after our experience of the day before. Our little friend, the mechanic, offered to lead us across the bridge, for it was no means safe in its unfinished state. With the help of my torch, we managed to jump from one plank to another till we reached as far as the bridge had been built. We found a ladder down which we had to climb into a boat. The river was fast-flowing, and the ladder, which was shaky and home-made looking, seemed to have been made for acrobats and not for ordinary people. I left my suitcase and two coats at the top of the ladder and asked the boy to carry them. No sooner were we safely in the boat than I heard a shout and knew that one of my coats had gone. All I could do was sit and watch it in the moonlight going very fast downriver. It upset me a bit, as I had knitted it myself, but it might easily have been one of us. Actually, I thought we would have reached Iran much more quickly, judging by the speed of the river current.

CHAPTER VIII:
GIRISHK HOTEL

Girishk was the name of the little town we came to. In the moonlight, we could see houses and trees on both sides of the road. Our friend had handed us over to two other men to show us the way. They both spoke English and told me that the hotel was only about a ten-minute walk from the bridge, but that can mean anything up to an hour in Afghanistan. It took us half an hour to reach the hotel, and when we arrived, there was no soul to be seen. But we soon persuaded a man to go to the bazaar to fetch the hotel servants. The hotel was something like the bridge. It would have been marvelous if it had been finished and looked after. The bathrooms were lovely, with fine wash basins, long baths, and up-to-date sanitary arrangements, but no water came, no matter how hard you pulled on the chain. It was the same with the taps.

We opened the big French windows on both sides of the bedrooms. We soon fell asleep on the comfortable beds whose sheets had been slept on by several people before us. Our sleep was interrupted when a servant knocked at the door and brought tea and some hurricane lamps. I am sure they thought we observed Ramzan too.

The night was cool, and we slept well until some more tea was brought, but this time to the occupants of a room across the corridor. They could do well on tea, for they were singing and talking as loudly as if it had been daytime. But I enjoyed the company as I felt rather lonely in the big empty hotel, for Tor was sleeping like a log. I must have fallen asleep again because I suddenly woke up alarmingly when two men passed our windows.

I immediately thought it was the driver and his mate from our bus and that the bus would go off without us. I woke Tor and told him, but he was not interested. He merely said: "Let them go," he rolled over and soon snored again. After that, I could only toss fitfully to and fro, for the servants kept talking loudly and laughing. Then the moon went down, and all the cocks in the neighborhood started crowing, and even the servants tried to keep them quiet. But the cocks in this country are mighty fellows who kept on crowing.

At half past eight, Tor awoke, and I think he must have suddenly realized the significance of what I had told him in the night, for he dressed in no time and ran out of the room. I thought I had been left behind and ran after him. The first thing we tried to find out was if the two other guests in the hotel had left but, thank God, they were still there. We were very relieved and ordered a big breakfast. I think the servants thought us rather peculiar, for we were so pleased with having bathrooms that we ordered buckets and buckets of water and thoroughly enjoyed a good wash, so much so that one of the boys asked Tor if he wanted tea brought into the bathroom. Breakfast was served without knives and forks or even plates.

We wanted to see what the town looked like in the daytime, so out we went. We found a clean bazaar, drains on both sides of the street, and masses of fruit in the shops. The main street led up to a fascinating little fort. I had the feeling of looking at something taking place in a marionette theatre. I saw enormous men handling dainty bunches of grapes, walking up and down to the little fort. But the fort, of course, was not placed there just for the day's show but was firmly fixed there forever. The whole effect was enchanting.

On our way back to the hotel, we heard a splash in the water channel which passed through the hotel gardens, and then we saw one of the guests enjoying a morning bath. He sang lustily and happily but whether it was to keep warm or because he was happy was difficult to say. I sat on the hotel verandah in the shade of the vines while Tor went back to bed again. It was a consoling reflection that if the bus left us stranded here by any chance, there would at least be plenty to eat.

I was busy thinking of some of the lovely fruits I had seen when five men from our bus came into the garden and strolled up towards me. I was very pleased to see them, for I still had a sneaking feeling that the bus had gone. I brought them right into Tor's room. They asked us how we were and if we had slept well, one by one. They all went over and felt the springs and mattresses and were most anxious to know if the hotel people had looked after us well. They were so pleased when we said the hotel was excellent and apparently very proud of having a hotel like that in Afghanistan.

After all that, I felt rather ashamed of myself for having accused them in my thoughts of being capable of leaving without us. They all were, hoping that we had a comfortable night, although I am sure they slept in the bus. They told me too that they had been diving into the river looking for my coat and that the boy who had lost it had asked them to tell me how sorry he was. After this, I felt I loved them all.

They sat around us, and I drew a map of Europe to show them where Norway, our homeland, was, but I might as well have pointed to the North Pole, for it did not mean anything to them. They told us that they admired us for our courage in traveling in their country as we did. We got on so well that they stayed around us almost the whole afternoon. Some of them had already decided to make themselves home, for they were lying on the floor in our other room.

For lunch, we had the well-known Afghan "pulao" made. I think, with one of the cocks which had crowed all night. It was served in a bowl with curds, but I could not help thinking of the struggle they must have had to catch the cock. Before they caught him, he must have been chased all around the compound, for it seemed that his leg muscles were still stiff and contracted after the run. I made my main course out of the fruit, which followed the pulao. The fruit was perfect.

We were not surprised when they came and told us that the starting time of the bus had been put back one hour. I asked for three teapots full of tea. I wanted to drink a lot before setting out on the sandiest part of the journey. When the servant brought it, there were no cups, no spoons, and no sugar, but I am sure the Afghanis prefer to drink it directly out of the pot as it would be cleaner. After consuming four glasses of tea and one of water, I felt ready for the road. The bill for the night and food came to about Rs.11 for both of us, and the hotel proprietor seemed very pleased.

We walked through the town to the bus, waiting in the shade of some trees in a little park. The hotel boy looked very surprised when we tipped him for carrying our baggage. Tor had left his hat bag the previous night on the bus and was worried as there were many things in it he did not want to lose. We asked them if they had seen it. I am ashamed to say that there was a suspicion in my mind that perhaps it had been stolen. Here again, the driver had taken extra care of it and handed it over to Tor with a broad smile.

CHAPTER IX:
GIRISHK-FARRAD

Outside the town, the desert was much in evidence. A hot, dry breeze met us. The mountains on both sides of the valley were pointed peaks. The sand looked like waves, and I felt that the sea had suddenly dried and that we were driving along the ocean bed. As I was sitting at the side of the bus, I felt the movement of the roof much more. Whenever I saw a hill or a curve coming, I put on my hat to guard against possibilities. The bus was like an old dhow* trying to battle her way to safety through heavy seas. I sat promising myself that I would be good even after all my life if only I could reach Herat without getting that roof on my head.

GIRISH

Now it was prayer time again, but the driver did not stop. The other people did not give in so easily and ordered him to stop. I was rather sorry that the prayers did not last long. The moon in the East had a lovely apricot hue, and the sky was azure blue above the pointed mountains that rose out of the brown, wavy carpet of the desert. It made a perfect picture of color and perfect line for praying and meditation.

I kept turning around to get a glimpse of the moon, and Tor did the same, upsetting the purdah ladies who now had removed their veils in the dark. Whenever Tor put his elbow up on the back of his seat, they gave me a push in the back and made a sign to indicate that I should tell him to face the front. I got rather annoyed eventually over the fuss they were making. I wondered if these women realized that traveling on this bus, they risked their lives. This wretched bus was perhaps now making its last journey, loaded with baggage, thirty-five people inside, and ten on the roof. I was sure they would have been only too pleased to get male help if the bus were to turn over and certainly would not mind being pulled out of the ruins even if their burqa came right over their heads.

When he was called to examine a woman's throat, an English doctor told me that he found her standing behind a curtain in the room and sticking out her tongue through a hole in the curtain. At that moment, I appreciated my freedom more than ever. I felt sorry for the women who looked like lost souls in their violet, black and white burqas. But they chatted and laughed and did not seem depressed in the least. When they slept, they slept soundly too, and one of them was sitting, breathing hard from inside her veil down Tor's neck and kept bumping up against his back. She probably would have fainted on the spot if she had known it was a strange man's back she was bumping against. Her little twelve-year-old daughter, who had known freedom up to now, did not realize what was coming to her in a year when she would need to go into purdah. She was probably longing to copy her mother and become grown up. Well, is there nothing like doing what your parents tell you? They are always right. I was too wide awake by now to be able to fall asleep and was pleased when we soon came to a rest house. The saloon was full, so we had a lovely view from the big terrace in front of the rest house. Tables were laid out on the moonlit terrace. It sounds very romantic, but usually, when you look at the tablecloth, it is quite unclean, and you do not think there can be an iron in the whole country. But here, things were really clean. There was a wash basin and out of the tap ran real clean water. I could hardly believe my eyes when the water continued to run; the flush worked too, and the water disappeared without first floating all over the room. The sheets and the beds were clean, where we could lie down to rest if we wished.

The tea set was clean and unbelievably intact. We enjoyed a good meal because we had brought Norwegian tinned sardines and good fresh tinned butter to put on the Afghan bread. After that, I lay down and tried to sleep, but everything went round in my head. The noise of the bus continued in my ears, and as soon as I had settled down peacefully, someone outside would shout so that I kept thinking the bus was going. But by this time, I did not care.

We were surprised to find spring water here on a small hill in the desert. I asked an English-speaking boy on the bus, and he very proudly explained to me the ancient water system of Afghanistan. There are apparently miles of underground canals (called carez). They were cleverly constructed. There are shafts down to the water here and there so that they can check if the water is running. Thus, a caravan can always know where to find water.

There was plenty of water here, so I thought there must be fruit. After a while, I got up and went outside to enjoy the moonlight and beautiful view. The old castle on the right echoed the voice of the person calling to one of our passengers lost somewhere in the desert, and we had to wait for him before we could set off. He had fallen asleep on the ground nearby.

Off we went again in the old scarecrow. After studying the question of how to avoid bumps while sleeping at night, I had a good idea. I put my small pillow inside my topi, put the topi against the door, somehow fixed my head inside, and slept soundly. I did not care if the driver fell asleep or not during the drive the night.

It was not until I woke up in a bed in a hotel after a good rest and looked out of my bedroom window that I realized that the country we had been driving through and the surroundings of Farrad looked lovely in the early morning sun. Did someone say, "*Bahut Achha Hotel*?" (very good hotel?) From the noise, it sounded to me as if I was still on the bus with the added application of twelve wasps, fifty flies, and ten sand flies.

The remainder of what had once been blue silk curtains did something to remove the glare from the room, but the heat was unbelievable. The opening into the next room had been blocked with wooden boards, but you could easily have seen through had you been interested. Tor could not stand either; he sat in the room or went outside, but I cannot imagine that he was better off there, for Farrad was undergoing a heat wave.

I placed a net over my face and imagined myself in heaven with all the angels buzzing around me. My illusion soon changed to one of being in the other place, and the small sandflies were devils that even got through the net covering my face. I wondered what I should do if I contracted sandfly fever now. This time the pulao was made with lamb. Even in this irritating heat, it tasted pretty awful, and we were pleased to return to our grapes again, which at least always tasted of grapes. We were not sorry to leave this hotel, for the bathroom was indescribable.

The town, surrounded by mountains, turned out to be very attractive with green trees and the river running through it. The car assistant was very pleased to see us again, especially as he wanted to call me a *"Memsahib,"* which was the only Hindustani word he knew, and of course, when he said: "Jaldi, Memsahib," I rushed into the bus. He was so amazed at the effect of his words that he laughed heartily.

We picked up the purdah women further along the road. My main thought was to get my old seat back again, not be forced to sit, and make sure that Tor did not turn around and invade the women's privacy. Outside the town, we came to a bridge that had looked all right while approaching it. Still, when we were on top of the bridge, I realized we would not be able to get down to the other side unless we all dismounted, which we did. We went a good distance ahead in case the bus heeled over, but we would have been very sorry if our dear old bus had broken to pieces.

Another rule in Mohammedanism is quite charming: you need not observe Ramzan when you travel. Some used that rule, for they had their meals before sunset. I concluded that this bus' passengers were not as orthodox as those in the previous one. For the latter had told me that in no circumstances could they eat before the last golden reflection of the sun had gone from the last floating cloud. They watched that carefully too. Or perhaps they watched each other.

CHAPTER X:
LAST STAGE TO HERAT

One of the women in purdah suggested sitting by the door again. I was determined to have room to stretch my long legs this time, and I asked her husband to explain to her that I would change later on. In my heart, I felt sorry for her because it was a very hot day, and it meant that she would be unable to lift her veil and breathe in the fresh air. They were all so sweet to us, so why wouldn't I be considerate to her just because I wanted to be comfortable? They never bought melons without giving one to me, the best one too. They never wanted money for the tea they brought us, and I felt I could live among these people and be happy all my life.

The car assistant took great interest in me, and I thought he considered me peculiar. He would sit beside the driver and stare at me for hours. Once, when I had fallen asleep, I woke to find him sitting straight up against the door, staring. The end of my *topi* had fallen over my face, and I probably wore the funny expression sleepers usually have. The car assistant was delighted over my appearance and was broadly grinning when I got up. I got confused about finding him staring at me, so I moved over to Tor's seat because the bus had stopped, and he had gone out. There was a loud crack as I sat down and realized I had sat on my *topi*. The assistant almost died with laughter, and very soon, I saw the humor of the situation, and we both doubled up with laughter. Now that it had been established that I could enjoy a joke at my own expense, he rushed out to tell the story to all the others.

On the road, we halted beside a car that had broken down. Everyone got out to see if they could help. Our driver, who had been driving all night, worked on the car engine for about an hour until he had put it right. It was another instance of their honest friendliness. We discovered later that a few roof passengers had gone on in the broken-down car. I was annoyed that they had not asked us to go in it for we would have reached Herat much earlier, but later on, I was pleased for we would have missed the next rest house with its Moghal garden. We would have missed the fun of wakening the servants and the fun of seeing what these bathrooms would be like. Once again, I turned on all the taps, but nothing happened until I found a big tap in the corner and turned it on. All taps started running at once like fountains, and the bathroom and I were pretty wet before I came out.

The ladies on the bus and I became more friendly than ever after I had told them to put their legs up on the seat in front of them. It made all the difference to their comfort. A little girl had sore eyes, which I had treated the night before with yellow ointment. She was already much better, so they had gained some confidence in me. At one of the stops, the same little girl came to me with a green leaf, and it took me a long time to think what it was for. Suddenly it struck me that I had seen the Kashmiris doing the same thing when they wanted medicine. I asked her in Urdu if she wanted medicine. Her smile was like the rising sun, and the little girl got a good amount of ointment from me.

We were drawing nearer and nearer to Herat, and excitement was growing. However, there was still some very pretty country to go through, and it was lovely driving amongst the pyramid-shaped mountains. On the way, we met a large number of camel caravans. At night or in the early morning, we could see the men sitting around a fire, and the saddlery was nearby. At the same time, the younger boys looked after the camels grazing around them. But how the creatures could eat those hard thorn bushes, I could not understand. But a camel's teeth are so long that it can chew cactus without the thorns sticking to its lips.

I happened to sit down on a cactus bush when I intended to lie down for rest. Even though I wore corduroy slacks, I jumped about four feet. What I loved seeing were the sheepdogs surrounding the sheep. Once, we came around a corner, and sheep were in the middle of the road. The dog came and soon barked them all off the road. He then hurried back and barked at us to show how annoyed he was that we had come on him too quickly to find him a little unprepared.

The tribes had terrifying-looking dogs, a mixture of bull and wolf. We were told that only a few had escaped their attack. I also loved seeing the tribeswomen. They were as strong as horses and looked straight into your eyes. Usually, they carried a baby slung on their backs, or it was seated in front of them on a camel or a donkey.

The donkey caravans seemed more jolly than the serious camel ones. The donkeys were loaded on both sides with chickens, or sometimes there was only one big hen or one cock perched on top of the donkey. It symbolized the making of a good *pulao* or perhaps a cockfight.

I could not help turning round once when I saw a donkey coming along with a boy and a big sheep seated on the top. Of course, the Karakul sheep of Afghanistan is something of a marvel. But I pitied the poor donkey. I touched these sheep's "broad tail" and sincerely regretted it. The smell was worse than anything I had ever known.

At last, in the distance, we saw Herat. The road ran in a straight line for about six miles. Hence, the last part of our journey was particularly monotonous. I was pleased to learn they no longer intended to go in long, straight stretches of road.

Tor and I sat and discussed how big the lakes were roundabouts and the size of the sea. As we drove along, the sea became smaller and smaller, and at length, I said I believed it was just a river towards Herat. The lakes amongst the mountains had changed too. I knew all about mirages in the desert, but I was certain it was water this time. Strangely, there were no trees nearby.

Another thing I was amazed to see was melons on the ground. The country looked so dry that I wondered how they could grow at all. But here, one finds the wonderful underground water system.

Delicious fruit, tobacco, and cotton are all cultivated in the Herat valley. Silk is manufactured from raw silk obtained from silkworms.

Herat, once the capital of an empire, is today a town with about 30,000 inhabitants. With or without a river, Herat looked fascinating with its mosque and lovely buildings. There was no river outside Herat as we had first thought, but we had to cross a bridge built in the same style as the Chinese one we had crossed outside Farrad. It was certainly not built to take motor transport.

I was told later that the long straight road lacked one bridge to be a perfect road into Herat. The bridge had been swept away by a flood and never replaced, so now we had to drive around the whole town over all sorts of bridges to get into the center of the town.

We were asked to show our passports again. They insisted on keeping them here as well. But this time, all our friends on the bus took charge of our case, and it was not long before our passports were given back again. We knew from this that the people trusted us, and we felt we were among real friends.

CHAPTER XI:
HERAT

When we arrived at the marketplace, everyone was most helpful with advice and brought us tangas. Still, they were slightly puzzled when we each set off in separate tangas. Tor's horse was much faster than mine, so he was soon far away. The hotel, situated far outside the town, looked like a palace. Inside we met a man we thought to be the hotel manager but turned out to be the Chief Engineer in-charge of roads in Afghanistan. He was a young man who spoke several languages. Still, the European engineer we met later easily surpassed him, for he knew nine languages. He had been in most countries in the world. When he told us about his experiences, he infused them with psychological insight and philosophical observations, which made his stories very lively. Still, my friend, the mechanic, followed behind me in his tangas to see that I came to no harm.

FROM HIMALAYA TO SOUTH PACIFIC

HERAT PHOTOS

FROM HIMALAYA TO SOUTH PACIFIC

He told us that everybody knew we were coming, and there was great curiosity as to why we were traveling in that unusual part of the world that no tourists had passed through for years. He advised us to call on the Governor, which Tor did. Unfortunately, the ladies were not supposed to call. My husband told him about our enthusiasm for his people and his country. As a result, the Governor put his car at our disposal. Indeed, a very convenient arrangement for us, as distances in Herat were great, and cars were few. Just as we were about to start on a tour of Herat that the European engineer had arranged, the Persian Consulate unexpectedly arrived. He had heard that we wanted to know about conditions in Persia. We really wanted to know if we could get through Persia. Most Persian officials we had spoken to so far in Afghanistan had led us to understand that it would be very difficult indeed. The Consulate spoke only Persian, so the engineer acted as an interpreter. Unfortunately, the Consulate had always traveled to and from Persia in his car. So he was unable to tell us anything about buses or lorries.

The Afghan engineer was more useful. He at least assured us that he could guarantee us a passage to the border in one of his lorries. It would be possible to come back if we could not get any transport at the border to take us further. We were quite prepared to travel by camel for a bit if necessary. Judging from the country we had been passing through, there would certainly be villages where we could have melons and water to sustain us on such a journey. Meanwhile, the European engineer was anxious to start the Herat tour before the sun set and said that his car was waiting outside. He suggested that the Persian and his family follow us in their car.

As a breeze blows in the early evening in Herat, it was by this time pleasant and cool after the heat of the day. Outside the town, we came to a Moghal Garden equipped with a modern swimming pool. Here we stood and looked over Herat. It lay in a valley which looked like a desert at this time of the year, yet Herat was very beautiful. I spoke of the beauty of the place, and the Persian said: "I like the place, but my wife does not."

"Small wonder," remarked the engineer, "the place is dead, as all the women are in purdah. When we go to a sports meeting here at our glorious new Stadium, it is very dull without our women to cheer for the men and give the place gaiety and color. It is like a bullfight in Spain with no women present."

We returned to the hotel for an excellent dinner. The Governor had specially asked the hotel to look after us well, and they certainly did. The menu consisted of meat cakes, two or three kinds of *palao*, vegetables of all sorts, delicious tomatoes, grapes, and melons. Later we lingered in enjoying comfortable beds as long as we could. We never knew when we would be able to do that again.

Our friend had arranged to take us to see some of the mosques. He had friends among the priests and spoke their language; I believe we were highly honored. He told me to put on stockings. I understood what he meant and put on a woolen suit, high-necked blouse, stockings and gloves, hat, and veil. I laughed when I saw myself in my bedroom mirror. I looked like a tourist in India thirty years ago.

First, we went to an old, ruined mosque with excellent

mosaic work. He introduced us to an aged Persian whose family had been mosaic workers for generations. He and his son had taken up the craft again and had been given the job of redecorating this ruined mosque. We were pleased that they were keeping this old art alive and resisting the encroachment of cheap factory-made work.

Our friend became very serious when we came to the mosque, and I pulled my veil tight around my face. "A year and a half ago," he whispered, "nobody was allowed to enter the mosque." We went round the corner of a big wall into a garden with huge old trees and a pond in the center. The entrance to the mosque faced this garden, and many priests were sitting on the steps leading up to the entrance. Some of them were old and toothless, with long grey beards, some enormous and fierce looking.

The engineer soon found friends among them, and he greeted them in their language and signified that we could pass in. Our friend walked up to the shrine in the middle of the garden in the gentle way the Chinese have. He put out his hand and said: "Behold the beauty," and turned round to watch our faces. The work in the shrine was like the most delicate Belgian lace carved in marble. We went from one tomb to another on an ascending scale of beauty and, at last, came to the most beautiful of all. My friend knew this tomb well. He fussed around it and showed us how it had all been carved out of one piece of black marble and how natural the carved leaves looked on it. The work was so delicate that it looked like it had been made from silk threads rather than stone. Still, in some way, I was dissatisfied, for there seemed to be a preoccupation with detail rather than a desire to achieve significant form. It was craftsmanship rather than art.

We stood for a long time gazing at the tomb, and at a distance, the engineer said: Why are we so afraid that we shall be forgotten? Why did this man make himself this wonderful tomb?"

I could not help smiling when I saw another tomb in the corner, plain white and inconspicuously placed on one side to make room for the magnificent black marble bursting with splendor. Vanity was surely the motive behind the black marble one. I could almost see the man, full of pride and pomp, allowing with some condescension a tomb to be carved for his wife and allowing it to be placed in the same room as his tomb. His wife's tomb was the plain white one. It was not his fault that the white one was much more artistic. I imagined that the plastic quality of the white one had been achieved by leaving the design to an artist. The result was a tomb of pure, lovely lines. I felt the woman had been much more aware of beauty than her vain husband.

As I passed the *Mullas* on the steps, I wondered if, by sitting meditating in this old mosque with its beautiful old stone carvings. They got more out of life than other people. Some *Mullas* looked grave and had a serious air about them. Others looked gentle, kind, and settled. Were they getting more out of life than we who walked out in the sunshine and breathed the fresh air? I felt like throwing off my veil to show I could face the sun.

CHAPTER XII:
AN ENGINEER'S TROUBLES

In the evening, we went for a long walk, and our engineer friend told us how difficult it sometimes was to work in a neutral country with potential enemies within her borders. He told us how one night, a party had been given. A group of three men sat drinking. He was one of them; they were drawn together by having the same profession. Still, they never dared mention their countries of origin and had learned to be very careful about how much they drank.

It appeared that it was difficult to get good drinks. Our friend said a bottle of pure spirit was standing on a table. One of the men thought it was water and, being very thirsty, poured out a glassful of it, and before anyone could stop him, he had emptied the whole glass. That evening the subject of war had been touched on. Everybody had felt a little embarrassed, and now there was an impression that the man who had drunk the full glass had been tricked into doing it. An atmosphere of mistrust grew, and because of that, a man of another nationality poured himself out a similar glass from the same bottle and emptied it in one gulp, as the first man had done.

FROM HIMALAYA TO SOUTH PACIFIC

Our friend said he just sat and waited to see what would happen next, for the atmosphere of mistrust grew rapidly. "I was terrified what the reaction of the whole thing would be," he said, " and I was also frightened that the Afghans would see them. I was sure they would run out, create merry hell, and cause a scandal."

Being of rather a slight build and no longer young, I wouldn't say I liked the look of the whole situation, and I wondered if I should phone a doctor. I hesitated over doing so. They were now both soundly asleep, and the immediate danger had passed. Still, I did not quite know which nationality of doctor to summon. I was suddenly acutely conscious of the intolerable situations which can arise in wartime. The strain of being a stranger in a foreign country, with my family in trouble at home and two dead-drunk bodies asleep on the floor, was certainly more than I could bear alone.

One of the drunken men was of the same nationality as me, so I decided, to even things up, that I would phone the doctor of the same nationality as the other man. He went on to tell us how he waited downstairs until the doctor arrived so that he could tell him what had happened. The doctor went upstairs while our friend went for a walk, greatly relieved to have passed the responsibility on to someone else. He could remember passing the doctor's car and thinking what a sickly yellow color it had.

After that, he walked like a mad-man along the road and thought of his suffering people in Europe and how his son and daughter had become slaves of the Nazi regime. Knowing they both had his temperament, they would have a bad time in an occupied country. He thought about his wife, whom he had not seen for many years, and wondered if she was starving in her advancing years. He walked and walked; for how long, he did not know. Then he suddenly wondered if he had done the right thing to come out of the room, away from it all. He rushed back and arrived just in time to see the dreadful yellow car disappearing. The color worked on him like jaundice.

The following morning, he had a telephone call, and a voice told him that the men were all right, but one of them had a big wound on his head and that it looked as if there had been a fight. "I recollected," he said, "that one of the men had fallen off his chair onto the floor and that there had been a bang on the table just as he fell, but there was no point in trying to explain all this, so the atmosphere did not improve amongst us after this. We sat watching the sun setting over the desert."

"Look," he said, "when the last tip of the sun goes under

the horizon and leaves a tiny little blue light behind, you can wish, and your wish will come true." Of course, both of us saw that blue light that day, and of course, we both wished and wished hard. I thought this man must have sat there for three years wishing and wishing the same thing, and yet he probably still believed that his wish would come true. Whether tomorrow or in ten years did not seem to worry him, no wonder he asked me later: "Why do you think we live on this earth?" All I could think of in reply was to say: "To learn and to be conscious of our being."

He said he would feel very lonely when we left. "I am so afraid," he said, "that I shall die without seeing my people, but then again, there are times when I feel I am one with humanity, one with the whole universe, and then I am so happy. I have a firm conviction of immortality."

I thought how funny it is that some people who long for loneliness and the meditative life cannot escape from the claims of everyday existence while others, like this man who was surrounded by the real meditative background of calm and beautiful surroundings and who was friendly with the philosophers of the country, would not find peace until he had returned to the hurly-burly of life and people again.

We were sorry to leave Herat, our friends, and the nice hotel. The lorry had been ordered by the Director of Roads and arrived at the hotel at about eight o'clock in the evening. The front seat was comfortable and roomy, so I managed to twist myself into a lying position with the help of a few cushions here and there. I quickly fell asleep. On the other hand, Tor had much more room but had to sit straight up against the lorry's side. He was rather pleased when we had a puncture, for he could get out and stretch his legs. It was a very cold night with a bitter wind blowing, and I felt sorry for the man who had to repair the tire by the light of my torch while I could stretch myself at full length wrapped up in a camel-hair coat and blanket.

We arrived at Islamkala early the next morning. If there is a place God has forgotten, I think this must be it. Nevertheless, the people were very nice and looked after us well. When we arrived at the border, we were anxious to know what would happen next and if there was any connection to the border station. There were several camels in a courtyard, and I felt certain this would be our next form of transport.

Our Director of Roads had apparently instructed his driver to do his best for us. We were made to sit in a waiting room, and the Customs people came and looked at us and our passes several times. After a great deal of arguing amongst themselves, they told us we could get on to a lorry.

With relief, we realized we were safe for another part of the journey.

Once again, crossing a border gave me a certain thrill, but here I looked hard to find something to make it exciting, but there was nothing. It was just desert and no rhythm in the desert either. It was the deadest desert I have ever seen. The only thing I remembered that marked the occasion was the driver's remark when we passed a telephone pole lying on the ground. "Now we know we are in Iran." It was a remark similar to the one the Indian driver had made crossing the border in the Khyber Pass. We all blame each other!

CHAPTER XIII: INTO IRAN

At noon, we arrived at Karez, and it was a relief to see women out of purdah. We were asked to rest in the house's drawing room belonging to the Customs officer and his family. The room was furnished in bad taste, but it was very clean. We had our food but were served tea in two cups as small as liquor glasses. It was worse than anything, but as it was served with an engaging smile from an unveiled woman, we were so charmed that we dared not to ask for more. Afterward, we laid flat on the carpet and slept for two hours.

In the afternoon, our hosts served tea out of small cups. Tor said he did not want any, and she seemed very pleased to be able to drink it herself with me. She left the sugar behind when she removed the tray and smiled at me very understandingly. She was very surprised when I refused to accept the great favor she had shown. Sugar was scarce in that part of the world.

The hostess had three daughters and a sister staying with her, so we had a grand time while waiting for the bus. They were interested in fashion, so I showed them my dresses and some Kashmir photographs. They could hardly believe they were photographs of real places as they had never seen mountains before. They were very interested in my children. I showed them their photographs, and we discussed their clothes greatly. We did not understand what we said to each other, so I had to explain myself with the help of drawings. When I pulled a face at my passport photograph, they cackled like geese. They were sorry when the time came for us to leave, and the youngest little girl kept holding on to my skirt to keep me back. I thanked God that I had not been born and did not have to live all my life in a town like that. I asked Tor to enquire once more when the lorry for Meshed would leave. He came back immediately and said he was leaving in a minute. We rushed away from the happy family, who refused to accept anything for their hospitality. I sat down and made myself as comfortable as possible again in the corner of the front seat. By this time, I had figured out a good technique for placing my cushions and blanket.

The lorry was surrounded by beggars who looked very poor and ragged after the proud Afghans. Here the beggars seemed to be a mixture of Russian and Iranian. I noticed a particularly sweet girl who was just an onlooker. She wore a black shirt, trousers, and a scarf. She had lovely blue Mongolian eyes and a turned-up nose.

The beggars were driven away by the police, and one

obstinate beggar was soundly smacked over the face, and he cried like a child. Our driver turned up, unshaven and wearing a big cap, but he spoke English which was a great blessing. He looked very wide awake and not in the least Oriental. He said he had been to Russia, and I think there was considerable uncertainty about his antecedents.

As we drove once more out into the desert, I saw two tribesmen galloping off up a side road on two magnificent horses. The horses around Herat, Meshed, and further north are supposed to be among the best in the world. I enjoyed seeing how well they carried their heads and how confidently the men in the saddle were seated.

I awoke from my daydream to hear the driver say in a dark Russian voice: "I am very afraid, very afraid, there are many bandits on this road." He always said everything twice. "Do you know bandits, plenty here? I have got money," he said, "have you got money?" he asked. We said: "No, very little." He asked if we had a gun. We said: "No," again. "Very bad," he said, "Very bad." " They come in the night."

By this time, I had pictured the whole thing in my mind. We would be stopped by at least six bandits armed with rifles and be robbed of all our luggage. I regretted I had brought a fur, amongst other things. Later on, when we stopped for tea, I put my ring in my shoe, and we put whatever money we had in a pillowcase.

We thought it was rather strange that he had asked us if we had the money, for he could easily have arranged the robbery himself if he considered it worthwhile. That was my first reaction because he looked like a rascal to me. We came to a village where he went inside the walls and stayed for about an hour. I felt certain that he had gone to arrange an attack for the night. It did not make matters much better when Tor said: "Of course, this is the worst part of the trip."

Every time I awoke in the night, I felt the ring in my shoe and was reminded of the bandits. I dreamt very vividly about giving them my wristwatch so they would not go for my ring, which was of more value.

Suddenly I got up and realized we were standing still. I hardly dared to peep out of my blanket. The door was open. Tor and the driver had disappeared, and the cold desert wind blew on me. In front of us stood a huge loaded lorry. Through some trees, I could see an old, dilapidated-looking house. A man was snoring on a bench outside it, underneath a red blanket. He looked like one of the Seven Dwarfs in "Snow White". I wondered where the bandits could be and where Tor and the driver had gone. In and out of the rest house walked sleepy soldiers, stretching and yawning. Out of the big lorry in front of us came a man wearing a dreadful yellow sheepskin coat, and it all looked a bit mysterious in the early dawn. I sat still, waiting underneath my blanket. Then I noticed two of the soldiers who came out of the house. I did not realize at that moment that I was looking at Russian soldiers-fair, strong-looking men for the first time. No wonder I was surprised when they carried rifles and fixed bayonets. They distributed ammunition and loaded their rifles. I crept still further down into my hiding place.

They walked hurriedly behind the lorry I was in, and all the others looked in their direction. I waited, tensed for a shot to ring out. Fortunately, it was all imagination shortly after Tor returned from a desert walk. The driver came stretching himself, still sleepy, from the resthouse. Some camels passed, and it looked as if they were loaded with big pieces of marble, but I looked again more closely and realized they were blocks of salt.

We drove on again through some desert country. The only fertile parts were the melon fields. The small huts where the farmers lived were very strange in shape; some looked like a good design for a hat box, while others looked as if they would be useful in covering up an old smelly cheese.

We arrived at a walled village that, from the inside, looked comparatively modern. The driver wanted to stay here for six hours, but as we wanted to reach Meshed that day, he had arranged for another driver. We were sorry to change our driver because we had learned to like him a lot. He was of Russian parentage and had quick intelligence. He rose in our estimation when he would not accept anything extra for the trip. It was strange to think that we had mistrusted him.

I was shocked when I saw the next driver, who turned out to be the man in the dreadful yellow sheepskin coat. He looked a nasty type, and I never forgave him for making me sit on that dirty yellow coat of his. It must have been made from a very old ram because the smell was unbearable.

CHAPTER XIV:
MESHED AND THE RUSSIANS

Meshed appeared surrounded by water, but as usual, the water disappeared as we drew nearer. Someone told me the country outside Meshed was full of blossom in spring. This time it was late autumn. It looked brown and barren. The town lay in an open valley bounded to the northeast by a range of mountains ten thousand feet in height. The town itself stands at the height of about three thousand feet. The two domes with the four minarets looked impressive in the glittering sun inside the high mud walls that surrounded the whole town. Before going inside, our papers were very closely examined by strongly-armed Russians. I wouldn't say I liked how they stuck guns right up into my face.

We arrived safely at the market, but here the driver asked an unreasonable price for the small journey we had done with him. We refused to pay and said we would talk to him in the hotel, hoping to find someone who could reason with him. We took another car and managed to get hold of a man who said he would show us the hotel. But when we arrived, we did not believe there was any hotel.

We passed through a gate into a courtyard with a garden with a pond. A verandah ran around the entire first floor of the building and was quickly filled with interested onlookers. They popped out of their rooms wearing dressing gowns, pajamas, or whatever they had on at the moment. A great discussion ensued, of which we did not understand a word, but we could tell that it was all about us and a room. In the middle of this discussion, we learned that there was another hotel somewhere in the town, so convinced that it could not be worse than this one, we went off to find it.

The man who had accompanied us from the lorry became anxious about his money, so he started a terrible argument which affected the taxi driver. When we arrived at the hotel, everyone argued loudly, and we could not have made a very dignified impression. Had we known the people of Persia better, we would have known this was quite usual. The hotel was most peculiar, and the front looked like the entrance to a motor car shop. They had a room, they said, but no furniture, and I asked if I could see it. On my way upstairs, I met a man who understood English and volunteered to help. Eventually, we were told we could have a furnished room if we waited for four hours.

The English-speaking man was, I thought, a Turk. He said that he lived at the first hotel we had been to, which he maintained, was much better than this one, and he wanted us to go back and try again. Back we went, but of course, they were rather hurt by this time that we had gone away, so our chances seemed nil. People on the verandah still stood discussing us.

The lorry driver had joined us by this time and kept following us closely, telling the whole world exactly what he thought of us. We asked our new friend what we should pay for the trip, and he said the driver's price seemed reasonable. Later on, when we got to know the proper value of the currency, it turned out to be not too bad at all.

Eventually, we got a room, sat down thankfully, and had tea with the Turk. What his job was, goodness knows. He was an engineer. We talked about roads. If there was a worthwhile business in the neighborhood, he seemed to run it. Later, we met him again in Teheran and he told me he had designed one of the big buildings there. I said I did not like the windows he had designed in the building. He answered: "Well, it is difficult. I designed modern square windows for that building, but the contractors who built it did not like the windows, so they just made high French ones. That is typical of this country."

He enjoyed frightening me by telling me not to put on my best clothes when I walked about in the streets of Meshed. "They will shoot you for a pair of good shoes here." When I stood on the hotel's verandah and saw some prisoners shackled together being led along by armed soldiers, I thought his remarks might have some point.

I went into the bathroom, turned on the water, and let it run for half an hour to remove some of the smell before I went in for a wash.

The Consulate had asked us to stay with him, but as we were so grimy, we thought it unfair to go into a private home.

I came to like Meshed for it is amazing how much difference the people can make to a place. After we had been to lunch with the British Consulate and his wife, they pressed us to stay on. Still, we had decided, acting on the advice of our friend, to leave Meshed as early as possible. We had already made arrangements for this. When we arranged the next part of our journey with the British lorry firm, they served us tea in the office and told us that living in Meshed was not much fun since the Russians had occupied it. Even the members of the firm had to have passes to go outside the town. Drivers who had driven through Persia with goods were changed in Meshed before going further north towards the Turkestan border.

We were also told that if the Russians came to official parties, there were always about three of them. They talked little and stood together-one could never persuade them to go to private parties.

When we had arranged with the lorry people, they offered to take us around the town by car. In particular, they wanted us to see the world-famous mosque. It looked gorgeous with its two domes, one covered with gold which could be seen from a long distance in the glittering sun. The other dome was of deep blue colored mosaic, and the two presented an imposing sight.

FROM HIMALAYA TO SOUTH PACIFIC

Thousands of pilgrims visit the shrine every year. Many walked to Meshed, the third most important place for pilgrimage after Mecca. The shrine is built over the remains of Iman Riza, a descendant of the Prophet. The gates leading into the courtyard were of rich eastern design, done in colored mosaic, but from a distance, all looked like a mass of very strong turquoise blue.

I am told the walls inside the shrine are studded with precious stones. When the kings in olden times feared their loot being stolen, the holy mosque was the safest place to keep the treasure. A double purpose was served. The rich donations to the shrine brought spiritual solace to the conqueror, and it kept the treasures in the country. But what a pity that such wonderful collections should remain unpolished, uncut, and unseen except by a few.

How I wished I could get inside! I heard about a European lady who, dressed up in purdah, walked in with a Mohammadan friend to have a look at the jewelry. "Walk right beside me," he said, "Otherwise, you will get lost in the crowd and exactly do as I do. If I kneel, do so."

It was several years ago. If she had been discovered, there would have been unlimited trouble.

Next, we went to a place where turquoise was polished.

FROM HIMALAYA TO SOUTH PACIFIC

The stones are found in the mountains around Subzewvar and are of very high quality with a dark blue color. I asked our friend if the story was true about the man with such a valuable blue turquoise that he dared not leave it lying about in his shop for fear of its being stolen. He locked it up in a cupboard for months, but when he took it out to sell it, its luster had gone because of lack of air and light, and it had changed from lovely blue to green. "That is quite true," he answered. "We reckon a stone is worthless when it becomes green and should be worn as much as possible to retain its luster."

CHAPTER XV: NISHAPUR AND OMAR KHAYYAM

The lorry was supposed to come for us at about two o'clock but did not turn until about 4:30 pm. It was a big American truck. The front seat was only made for two, and it was not so pleasant to have three people in it. But to sit m the back of the empty lorry would have almost killed anyone, as we found out when we set off. We had become used to the speed of Afghanistan driving, about ten miles an hour. This was nearer fifty. I hardly had time to collect myself before we were outside the town. I had to look around quickly if I wanted to have a last glance at the lovely golden dome of the mosque.

Outside the town, the road improved, but I could hardly believe that the driver intended to keep up this terrific pace, driving an empty eight-ton lorry. My liver and kidneys had a good shaking. Then he pulled up with a jerk and came to a dead stop outside a tea house. The tea house looked very dirty, and we preferred to sit outside. The tea was undrinkable and served in very dirty cups. A mad-looking boy served sugar from old rusty tin, and he selected sugar lumps carefully one by one with his fingers. Finally, a cow arrived and went inside the house by a side door. The calf was accorded a special honor and allowed into the cafe. I was glad to be away.

NISHAPUR

We reached Nishapur in the evening. Here is the mausoleum of the war-famous Persian poet Omar Khayyam. He was born in Nishapur in the eleventh century, but he was introduced to Europe nearly seven hundred years later when Fitzgerald translated his poems into English. Unfortunately, very few Persians recognize Khayyam as a poet of any high merit.

He was known as an astronomer and to him goes the credit of having revised the Persian calendar. However, I wonder if he was responsible for the strange way in which the Persians record their time at present. Their day started from sunset and not from midnight to midnight. This method was rather confusing. For instance, what we called Sunday evening would be Monday evening with the Persians, and many funny situations resulted when engagements were made with them.

Just as most of our engagements were subject to the clause "Weather permitting," the Persians have "*Insha Allah*" attached to all their promises or ordinary talks about the future. This is because "*Insha'Allah*" means "God willing." Similarly, when they have to refer to something of the past, they supplement their saying with "Mashallah" which means "By God's grace."

We drove so quickly that I barely had time to enjoy the blue mist as the sun set behind the golden brown mountains. The country here was well irrigated by canals that ran down towards the villages. Suddenly we stopped again. As we again were tearing along in the night at a breakneck speed, we were suddenly stopped by a flashlight signal. Two well-armed Russian sentries appeared, one pointing a gun at us while the other cross-examined our driver, who, by the way, spoke Russian fluently. The soldiers were apparently not satisfied with his explanation of our identity because he made us get down from the huge lorry and stand in the beam of the strong headlights. This time at a very small tea shop in which lived two friends of our driver.

Despite our special Russian road travel permit, we were thoroughly cross-examined, and our replies were taken down word by word. These stern Russian soldiers left nothing to chance. Eventually, they became reassured as to our bona fides, accepted a cigarette, and wished us good night. I now saw the driver's point in going so fast. He drove madly to finish with the monotony of those miles of long, boring roads and to have a longer time at every tea shop or village. He must have been quite a lad in his way, this driver, for all the girls received him with great enthusiasm.

At one o'clock in the morning, we arrived at a village with a very pleasant little Bulgarian cafe. It was beautifully clean. Two women-mother and daughter-served the loveliest beef stroganoff, and the father served wine. The driver said he would stop for twenty minutes, but as we had already experienced his interpretation of twenty minutes, we did not wait in the car for a moment but went out to try and sleep.

After some time, I heard a violin playing polkas and someone clapping in rhythm. I went over to the window and peeped in. The son of the house was playing the violin, and the father and the driver were clapping their hands in rhythm and singing. At two o'clock, the driver came out to the lorry, followed by the other members of the household. The son was still playing the violin.

We had another mad drive through the dark night, but after half an hour, the driver stopped again at a house. This time he said he wanted to sleep, and we took him seriously, for he went inside the house, taking his big coat with him. I climbed up on top of the lorry, rolled out my bedding, and slept under four blankets.

In the morning, I learned that it had been below the freezing point that night. No wonder I thought it was a bit chilly, but the air was lovely and dry.

The stars and the moon did not keep me awake long. As I still wore my shoes, I did not put my feet inside the bedding, with the result that I awoke to find them as cold as ice. I was just awake enough to have the sense to put my hands under the blankets, for they were very cold, even with gloves on. So I forgot about my feet again.

The driver awakened us in the morning. I say 'us' because the car assistant was asleep underneath a sheepskin coat in the corner of the roof. He must have come up during the night, for I never saw him there when I climbed up to go to sleep. The sun was up and shining, but when I got on to my feet, I fell again, for they were quite numb with cold.

Standing on top of the high bus, I could see right over a wall into the funniest little village. It was an ants' hill enlarged a thousand times, only in this case, the ants had used mud mixed with water to build their small compartments inside the wall. I could not help being reminded of the small ants again when we were stopped on the way by some small boys who held up big melons for us to buy. As soon as we stopped, the small boys ran into a mud hut built underneath the ground and brought us up ice-cold melons. They tasted delicious and were most refreshing in the dry, dusty climate.

The sandy brown mountains looked lovely in the morning light, which infused them with varying shades of green and turquoise. Some were very high, and suddenly it dawned on me why the people had adopted beehive-shaped buildings. The mountains were terraced upwards in the same shapes, each beehive a bit above the other.

We passed tea place after place, and the driver popped in and out at each one and made witty remarks while having a quick cup of tea. I never saw him paying for his tea; he appeared to pay with his good humor. He was liked by both old and young.

He asked us to sit down and have tea with his friend at one tea spot while he carried out a little repair job. We were seated in a kind of office, and after I had finished my tea, I watched the Russian soldier walking up and down outside. He was Turkoman and was wearing big Cossack boots. Then I looked at some pictures on the wall. There was a photo of Stalin in his long overcoat, and beside it was a photo of a plane and another which I could not understand from where I sat. It looked interesting, so I walked across the room and had a close look. It was a photograph of some Russian pilots dancing to a balalaika in front of their plane. It was a charming photo. I suppose I looked for quite a while, for they were such a gay, happy lot to look at, and I thought of how Russian dancing and music were among the best in the world. Eventually, I went back to my seat again. I had hardly sat down before the Russian soldier came in and looked at me. Then he, too, walked over to the two pictures to see what it was which had attracted me so much. He stood looking for a long time and then walked out. It was a good thing I had looked at the right kind of picture. I felt uncomfortable, reflecting on what living in a country must be like where every action was closely watched.

By now, I had begun to enjoy the fast speed at which we

were driving and liked the way in which the driver made the best out of every small stop we had. At midday, we arrived at a village where the bazaar shops were filled with fruit. Once again, we had a collection of curious children around us who were very pleased when we gave them fruit. Four small boys sat round half a melon and dipped their fingers into it, eating only the seeds. Unlike Europeans, they ate nothing of the solid part of the melon.

Only one little sensitive-looking boy was not as shy as the others, or perhaps his longing for something novel was stronger than the others. He followed me wherever I went while the other little boys sat in a corner and ran every time I looked at them.

He was pleased when I took out a pencil and drew a cat on a piece of paper for him. I also drew a picture of his friend who wore a national costume. They did not seem to be very impressed with the drawings, but when I drew a lorry, they both cried with delight and asked for another drawing. I had struck the right thing, for now, all the other shy boys came too, and all wanted lorries. So I drew as quickly as I could, lorry after lorry, and they snatched them out of my hands even before they were finished.

Luckily I had sufficient paper, but my lorries had to become smaller and smaller to economize on the paper. A little girl came and held up her hand for one. By now, the boys had a fight every time a drawing was ready. So I made sure the little girl got hers by placing it right into her hands. The little girl's mother came up, and she and the little girl went away with the piece of paper as if they had been given some contract and had to hurry up in case it would not be implemented. The boys looked at the little girl as if it was hardly fair that she had been given an advantage because of her sex.

I was scared to death when one drawing fell underneath the lorry, and the boys tried to get it. The lorry assistant had to climb down and remove the boys forcibly, as, by that time, there were about ten lying underneath the wheels.

We stayed in this little village for four hours, so I had time to study each little boy. Even with the same education, I could see how they would all grow up differently, developing separate characteristics which were already apparent in them. Two of them had clever, intelligent faces, while one or two looked like they would turn out rascals. It must be a difficult task to be a schoolmaster in Persia.

We were stopped at the crossroads into Sharud to have our permits examined. Here again, there were Russian soldiers armed to the teeth, watching the crossroads and stopping every car and lorry. The drivers' passes, too, were examined. There was another lorry at the crossroads, and a rather attractive-looking officer stood talking to the driver of this lorry. We thought he looked as if he would be able to speak English, so Tor spoke to him.

He turned out to be a Russian, and what little English he spoke, he had learned in the last war. But really, he spoke it so badly that it could hardly be called English at all.

A lot of remarks were made about our red-colored passes, and they wondered what nationality we were. We told them that we were Norwegians but never expected them to know where Norway was. Then to our surprise, the Russian officer drew a circle on the road, pointing to the North and South Poles said, "Nansen" and "Amundsen." This officer was the only Russian we came across who spoke to people other than of his own nationality.

CHAPTER XVI:
END OF THE ROAD

Not far from Sharud, we went through an attractive pass that reminded me of the Khyber Pass. If I had known at the time that a bus had been attacked at this very spot on the previous day, perhaps I might not have enjoyed the pass so much. The story was that six tribesmen, with one rifle, stopped the bus and thoroughly looted it, extracting about a thousand tomans from the poor people who were traveling. Unfortunately, another car came up just as they had finished looting, but the tribesmen managed to escape.

Although there was a watch tower at the summit of the pass, which gave a good all-around view, it was a good place for a hold-up, for the dacoits could easily make a quick getaway among the hills. From the top of the pass, we could see Sharud not far away, nestled in the valley surrounded by mountains.

Sharud meant the end of our journey by lorry. We would proceed by train from there, and you can imagine how pleased I was to catch sight of the little town. The driver, of course, told us that if we wished, we could go on Teheran by lorry, but I would have been shaken to pieces had we done that.

Our permits were examined again outside town, and we were driven right up to a hotel. Our expectations in this direction were not high after our previous experience, so we did not question Toman, a Persian silver coin worth about one rupee, where we were told to go, which was through a wine shop, down some steps, and into a garden where a group of people stood talking.

As far as we could make out, there was no room once again. We talked and talked, but no one could understand us. Then, at last, a young boy who could speak English told us there was only one room available, but it currently contained three men. We told him we could sleep in the garden if necessary, but he said: "It is very lucky for you because my friend and I will give you our room and move into the other room with the three men." I agreed with him that it was very lucky, and I also thanked him very much for his officer and told him how kind he was. He was so delighted to be able to do us a favor that I started liking the Persians from that moment.

The young boy and his friend moved out immediately, and we moved into the vacated room, which had the only bathroom in the hotel and the only wash basin. But you can imagine what it was like when all the guests brushed their teeth and washed themselves immediately outside our door, which would not close properly. So I put all my suitcases in front of the door before we went to sleep that night.

It was still early in the evening, and we went for a walk in the town, which had attractive broad streets with water channels on both sides. Everybody stared at us, and it was unpleasant when nobody could understand us when we talked to them. I suppose the Persians thought we, too, were Russian, for the Russians occupied a whole street of houses. We were just on the point of turning back when approaching us up the street came two young men-one I guessed to be a Turk, and the other could be nothing other than an Englishman.

They came up to us, and it turned out that they were employees of the company in whose lorry we had traveled.

It was good to talk with someone who understood us for a change. They pressed us to come and stay at their bungalow. But after all the trouble we had had in getting a room, we did not like to hurt the feelings of the two young men who had moved out of their room for our sake.

They were on their way to the telegraph office and asked if I would like to go with them to see a little more of the town. I accompanied them while Tor said he would be happier near the hotel, for he had eaten too many melons lately. We had to wait for about two hours to contact the nearest town by telegraph. The man who was supposed to be operating the telegraph service kept going out first of all for a meal and then for a smoke. I realized that patience was more necessary than ever before. So the three of us sat down, content to wait, and began to talk about other things.

I told them about the terrific pace at which their lorry had been driven, and I said that I thought their lorries would not last many years. They both laughed. "Years!" they said. "We put them into the workshop for repairs after a month on the road. The drivers are well paid, for they are scarce and do exactly as they like on these long roads. It is quite impossible to control them, but if they have an accident, they are put in prison for six months." They told me that tires in Persia cost five thousand tomans each, and one could easily understand what a temptation this was for the drivers. A whole lorry sometimes disappeared, and no trace was ever found.

On the following day, we had lunch with the Englishman and the Turk at their bungalow. They had a woman to cook for them, but it did not seem to make the food much better than the normal fare served to us in Persia. The fruit was lovely, as usual.

The fact that from now on we would make our journey

by train did not mean that we had left our troubles behind, for we immediately met the problem of how to get a ticket and a seat on the train. Unless we happened to be personal friends of the station master, it seemed almost impossible. We were told that we might be able to get a seat for the following day, but we would have to pay twice the normal fare. We decided to chance to wait until the following day and returned to the hotel.

Quite a number of people intended to sleep in the hotel garden, and as I lay in my bed in the stuffy room, I envied the fresh air and the clear moonlit sky. I fell asleep thinking of all the people who would come in the morning to disturb me with their morning wash, but I could have spared myself that worry, for they never appeared. Whether it was that they did not wash at all in the morning or if it was that we were early risers, I do not know.

The Turk came in the morning with a lorry to take us to the station and to help us with the difficult process of obtaining tickets. Somehow he looked as if he was very proud of being able to drive such a big lorry, so I asked him if it was more difficult than an ordinary car. He had asked the driver to sit behind and said he had intended to drive. The driver looked slightly surprised and saw his face change, but he went behind without a word.

We went on talking as we drove along. The road was flat except for a little incline down towards the station. I think we were going at a good speed to show off, and as we went downhill towards the station, the Turk put on the foot brake, but it did not work. He then bent forward to put on the hand brake, but that did not work either. He then naturally turned round to curse the driver for the state of the brakes, and by this time, it was too late even to change down into a lower gear. We were very near the station buildings by this time, where there was little room to maneuver, and the only thing he could do was to steer right into some bales of cotton lying on the road. We went right into them with a terrific bang, and they acted as a spring buffer. We were lucky. The big lorry just seemed to shake off something unpleasant, and that was all. I enjoyed the exchange of looks between the driver and the Turk. He did not say a word to the driver, which rather astonished me. Still, it certainly demonstrated once again the strong position of the driver.

I was asked to stand and watch the luggage as already there was around us a collection of boys whom, from their looks at least, one could hardly trust. One of them impressed me. He was a cripple with no legs, but somehow he had managed on his own to climb onto our lorry when we started and had come down with us to the station. He was first out of the lorry again and appeared right in the center of the other boys. But his habit of pushing himself forward was, I think, a part of his technique as a disabled person so that people should not forget him. He had a very intelligent face, and I was told he made a lot of money.

I was sorry to miss the argument which must have taken place over the tickets, but anyway, the most important thing is that we got them.

CHAPTER XVII: TEHERAN TRAIN

Eventually, the train arrived, and we all rushed onto the platform to get a seat. We were lucky to get two window-seats. The boy from the hotel sat down in the compartment with us to prevent people from filling up the compartment- but the contrary happened for everyone. He seemed to come and talk to him, and the compartment was overflowing in no time.

TEHERAN

A young mother entered, accompanied by her five-year-old son and carrying a baby in her arms. The boy was ill, and when I tried to make him smile, he only looked at me with hungry eyes and seemed to blame me for having taken the best place in the compartment. We found out that he had dysentery and was going to Teheran to be cured. Tor, sitting next to this family, was suddenly surrounded by the most intimate baby clothes hung up anywhere to be dried.

Whether they were washed or not, it did not matter, and I shall never forget his face when a white nappie was placed on a table right beside the grapes he was just about to eat.

Later, the mother tried to fasten the nappie outside the window so it would dry in the breeze made by the moving train. The baby's trousers were hung up right above Tor's head and fell down every few minutes.

We did not want to tell them what we thought about it all as it would only have created an unfriendly atmosphere towards us, who were foreigners in a foreign land after all. But it was difficult to restrain ourselves.

People kept on coming in from the third class

compartment to have a sleep in our first class one, but how they could sleep, I cannot understand. They talked and shouted at each other and seemed to go through their entire life story to every newcomer.

Suddenly a waiter came with a tray loaded with tea cups, and apparently, this heralded meal-time. Everyone became very busy pulling out parcels of food. One man was a bit clumsy when he reached for his bundle on the rack, and the contents fell right on the head of the mother and her sick children. Later I wondered if he had done it on purpose, for the woman sat and blamed fate that she already had two children at the age of twenty-one. She blamed the whole world, too, for her children's illness.

The poor child was so hungry that he threw himself at his food and ate like a little pig. I looked to see what he was eating, and to my horror, it was curry and rice with meat. I was very upset and did not know how to tell the mother how wrong she was to give that kind of food to a child suffering from dysentery.

I had hardly had time to look out and see if the country through which we were passing was interesting, but it definitely was not. There was only salt desert. The salt gave the effect of patches of snow lying here and there. It looked as if *Lut's* wife must have traveled this way and turned round a couple of times for all this salt to have been left behind. Big lakes appeared here and there and occasionally relieved the monotony, but these always turned out to be mirages.

Now the train rolled into a town, and one could see the gorgeous domes and mosques. The town was Semnan which is one of the great caravan centers of Persia, lying halfway between Teheran and Meshed, with Mazanderan to the north and the vast salt desert to the south. It is curious to think that there were forests and cultivated land in the olden times where now we find the salt desert. The country must have benefited in those days from the Carez system, which even to this day is found· all over Persia. If modern engineering methods were applied, it should be possible to make the desert into fertile land and restore the famous old Persian gardens.

Here again, we thought it best to limit this compartment, if possible, to only the fifteen of us who had been there all the time. The compartment was, of course, really only built for eight. But alas, a servant carrying a huge basket overloaded with fruit came first. I was anxious to see to whom this belonged. · As I had imagined, following the basket came a jolly fat woman with red lips, high-heeled shoes, and dressed in a silk frock that fitted like a glove. As she came in, she talked and laughed with the two women who were following behind her. They looked prosperous and happy. All three sat down and occupied the whole bench, but they told me I need not worry, for only the first fat, jolly woman was traveling on the train. Then this woman's husband arrived, and we were introduced. In less than five minutes, we knew more about her husband and daughter than I knew about people I had known all my life. Her husband was certainly a fine-looking man, six feet tall, and the jolly woman told me that she married him because he was so attractive to look at. She herself was a Catholic and had great difficulty getting permission to marry him-a Mohammadan, but "Never mind," she said in her broken English, "I like him very much." She liked her only daughter, too, just enough, I understood to make life a bit more interesting and not too troublesome.

She told me that she did all the cooking in her household, and as her husband was a fairly high Government official, I was rather surprised to hear this. When, later on, I saw what food meant to her, I could well understand that only delicacies created by her own hand could satisfy her appetite. Moreover, she told me that she kept traveling between Teheran, where her daughter attended school, and Semnan, where her husband lived.

Her daughter, of course, was more or less a genius. Her

husband needed a great deal of looking after her. The servants, she complained, did not give him enough to eat when she was away, but judging from his healthy appearance, I reckoned she could easily have stayed away for a couple of months before any ill effects would have been noticed.

She explained to me that she kept her basket of food handy so she could dip down periodically and pick up a biscuit. If she did not have something to eat every half hour, she would feel some stomach pain. The child with dysentery looked at her with large hungry eyes every time she put a biscuit in her mouth, for biscuits could not be bought by ordinary people.

There were many halts on the way. Once, the train stopped in the wilderness and, looking out, I found everybody running as fast as they could across to some men selling bread and melons.

Bread in Teheran was dear, I was told, and almost unobtainable. In Afghanistan, they roasted the bread. In Persia, they had the same thin bread unroasted, and when they went shopping, they hung the bread over their arms like a hand towel.

At another station, we heard raised voices outside our

compartment. Apparently, a girl had been given a second-class ticket for the same amount of money as one should pay for a first-class one. So, naturally, when there was no room in the second class, she wanted to travel by first class. But the train police and the conductor insisted upon her paying more. She was a most attractive Persian girl and used all her womanly charm on the railway officials. She might have been successful too, but she had a friend traveling with her who had five children, and this friend said she could not afford to pay more than second class. So the loss of money on seven tickets was too much for the police and the conductor. Still, eventually, of course, they all landed in our compartment.

The train moved, and in no time, all sorts of discussions were going on in high gear. The woman beside me said that she was sure all the railway officials tried to squeeze more money out of people who had to travel by train. Her husband, she told me, had tried to stop this racket on the tickets, but it was difficult for everyone involved. I could understand how it arose, for they all seemed to me to be very underpaid. How could they possibly live on fifteen tomans a month when a pair of shoes cost one hundred and twenty.

The good-looking Persian girl entertained the whole compartment, and the corridor was packed with men looking at her in no time. She seemed to speak most languages and was a good representative of young Persian womanhood who had emerged from *Purdah* many years ago. I was told by a European who had been in Persia during the first years of freedom that the Persian girls had no idea of how to dress in European style at that time. If a European woman came into a shop, all the Persian girls rushed after her to see what she bought. Whenever she touched a particular piece of material, it was sold out in less than ten minutes.

Once again, I made an attempt to concentrate on the scenery. It was still desert, but it seemed to be varied now and again by green hillocks. I am not sure whether grass gave the green color to these hillocks, but I think it was the stone itself. It was very soothing to the eye and looked magnificent in the setting sun.

It was growing dark, and the conductor came round with electric bulbs which were taken out during daytime; otherwise, they would all have been stolen, like everything else detachable on the train. One could not open the window because the handle had gone.

With her five children sleeping all around her, the mother looked like mother earth. She was so happy and gay and, by comparison, made the other mother. The latter constantly complained about her two children, ashamed of herself.

However, we were by now all very friendly and knew everything about each other. Because for a long time we had been shouting at each other above the noise of the train and the other passengers. By this time, my head felt quite dizzy, and it was with relief that we arrived in Teheran at about nine o'clock in the evening.

CHAPTER XVIII:
OVER THE HILLS TO THE CASPIAN

We had been told that it would be difficult to find hotel accommodation in Teheran, and so it was. The driver who took us from the station realized that we had not been there before and drove us around the town at least three times before stopping at the hotel. For this, he charged us a small fortune and, at the same time, tried to convey the impression that it was only because of him that we had managed to get a room in this small, peculiar hotel.

We were very pleased, however, to get accommodation at all. By comparison with the hotels we had become used to, it was like paradise.

There was a wash basin and a tap, and I looked forward to washing all my clothes. Still, I was somewhat disappointed when I had to call a servant whenever I wanted to let the water out, for it would not run away.

The other hotels in Teheran turned out to be really excellent and up-to-date. A Norwegian whom we met the following day asked us to come and stay with him, but as we intended to go right on to the Caspian Sea as soon as possible to live in a green country for a change, we did not think it worthwhile to accept his offer. Thinking of the future, however, we said we would be delighted to stay with him on our return to Teheran from the Caspian.

THE CASPIAN SEA

Once again we were offered help with the problem of getting train tickets for here we met the same delay. But our friends were very proud that they managed to get tickets for the following day. The secret to success in obtaining seats was to get to the station early, and we were lucky to find comfortable first-class window seats. We sat there for about three-quarters of an hour, waiting for the train to go. Our compartment soon became filled with Russian officers. Amongst them was a Russian girl who interested us very much. She, too, was dressed in uniform and had short cropped hair. A boyfriend sat next to her, talking in whispers for a long time. We soon attempted to strike up a conversation with the officers, but by their curt replies we realized they did not wish to talk to us.

Five minutes before the train was due to leave, a Russian guard came into our compartment and asked if we were Russians and added that all first-class compartments were reserved for Russians only. We realized we would have to be quick and rushed out and found an empty compartment in the very next wagon, but it was locked. On our request to the guard to open it, he replied that it was reserved. We asked:

"For whom?" But he would not answer. Later we found that the Persian guards had reserved the whole compartment for themselves to sleep in. He was furious when we ordered him to open the door for us.

The first part of our trip went over the same route we traveled when coming into Teheran from Sharud. Still, this time it was in the day- time and therefore much more interesting. I could watch the lovely volcano-shaped mountain stand out quite alone, rising to a height of eighteen thousand feet. It reminded me very much of Fujiyama in Japan. Standing in dry desert country, the wisps of cloud around it were broken by the sun's rays to make the most delicate pastel colors. Its peak, which was just visible, was covered with snow, and sometimes the snow cap shone golden pink.

Looking at it, I wanted badly to climb it. Why I did not do so, I cannot understand. It could easily have been done from Teheran in two days, just by sleeping in the open at night. The weather was ideal at the time for the purpose. Still, the idea of having a bath in the Caspian had entirely possessed me. I was frightened that something would prevent me from feeling the Russian salt water which I imagined at that time would be just as salt as the Dead Sea. One of the Norwegian engineers of the company, which had built the railway through the mountains over to the Caspian Sea, had told me some of the difficulties they had met in building the railway, so we followed the passes with great interest.

I loved watching the twists and turns that the railway took as it climbed slowly upwards. Somehow it created in me the same feeling that I had felt when I read of the introduction of the train up to Trondheim in Norway as a child. It disturbed the Dovregubben. He was a big giant who lived in the mountains before the advent of civilization. Our present engines were having great difficulty pulling the train up the hill. Had I been a child, I am sure I would have thought that once again, it was a giant and his family pushing the train back.

We reached the seven thousand-foot summit, and the engineer had told us to watch the landscape as we went down the other side. It was extraordinary how the country running towards the Caspian Sea at once changed into the most green and fertile hills. It was a kind of vision for us, for we had not seen so much green since Kandahar. What a railway! When I looked at it, I felt very proud that so many Norwegian engineers had had a hand in building it. I had seen pictures of it and had heard a great deal about it, but to be able to see almost at once the whole railway descending from seven thousand feet to below sea level within a comparatively few miles was worthwhile. I enjoyed running from one window to the other as we went round curves to be always on the side, which gave a view. Sometimes the curve was so sudden that I became confused and finished by looking straight into the hillside.

Sometimes the train would go into a tunnel and, before it emerged again, would almost complete a circle inside the mountain. I knew when a circular tunnel was due, and I had a big glass of water ready to see the water turning round inside the glass. I had cloned the same thing at home once on the Romsdal railway, and it was fun to do it near the Caspian Sea.

As we went downhill, the night was falling, so now, as we drew near the sea, the whole valley became like a dark green picture disappearing out of focus.

For several months before this, we had been living at the height of about four thousand feet, and coming out of the train below sea level was like coming into a beehive, for my ears sang. My head felt three times its size. It made us tired and bad-tempered. The station was Chahi, the nearest place to the big hotel by the Caspian Sea, which we wanted to see. We had meant to go straight to the coast, but it was dark now, and as all the taxi and bus drivers looked rascals to us, we did not feel like putting our lives and luggage in their care. So we made up our minds to go straight to the nearest hotel.

All our possessions could easily have been stolen that night, for we could not lock our bedroom door, and our heads were too thick to hear anything. There was something we heard most of the night, however, and that was the Russians singing in their barracks right across the road. I did not mind it at all, and I managed to tune it in with the rest of the noises going on in my head, so I had a full orchestra right up to three o'clock in the morning. Anything was better than that terrific pressure on my ears and eyes.

We rose early the next morning to try and get a bus, a car, or a lorry to drive us out to the Caspian Sea. I did not get any further than the corner of the hotel. From there, I could see lovely Demavend still surrounded by its dreamy atmosphere, and I stood and watched the mountain for a long time. Eventually, we heard of a bus or car bound for Babolsar. Still, getting anything fixed for a certain time in Persia is extremely difficult. It must be an ideal country for a philosopher. They say "morning", which means "afternoon", and turn up the following day or, if you are lucky, the day after that.

So we resigned ourselves to having breakfast. But, unfortunately, the plates were dirty, one egg was bad, and the tea was cold served without sugar or milk. The pressure on our ears was still unpleasant, and it did not make things any better when a man came and stood outside the window making faces at us.

When we signed him to go away, he laughed like a maniac and rushed off, only turning up at the next window with a new idiotic expression on his face. The whole thing did not even raise a mild smile, especially when we were grossly overcharged for our room which had dirty sheets on the bed and no place to wash in. The food too was very bad. When we came to pay, we asked them why they had kept the hotel at all. Still, I regretted saying it, for it looked as if there was a kind of understanding between them and the driver Tor had gotten hold of. When the driver saw that we did not give the hotel people big tips, he was not too keen to take us to Babolsar.

We were dying, however, to get down to the sea to the comfortable hotel in Babolsar, which we had heard so much about. Eventually, we succeeded in getting off. The road went through rich fertile country, and my old love Dema, turned up now and again as we swung along the road. Soon I could feel the smell of the sea in the air.

CHAPTER XIX: BABOLSAR

When I saw the beautiful blue-greenish water, I could hardly believe that I had finally arrived at the sea I wanted so much to bathe in. My headache disappeared in a flash, and I looked for something new and exciting. I was surprised when the scenery again reminded me of something I had seen before, for here were the sandbanks of Denmark's coast. Only the color of the sea was different. It was quite unique, and I had not seen anything like it.

We arrived at Babolsar. The hotel looked like a palace with nicely laid-out gardens. It was situated quite close to the sea-about ten minutes walk down to a white sandy beach, where a most luxurious casino, built in the form of a ship's bridge, lay as if floating in the sand. The small town had grown up very discreetly at the back of the dominating hotel. The whole place was meant to cater to the idle pleasures of peacetime, of course, while now it looked rather war-minded, with all the Russian troops marching up and down in rhythm to their war marches.

Russian soldiers and soldieresses were peeping out of most of the bungalows in town that they had occupied. There was only one road where we were allowed to walk down to the beach, as the others led to spots reserved for the physical training of troops.

The hotel looked grand as we entered a big hall covered with some of the best carpets in Persia. The ex-Shah had made a hobby of building magnificent hotels all over Persia- which he had filled with priceless carpets, good old Persian paintings, and the finest antique brocades. Each hotel was like a museum of Persian arts and crafts. The bedrooms were a dream with comfortable beds into which you just sank and fell immediately into a state of coma and were not aware of anything until the following morning when you suddenly got up and thought: "Oh yes, this is the place for caviar alright" but your dream of caviar disappeared when you heard the price of it. Our luck was in, however, for on the night of our arrival, we met a Danish couple who asked us to join in celebrating their wedding anniversary in caviar and champagne. The caviar was just right-big black balls like gunpowder.

The food was excellent: the fish was fresh from the Caspian Sea, and we had a wide variety of vegetables and fruit, all of which grew on the spot.

The hotel manager was a most interesting Swiss, and he seemed to know everybody worth knowing in Southern

Europe. I had tea with him and coffee after dinner, and I enjoyed his stories very much. But, when we got a bill of five tomans for the same tea and coffee in addition to our daily bill, which was far above normal, I thought his stories were a bit expensive!

I was dying to have a bath in the green sea, and we walked down to the beach, carefully avoiding the pieces of land under the control of the Russian Army. The sea was lovely and warm, even in October. It was not as salty as I had expected it to be. One Persian boy on the beach had invented his own patent for shelter against the sun. From a distance, it looked like a sail, but actually, it was a piece of cloth put up between two sticks, and so long as the sun did not shine vertically, it was very effective.

There was quite an international crowd on the beach - English, Russians, Swiss, Danes, Norwegians, and Persians. The Russians, of course, did not mix with the rest of us, but I do not think I could have mixed easily with them in their nudist attire.

It was pleasantly warm after Teheran, where a woolen suit would have been the right thing to wear. To be sunbathing on this magnificent stretch of sand with the Caspian Sea, caviar, and Russians all around us was life at its best. Nevertheless, we were always conscious of the

Russians as they sang day and night. Their regimental march had an unmistakably Russian motive about it which fascinated me. I lay awake at night listening to their songs. They conjured up in my imagination the Russian scene, big boots, huge coats, and Cossack caps.

The new regiments, however, had to catch up with the old ones in their ability to sing and march properly; sometimes, their singing did not sound too good. Now and again, we tried to strike up a conversation with them, but they always avoided us. The soldiers themselves looked more Turkoman than full-blooded Russian. On the other hand, the uniformed Russian girls looked big and strong enough to move a house if necessary.

On the beach, I met a young English officer who was there on a short holiday from Iraq. He had had great trouble getting a pass and now wanted to stay longer, but as his pass had expired, he dared not take the risk of staying for another day. He was interested to hear that I had come from India and said that that was one place he wanted to go, for one of his ancestors had been an important man there. "My grandfather," he said, " was the Englishman who started the Congress party. So it goes without saying that I would not be too popular there nowadays."

We talked and talked so much that I forgot I was still in

a wet bathing costume. I lay in the shelter of a patent tent but did not realize that a strong draught blew through between the sand and the sail. I caught a bad chill in the stomach.

We lay and listened to the Russian soldiers singing inside the unfinished ultra-modern Casino on the beach. It looked lonely and deserted but could have been a lovely place in peacetime. Here full advantage could have been taken of the sea air, the health-giving sun, and the eastern moon. Still, gambling in such surroundings did not appeal to me. Yet, I suppose some people must always indulge in some form of excitement to feel they are alive.

I had to sit in the hotel that afternoon because of the chill I had caught, and I sat and talked to some Persian businessmen from Teheran. One of them told me that there were few carpets in the hotel worth less than ten thousand tomans each, and one, he knew for certain, cost sixty thousand tomans. So we went and looked at this one, and it looked well worth the price.

The sun was setting, and one of the Persians suddenly interrupted the conversation to ask me where my husband was. I told him that he was walking outside. He looked very worried and said that it was growing late. I told him that he would be alright.

"Well," he went on, "my friend and I went out walking the other night to visit some friends. As we were late, we took a shortcut over a meadow when suddenly, from the shadow of some trees, stepped a huge Russian soldier who pointed his rifle and bayonet towards us and shouted, 'Hands Up.' I looked rather stupified as I did not understand any Russian, but my friend did, and seeing him raising his hands, I understood and followed suit. Although we still held up our hands, we could not see the Russian sentry clearly, for he remained in the shadow of the trees. We were both wearing white suits, and when our friends from the boarding house came out to meet us and saw us standing in the dark with our hands up, they shrieked and ran back to their bungalow, thinking they had seen two ghosts.

I was not inclined to take the situation too seriously, so I asked my friend what Russian meant. The Russian shouted again at this and told my friend that if we talked to each other, he would fire.

Apparently, the Russian was frightened, which was the dangerous part about it. My friend's wife and children were living in the town, and probably at the thought of not seeing them again, he started crying so much that he shivered all over his body. Again I heard the sharp note of a Russian command, and my friend stopped crying. It was very tiring holding our hands up in the air for so long, but as soon as we moved them, the Russian shouted again.

Standing there like that, it seemed as if we stood all night. Two hours had passed, and it was getting very dark. At last, it seemed to be time to change the guard, for another sentry appeared, and he was sent off to report the case. An officer arrived on the scene at once. He laughed and told us in Persian to put our hands down, but by this time, we could not lower our arms, for they were quite stiff, and the officer had to help us.

The whole of my body was stiff too. The officer apologized and explained, "This soldier was very keen on carrying out his duties and apparently had thought we intended to attack him. Unfortunately, the events of the evening proved too much of a shock to both of us, and I had to stay in bed for two days and be constantly massaged."

As soon as the Persian had finished his story, I rushed up to see if my husband had come back and found him singing happily in that lovely long bath attached to our room.

CHAPTER XX: CASPIAN LUXURY

The Danish couple had a car they told us they intended to sell in a short time for sixty thousand tomans. A *toman* is about the same value as a *rupee*. The car was a small five-seater, well-kept car, but it seemed a small fortune for anyone to pay for a car. So we went in their car to the next place along the coast. Chalus was also a very large hotel, but it was not quite up to the standard of the one we had been living in. Chalus was the Caspian Sea end of the road, which ran over the mountains from Teheran.

The drive along the coast lay through miles of green soft fertile country. To seaward, a mixture of seaweed and sand stretched right out to meet the sea. We chose a beautiful spot for a swim. The shore was covered with gorgeously colored shells, and on our way back to the car, we picked red pomegranates from the bushes. They were wild pomegranates. So the taste was not exactly sweet, but I felt I had to eat one after the terrific effort I had made to break the skin almost as hard as a walnut.

The hotel in Chalus had much better food than the previous hotel and a friendlier atmosphere. We had sent a letter to Teheran with one of the Persian businessmen to our Norwegian friends there, who said they would come in their car to meet us at Chalus. We heard later, however, that the letter never reached them. Even though the Persian businessman had promised that he would deliver the letter personally to our friends. This meant that we would have to revert to our lorry mode of transport once more. I had quickly got used to living in luxury again, so I dreaded the thought of a dusty, bumpy lorry. We could not get in touch with Teheran either because there was no telephone or telegraph office in Chalus.

In the hotel, we met a Persian who was an engineer in charge of lorry convoys, and he promised us a seat in a lorry if our friends did not arrive. This Persian had been brought up in France, where his father had been an ambassador, and later, he had spent some years in New York. He had a most attractive personality and an interesting face. We had our meals together, and he told us about some of his experiences. His manners had a diplomatic trim. He gave us wine for dinner, saw to it that the table was well laid, and tipped the servant so that dinner would be well served. He called me madam and kissed my hand. Sitting on the open verandah of the hotel, with the lovely garden full of flowers stretching in front of us, we felt as if we were sitting in a little cafe somewhere in France.

I asked him if he wanted to go back to Paris and New York after the war. "No," he said,"I love my country and my people. I could look at them from a distance and compare them with the Europeans and Americans. When abroad, I found a lot of similarities between my people and the French. Admitted that my country does not enjoy the same high standard of modern comfort, nor do I think they have an appreciation of the poetic and romantic side of life." I said: "The Persians always seem to enjoy their conversation."

"It is considered a great art to show wit, humor, and sarcasm in one's conversation," he said, "You will find the ordinary people, I mean those who can hardly read and write, quoting long passages from classical poetry. On the other hand, I like the sweet, cultured talk and the joy of the people when they greet each other. I know we are dreamers and sometimes very happy over a glass of wine or smoke of chukka. And at such times, poetry flows fluently."

I noticed that Persians pick up languages very quickly. In the streets of Teheran, you may meet a Persian-speaking Arabic, Turkish and Russian in his own language. Among the continental languages, French is the most usual. The American University in Teheran is responsible for making English popular. Is it because of the geographical position of

Persia that the Persians are polyglots, or has it anything to do with the Persian language itself? I was told that the Persian language's prime words and prime numbers are practically the same as in Sanskrit. In fact, there is a very close affinity between the two languages.

At the moment, we were enjoying a tasty fish from the Caspian seat. I said: "I am pleased the Ramzan is over." He laughed and said: "Do you know, one year, when I came back from Europe, I made up my mind to go through Ramzan as the others did. That was for the first time in my life. I realized what hunger and thirst really meant. Perhaps it seems a cruel and exacting form of fast for a Prophet and legislator to impose on his followers. But in actual practice, it is of great value. It is enjoined on everyone. The rich are thus made to realize what some of their brothers suffer when they don't get a meal and are brought to sympathize with them. Then, of course, the Prophet gave us our Laws through religion.

Hukka is an oriental device for smoking in which the smoke is passed through water before the smoker inhales it. The noise made while smoking is also known as "hubble-bubble."

For instance: *Madar, pidar, dokhtar,* and *biradar* in Persian are *matar, pitru, duhitru,* and *bhratar* in Sanskrit, meaning mother, father, daughter, and brother, respectively.

At Bandar Pahlavi on the Caspian, large fisheries supply fish to areas hundreds of miles away. "But doesn't the Quran tell you not to drink?" I asked, "and Persia is full of wine shops......and very good wine too!" "My people have another charm," he said, "and that is that we usually observe the laws with exceptions." He raised his glass and said, "Skaal." Because he had already been taught the Scandinavian custom when we drink wine.

Outside the hotel stood Russian guards on both sides of the road, which in one direction led to Babolsar and in the other to Teheran. As we liked to call our Persian friend, our ambassador said that a Russian officer had refused to pay his hotel bill, for he considered it unreasonable. He had paid what he thought a reasonable price and had gone out to his car, ready to drive off to Babolsar. But he had to pass the Russian guard, for the hotel proprietor had already been to the local Russian headquarters to complain, and the officer was not allowed to pass before he had paid the unreasonable bill.

The ambassador came with us to the transport company in whose lorry we were going to Ramsar. Everyone told us there was a hotel in Ramsar that was still more marvelous than the one in Babolsar. We talked to some people at the transport company and found out that it was difficult to go and return in one day. We dared not risk staying away any longer as the Norwegian engineer might turn up and think we had gone. Instead, we rested in the afternoon. A servant knocked at the door shortly after we had decided to rest and told us that there were some people to see us. We went out, and there stood the engineer and his wife. They had come all these miles over the mountains to fetch us. I was very touched and more so when I saw the dust and the nature of the road they had traveled over the following day.

They suggested that they would take us along to Ramsar and off we drove again along the beautiful sea-coast road. It was not far away, and soon we were driving through the avenue of orange trees, which led up to the famous hotel.

Shah Riza could have received any royal person at this place, and I suppose that was really his idea, for he had built his summer residence close by.

The hotel was situated on a hillside, at the edge of a forest. From the hotel, broad steps led down to the garden, from which a six-mile-long avenue led right down to the Casino on the seashore.

A Norwegian we had met previously had told us that he thought there were too many statues in the garden. He was right, for the garden was full of statues, and I could not stand being stared at by so many faces as I walked down the length of the garden. The statues seemed to spoil the whole effect, at least to me at close quarters, so I hurried through the garden. But when I stood on the terrace and saw before me the whole plantation of a hundred thousand orange trees, overshadowed by the forest-clad mountains, I really thought it was what a Shah's summer residence ought to look like.

The Casino repaid closer study. The furniture was upholstered in colored leather. The fittings on the doors and windows were chromium-plated. There was a bar in the latest American style and a neat American kitchen. There were dressing rooms, restrooms, massage rooms, and everything to make life worth living.

There were only about ten people staying in the huge hotel, but who cared if it paid or not, for it was all kept up by the State. The manager once complained to the old Shah about the small number of people who stayed in the hotel and suggested that they should reduce the prices; otherwise, nobody would come at all. Shah Riza answered that it was the best thing to happen because guests would not wear out the furniture and carpets. Throughout the journey, I noticed many opinions about how a hotel should run.

The food was good, and we thoroughly enjoyed our dinner and our breakfast the following day. After that, we returned to Chalus.

On our way back, we stopped at a little village to buy some salmon for dinner, which we had hoped to have in Teheran. The marketplace was a model of modern town planning. It was built in a circle with streets leading off from it. Another of the Shah's inspirations. Everything looked very tidy and clean, but the people did not seem to fit in their new surroundings. Here they lived in an area where they had all the necessary food for building strong and healthy bodies. Yet, as we looked at them standing helpless, staring at us around the car, they all looked like mummies brought to life or dwarfs. Many seemed to suffer from goiter, and most had enlarged spleens due to malaria.

I thought of the giants I had seen in Afghanistan, where every food scrap is obtained only with a struggle. There was an abundance of vegetables and fruit and as much fish as anyone could wish in the sea nearby and still they were stunted in growth.

We stopped and enjoyed our last bath in the Caspian Sea. Our friends warned us not to venture too far out to sea, for the waters here were frequented by a fish like a swordfish which had been known to attack human beings. One man, in fact, had recently been killed by one of them. So we might easily have been turned into some sort of caviar.

Eventually, we arrived at our hotel in Chalus and had lunch there. Then we started off on the road to Teheran up through a thicket. Soon we were out of the forest, but the road still climbed, and the summit of the pass was almost as high as the railway pass over which we had gone on our way to Teheran. Sometimes the road was very narrow, and guards controlled the heavy traffic.

At the top of the pass, we went through a mile-long tunnel. The tunnel had its uses, for it kept at least the highest part of the road free from snow in the wintertime. There were guards at both ends of the tunnel who were in telephonic communication with each other to be able to control the traffic, for this part of the road was very narrow and did not allow two cars to pass. Unfortunately, one lorry had broken down on the way through. It almost completely blocked the tunnel, and we managed to pass it with great difficulty.

When Shah Riza built this road, little did he know that the advent of the war would turn it into one of the most used roads in the world? He had brought it into being in the first place just to get to his summer residence once or twice a year.

FROM HIMALAYA TO SOUTH PACIFIC

On the way down the other side of the pass, we intended to have tea at an attractive old house where the Shah used to stop on his way to and from his residence. Still, we walked all around the house trying to find someone in charge but without success. A little way back up the road, we had passed a big stationary convoy of lorries. We noticed that the convoy had already started moving, so we rushed to our car to try and get ahead of them. Some of them managed to get in front of us, and we suffered their dust for a long time before we managed to pass them. We were thankful that the engineer and his wife had come to fetch us in their car. Otherwise, we would have had to travel in one of these big lorries in convoy, and I hate to think of the dusty condition we would have been in at the end of the journey.

The countryside gradually faded as darkness came. I fell asleep and did not awake until I found myself at the entrance to our friend's house in Teheran. Our appetites grew as we smelt the salmon, which we had brought, being cooked. It was served in the good Norwegian style. There were hot curly pieces of red salmon with melted butter and freshly boiled potatoes. Our friends were famed for having one of the best tables in Teheran, and I could well imagine why.

FROM HIMALAYA TO SOUTH PACIFIC

They had a charming old-fashioned bungalow with a big garden, and it was a dream to have breakfast on the verandah, sitting in the morning sun and starting off with caviar and good Norwegian coffee or should I say Scandinavian?

CHAPTER XXI: IRAN'S CAPITAL

My previous impression of Teheran was of a beautiful town in a lovely setting of snow-clad mountains. Parts of the town had an unfinished appearance, for some of the big modern official buildings had been left incomplete. The architects seem to have enjoyed themselves by experimenting with many different styles. Still, the residences belonging to the various Legations were probably the most magnificent.

I was surprised to find that what I had heard about the water supply system was true. At certain hours of the day, water was forced up through the open drains on both sides of the street. At these times, it was in every-body's interest to collect as much water as possible from the drains in receptacles. The water was then transferred into big tanks in the gardens or on the roofs of houses.

I was sure this water, meant for ordinary gardening purposes, was also used as drinking water by those who did not take the trouble to fetch drinking water from the British Legation, which has its own water distillery. I saw water being carted around for sale in big barrels. I thought it was strange that the Government had not prioritized arranging a proper water supply before all the magnificent buildings and hotels had been put up.

When I saw people sitting washing their clothes and bodies, their pots and pans in the open drains, I was not surprised to learn that there was a good deal of disease in Teheran.

But the town is making some progress during the war, for it has become an important center. The advent of modern methods and equipment is rather a new thing for Persia. Still, one can see how it is already breaking up long-standing systems.

I heard a story of how not many years ago, a royal party was touring Persia. They had to stop at a small town. The Persians had overlooked the question of beds for the royal visitors and their servants, so they asked the British Legation to help them out of the difficulty. Lorries loaded with beds were sent to the small town and arrived just before the Royal party.

As I said before, *Purdah* was only recently lifted in Persia, and one could see that some of the older women had not yet got used to the sudden change.

The old Shah, Riza Pahlavi, was very strict that the

women should obey when he first gave them the order to discard the *Purdah*. When the Shah had to leave during the last trouble in Persia, the women who were still a bit shy about their uncovered faces adopted a sort of skirting hood made very often of flowery cotton. This they wore on the head, hanging down on both sides and at the back. They could easily cover up their faces in a hurry that way. It looked extremely ugly and did not fit into the picture of the town at all.

I suppose I looked rather out of place when I went into town in my slacks. It was a bit of an experiment which I only did once. I was made so uncomfortable by the persistent staring of the people and sometimes by their open laughter that I soon rushed home again through the back streets.

I heard a story of a certain astute businessman who anticipated the day on which t was decided for the removal of Purdah. He had taken into stock masses of European-style women's hats. He made a fortune out of them, for no matter what the hats looked like, he was completely sold out in no time. I believe the sight was one which feminine eyes at least could not easily forget, for many did not know the back from the front of their hats.

There was an attractive bungalow with a big garden made into the Scandinavian Club. It was excellently run by a Scandinavian girl, and I was told that at the time when Scandinavian engineers were working on the railway line to the north, it had been a very lively spot. But by this time, the railway had been completed, and the engineers scattered all over the world; they had left a certain heritage behind, and it was strange for me to find Ibsen and other books in my own language for sale in the secondhand book shops.

Being in Persia, we naturally wanted to buy some Persian carpets. So we hunted around, but in all the shops we visited, we found that the carpets were all new and were fabulously priced. One year ago, a shopkeeper told us everyone bought carpets as a method of investing money, and that was why all the best old carpets had gone.

One of my fellow citizens showed me a beautiful old Persian carpet he had been lucky to buy in Persia before they were sold out. He was looking forward to taking it home to his wife in America. However, when he came back again after several months, I asked him how he got on with the carpet, and he told me he had to pay a lot of duty for it. "My wife was disappointed," he said, "She asked me why I had bought an old carpet when there surely were plenty of new ones to be had."

As far as I could see, the only thing at a reasonable price was Persian silver. But none of the designs appealed to me.

They were all too overworked and intricate. I imagined it would make any housewife or servant furious at the idea of having to clean them.

I can at least boast that I had a glimpse of one of the world's most attractive women. One day, as I passed the palace garden, I saw the beautiful Queen of Persia standing and looking at her children. The new architectonic palace, surrounded by lovely gardens, gave the mother and children a lovely setting. Every house throughout Persia had a picture of the royal family. If they did not understand my Persian, they certainly understood when I told them they had a beautiful queen.

Our hosts took us for a drive outside Teheran. Two first-class roads led out to a summer palace built on hillside some hundreds of feet above the town, which stands three to four thousand feet above sea level.

There are many Europeans and Persians who have beautiful bungalows where they go in the hot weather, some of which have swimming pools in their gardens. But as I have said, the Legations claimed *pride of place* in this respect. We motored past garden after the garden and caught a glimpse of Demavend on the way up. Next, we passed the Summer Palace, which belonged to the Shah and on top, arrived at the lovely hotel also built by him. The garden resembled the one in Ramsar, with a superabundance of statues and big vases, so many that we could hardly see the flowers.

The hotel, like the others, had beautiful carpets and paintings. The verandah gave the most lovely view of Teheran, which looked as if it lay in a valley. Behind the hotel, many refreshing walks led up the hillside, and I was told that it was from here that one could climb Demavend.

A little stream came down from the mountains, and beside it were paths which crossed the stream by small bridges, and here people used to walk out from the town for a breath of fresh, cool air. Here also was the place where people skied in wintertime.

CHAPTER XXII:
THE PEACOCK THRONE

It was Sunday when we went to see the Peacock Throne, which was in the Old Palace. I was thrilled as we made our way to the Gulistan Palace, for here, at last, I was going to see the Indian Moghal Throne, so you can imagine my disappointment when they said the palace was closed and would not be open until the afternoon.

I was thought to be rather mad when I wanted to set off again to see it immediately after lunch. So I said: "Why should I not miss an afternoon's rest to see the treasure when I have traveled the same long road as the Throne was carried, all the way from India? "

Off we went to the Old Palace garden. There a guide offered to take us around. It struck me that our guide was just like old Uncle Bille in Delhi. Judging by the authoritative way he spoke of olden times, he could well have been one of Shah Jahan's own private bodyguards. He walked around, dressed in a big cloak, with an air of tremendous importance and dignity, making us walk tip-toe along the well-polished floor. As we walked up the steps to the hall on the first floor, the picture of the Durbar Hall in Delhi flashed across my mind. I heard the old guide's voice saying: "....and here was Shah Jahan seated in all his glory, surrounded by his people and greatly admired and respected by them."

I thought of the green emeralds, the peacock blue sapphires, the pigeon, blood-colored rubies, the sparkling diamonds.

The Old Palace looked like a museum, and as I passed along, I could see that there were many valuable and interesting articles in the glass cases lining the walls. I did not have time to investigate them as I was too anxious to see the throne first. So I whispered: "Where is the Peacock Throne?"

The guide pointed to the far end of the enormous hall, and there was "the throne" between mirror-covered walls, making it look more imposing than I had ever dreamt of. "Takhti-Nadiri" means Nadir's Throne. I was told that when Nadir Shah came back with the throne to Persia after looting Delhi, he was so fascinated by its beauty that he had a copy made of it. Nadir Shah's reign did not last long; he was killed by his own officers. His successors sold the valuable stones wherever they could. The throne was so badly dismantled that it was almost irreparable. But Aga Mohammed Khan utilized what was left and constructed a new throne.

So here we were standing looking at the throne of all thrones, once so glorious and so envied. . . . . . It was certainly made in peacock design, inlaid with large emeralds. It looked so marvelous and fascinating.

The design of the throne struck me as being Europeanized and not as oriental as I thought it would be. Surely the Mughal Emperors sat cross-legged on their thrones and not as we sit in our chairs.

Shah Jahan had such immense treasures in his palace that he invited suggestions from artists to choose some elaborate designs so that all his colored gems could be used.

The peacock is a sacred bird in many parts of India, even today. It signifies royal splendor. Taking their inspiration from this fact, the artists suggested the design of the Peacock Throne. It gave them unique scope for utilizing a variety of colored precious stones. The rich pattern pleased the pompous and art-loving Shah Jahan. The famous Koh-i-Noor diamond - Mountain of Light was also brought to Persia by Nadir Shah. Later, in the course of history, it went to Afghanistan and then to Ranjit Singh, the last ruler of the Sikhs. Eventually, it passed to Queen Victoria.

I think the guide suspected me, for I knelt down several times to look at the throne. Some stones had been extracted, and I could well imagine the temptation to most people if they got a chance, especially to some of the poorer people in Persia, for any one of these stones, if real, would enable a man to live all his life comfortably and would allow him to sit smoking his *hukka* all day long. Certainly, these stones, if not real, were all good copies, and I felt sure that the real stones had been cut in Jaipur, where the Mughal Emperors used to keep hundreds of stone cutters. Jaipur is, in fact, a center of Indian stone-cutting to this day.

The pearls on the throne were enormous and must have been of great value before they were replaced. I had taken such a long time around the throne that the rest of the party was getting impatient to see some of the other things.

There was a lovely carpet which I shall never forget. It had a sort of silky surface; the design, in colors of rust and pink, was of small roses-a carpet for a Queen. But I could not help thinking of the artisans who perhaps had given up a great part of their lives or offered their children's eyes for this carpet so that a grand lady could place her feet on it for a minute or two each day. The past is full of such anomalies. One of the worst was when Alexander the Great ordered a beautiful Persian town to be burnt to the ground just to satisfy the capricious mind of one of his mistresses. It showed the capacity for vanity, cruelty and sadism most conquerors have. Cleopatra, on the other hand, when she swallowed a very valuable pearl at a dinner party, probably ate it because she lacked calcium.

Before leaving Teheran, I wanted to see the hotel and garden where our Norwegian boys escaping from Norway celebrated their 17th of May, Independence Day in Norway. They had told me about it in Bombay. Apparently, there was rioting at the time in Teheran, so they could not celebrate the National Day by the usual method of holding a demonstration in the streets, so they just had to be content with walking up and down the hotel and around about the garden where they finished off with a very inspiring speech by one of the boys.

I saw the garden and wished I had been there at the time. I could picture one of the young boys giving his enthusiastic speech, all the while, the crowd waving their sticks and threatening the enemy and expressing a determination that they and they alone should be allowed to win their country back again. I am sure Teheran had never before seen more enthusiastic patriots than this small group of Norwegian youngsters who escaped through Sweden and Russia to reach Teheran and from there to go to Bombay and on to England in order to serve their King and country: Our hosts saw us off on the train, which again was very crowded.

However, I was pleased that the country around Teheran was uninteresting to look at, for I was very tired.

It was a pity that we went through the mountains at night, for I had always wanted to see this part of the railway. In fact, I sat up most of the night, peering out the window to see what was to be seen in the dark. It was very similar to the line down to the Caspian Sea. However, the moonlight gave a certain magic beauty to the scenery.

It was strange to see Americans driving the train at every station. Americans appeared on the scene to welcome us and see us off again. The Americans drove the train, the British Government looked after our passes and the Persian Government our tickets, so we could not go far wrong. The following day we were dropped off at a little station in the middle of the desert. It was Awaz. Two soldiers came up to me and asked if I was English. I said I was Norwegian. "There you see," said the smaller one to the other, "Talk in your own language now."

The boy he referred to was a tall Swedish American. He had lived in America for fifteen years and almost forgot his language. The smaller boy told me with some pride that he was a Red Indian. One could have told that from his profile and the shape of his head, and he just lacked the feathers on top and hanging down his back to be an advertisement for the wild and woolly West. He made the same sort of noise, too, from the: films one expects to hear way out West-" Ko-i-i-i-Ho."

They were very pleased to find out that we were taking the same train to Khorramshahr, and they asked us to join the rest of them. They almost carried us into their compartment.

The Red Indian boy introduced the whole compartment to us, adding: "If you have not seen the American Army before, you will certainly see it now." I think he had already drunk quite a lot of vodka, and later I saw some of the boys very drunk.

It takes a good stomach to stand that sort of thing in such terrific heat, or anywhere for that matter. The Red Indian enjoyed calling attention to a soldier in the corner who looked rather embarrassed, for he knew that the Red Indian was liable to say anything. The Red Indian went on: "He used to be an Irishman-a good type too," and added: "Here is a Scotsman," but he need not have told me all that, for I can always pick out a Scotsman in a crowd. It was interesting to see how many countries of Europe were represented amongst these American soldiers and how one could almost tell which country they came from, for most of them had not yet lost their national characteristics. The Red Indian was very proud of his Swedish-American friend. He had a delicate build, fair color, nice hair and lovely blue eyes- a fine Nordic type.

After this lengthy introduction, they shared their tinned food with us. It was excellent. Peaches in six-pound tins, biscuits, cheese, chocolates, chewing gum, of course, and cigarettes. At every station, the Persian children lined up and threw food out of the window.

Later I heard that some of the Persians took advantage of the generosity of American soldiers and went from one American camp to another, collected tinned stuff from the soldiers' daily rations, and sold it again, sometimes to the Americans. But, of course, then they paid very high prices. The American soldiers had adopted the Eastern way of cooling water. Still, instead of using mud jars, they had made long canvas bags which hung outside the carriage window. It tasted very cold in that terrible heat.

The distance from Awaz to Khorramshahr is only forty miles, but the journey seemed to take a very long time. In the dust of the desert, it was difficult to see much outside. Hundreds of dust devils, which started by picking up the sand in a big ring, went higher and higher skywards in a spiral shape until the centripetal force no longer held the sand together when billions of microscopic pieces of sand would fly off in all directions. It looked as if there was a continuous sandstorm at some places, and I fancied I could see lakes and other shapes in the landscape, but they were only mirages.

CHAPTER XXIII:
OIL CITY

Coming into Khorramshahr, I saw no stations, only a few warehouses. So we were rather lost here amongst the railway tracks. Nor did there appear to be any taxis or horse carriages. So we were very pleased when the Swedish-American offered us a lift.

The jeep took us through Khorramshahr to the oil company's rest house on the riverside, where we were asked to stay. The driver of the jeep said he had not spoken to a woman for two years, so instead of us thanking him, he thanked us for coming with him. The rest house was built in a square with a nice lawn in the center. The idea, I suppose, was to protect the rooms from the dust of sandstorms. Khorramshahr is situated along the bank of the Karun river overlooking Abadan island. I went round the place, but the dust spoiled any attraction it might have had. The silverware in the *bazar* looked interesting, but shopping was impossible as the prices were shocking. Even old clothes were bought up at high prices. The sailors told me they got about twenty *tomans* for an old pair of shorts.

The British Club was very nice, and the Consulate

garden was full of flowers. Elsewhere that part of the riverside was covered with date baskets brought in by native dhows from the date groves on both sides of the river and gulf.

With its rough trunk, the date palm has a gay and romantic life. In its habits, it is polygamous, and there are two sexes. When the trees are in flower, the so-called wedding takes place. Flowers from the male palm are taken to be sprinkled onto the blossoms of the female every year.

Unless they are brought together, good dates cannot be grown. Around Basrah, the date palms are planted in groups of thirteen, one male to twelve females. The dates were taken into big old storehouses along the riverfront where they were stored, dried and packed in attractive Arabian boxes untouched by hand, but not by feet, for the baskets were stamped on by all sorts of people and creatures as they lay on the bank. The fascinating old paddle boats, used as ferries over the river to Abadan, had mostly been replaced by motor boats and, more recently, by fast-moving speed boats and later still by amphibious vehicles. It was the first time I had seen them. As I watched them rolling into the water, I thought it was a motor accident and rushed off to see what would happen to the people inside the car when they reached the bottom of the river. The motor tripped up to Basrah, which did not take long, was interesting, as was this age-old port of Iraq.

These places up in the corner of the Persian Gulf are the home of the Iranian navy. The colorful uniform of the police gendarmerie, customs officers and naval personnel lent a gay atmosphere to the khaki-colored riverside.

We had to cross the river to Abadan, which lies on an island. As we drove along towards the oil town, we were told all about the famous oil pipeline, part of which we could see as it carried millions of gallons along the Karun valley, down from the mountains north of Awaz, right across the desert and the Bahmashire river to the refinery at Abadan, where it was refined into kerosene, benzene, petrol, heavy oils and most important of all in wartime, aviation spirit. This oil refinery is now one of the largest in the world. I was taken aback by the little paradise they had created out of what had been nothing but a swampy island many years ago. Here stands now a modern town.

The heat in the summer months is terrific, but the Europeans live very comfortably in air-conditioned bungalows. There are air-conditioned canteens and restaurants. A big open-air cinema accommodating about a thousand people attracted me very much. There was a sweet dancing club on a ship in the river, with a most romantic mile-long bridge leading out to it through weeds and swamp land. The rose gardens were lovely, too, and a good place for a cooling stroll after the exertion of dancing on the upper deck. But I did not like the sharks swimming around in the water.

There were many swimming pools and a big one at the sailors' home with air-conditioned rooms. There was an eighteen holes' golf course in the desert, tennis and cricket and speed boat races on the river.

Abadan has a polyglot population-Americans, Europeans, Persians, Indians and Arabs. In the air-conditioned hospital, we found ten Norwegian sailors. They were very happy and told me they felt just as much at home as in a Norwegian hospital. I think this was to be expected, for one of the doctors was a Scotsman who was very attached to the Norwegian sailors, for he reckoned the Norwegians and Scots to be related. We had dinner at this doctor's bungalow, and his wife told us that the Norwegian sailors were among the best-behaved patients in the hospital.

Even though most people reckon Abadan to be the most God-forsaken spot, I certainly enjoyed my stay there. As I walked along the riverside, I was reminded of the strenuous efforts made in India to collect scrap metal. Here on the beach were thousands of empty tins washed ashore. In fact, the Persians went around and picked out the best ones amongst them, whereas further north in Persia, one hardly saw metal or tins at all. The poor women who washed their clothes in the river had to place planks over the tins to avoid cutting their feet.

CHAPTER XXIV: TANKER PASSAGE

We had made arrangements to go back to India on a Norwegian cargo ship, but the ship was delayed and would not leave for some time. However, there happened to be another Norwegian ship there, an oil tanker. Although we had to travel on this ship at our own risk, we thought it better to do this than wait for the other ship.

When I came on board, the Captain said to me: "You know this is a tanker. How do you dare take such a risk and come with us? I certainly would not unless I absolutely had to." I must admit I felt a bit nervous after this and also because we had heard rumors about the presence of submarines in the waters through which we would have to pass. Moreover, the two oil engineers who lived in the bungalow enjoyed frightening us when they heard we intended to travel in a tanker. But we had made up our minds, no matter how much we feared the consequences we committed.

Actually, we had been offered a lift by car down to Quetta, which was very tempting at the time. However, if I had changed my mind and not gone by sea, I should never have been able to look our sailors in the eye again, for why should not we, for ten days, go through the dangers that they were going through nearly every day in the year.

The tanker was one of the latest in the Norwegian fleet, beautifully designed and most comfortable, and our cabin was like a pleasant little home. We were assured that there was no danger, at least for the first six days of our voyage, so we could relax and enjoy every second of it. All night, as long as we were in smooth water, I used to put my bed on the deck, watch the stars, and try to fall asleep. Every Norwegian ship has a well-equipped library. Here was my favorite collection of Wildenvey poems; in the daytime, I would learn them by heart and repeat them when I lay on deck under the stars. But all the time, as I lay, I could not get rid of the fear of being torpedoed at any moment.

Fear usually dispels concentration, but I found that I was able to concentrate on these poems better than I had ever done before. As I repeated it to myself, each line seemed to have a significance that I had not grasped before. In the end, I had to adopt an indifferent attitude towards the danger. Why does it matter, I thought, if our body dies? Why does it matter as long as the effort we have brought to bear in life and the goodwill we have created is somewhere and somehow preserved?

When I lay there thinking and reciting Wildenvey, I could not help thinking of my children at home in Norway. I knew that nearly everyone on board had similar thoughts. They all wanted to come through alive, so they could see their families at home once more. So we were, in fact, all in the same boat.

I got to know all the sailors on board as they came to do their daily rounds of work. I used to talk to them during their off-duty period, which they used to pass lying on the deck listening to a gramophone or reading books.

The opening remark was, of course, always to ask what news had been received from families at home. Every Norwegian naturally is very interested in his own people and in the resistance to Nazi aggression the people in Norway are putting up. One of the sailors said: "I wish I were at home so that I also could suffer with them and help them in their resistance. I feel ashamed," he went on, "We do nothing compared with them."

I told him that I was sure that had he been at home, he would not have failed to help to the maximum. I pointed out to him that, in any case, the danger that the people at home ran could not be worse than that in which he constantly lived by sailing the seas on an oil tanker. Sailing down the Persian Gulf was pleasant, and I enjoyed every minute of it. At one place, we waited for other ships to join our convoy; it looked as if we were going to be thirteen in convoy. I always seemed to strike that number, or perhaps I always noticed that number when I came across it. In contrast, other numbers did not attract my attention at all.

The Captain used the opportunity to practice boat drills when the convoy was being assembled. The lifeboats were lowered into the water, and everyone had put on life jackets. The sailors told us the water usually caught fire when a tanker was torpedoed. So the best thing was to remove the lifejacket and keep it underneath the water for as long as possible. I told them I was a good diver; it was a lie. Anyhow, if I had met any of the black and yellow snakes I saw swimming about on the surface of the water, I think I would have drowned straight away from terror. All the equipment on the lifeboats was checked up, food, water, compass, etc., and it all seemed to be in first-class condition.

The equipment in these lifeboats had been thoroughly tested, particularly in one case where a Norwegian captain and his crew had stayed afloat in their lifeboat for thirty-two days and had lived on the rations they had in the lifeboat, occasionally supplemented by raw flying fish, which landed in the boat. As we rowed away in lifeboats from the ship, I liked the direct way in which the sailors could talk of our chances of survival in the event of something happening to the ship. I talked to the officer in charge with the intention of getting something out of him. I asked him what he thought our chances were.

"None whatsoever," he answered, of course. When you are blown up that way." I said to him: "If the petrol burns on the water would not the flames reach very high?

"Oh yes," he replied. "It is surprising how high the flames reach." He told me of one sailor who was on board the ship and was the only survivor from a petrol tanker which had been sunk. He was a good swimmer and escaped by swimming mostly underneath the water. He had been lucky in reaching a patch where oil covered the water instead of petrol. He stayed in this oil patch until the flames covering the water all around him had gone out.

I saw a chance to console myself here, and I said: "I am sure the oil would cover most of the water in our case." "How could it?" he replied, "When we carry no oil whatsoever, it is all petrol."

"Anyhow," I said, trying to console myself again, "There are no sharks just here."

"Perhaps not," he said, "But the fish in these waters are much worse." I looked at him; he was quite serious and calm.

I said to him: "But when you know of all these dangers, and you go through them every day for years, do you not still feel very frightened?"

"Oh," he said, "We just put off thinking about it till it happens, and at that moment, we are all too busy to worry about our fear."

He laughed at that and said: "Let us try the sail, boys, and whistle up a breeze." It was a gorgeous day, and it was difficult to imagine the possibilities which were always present. So we sailed back to a good cup of coffee and a lovely soft cake made by the excellent Danish cook we had on board.

After coffee, I went up on deck again and stood watching the different kinds of fish I could see. I liked, in particular, to watch the flounder when they came up to the surface. They moved so slowly that I shouted to the boys, who ran for their fishing nets and succeeded in hauling in quite a number in no time. Finally, the Captain came along and told me that he had just received a report of the presence of a submarine somewhere out in the open sea. I was proud of the fact that he had told me at all, but I could not help feeling a bit upset.

CHAPTER XXV:
LIABLE TO BE TORPEDOED

It was a new thing to me to have to face the definite possibility of death. I was trying hard to get used to it. Still, of course, even when I kept telling myself that there was no need to worry, I only succeeded in making myself even more conscious of the danger. We usually had a drink before dinner every night with the Captain and the officers. At this time, we used to listen to the European war news.

I liked the first engineer, who was a pleasant, typical old sailor who thoroughly enjoyed telling stories over his whisky and soda. He told me how once he was sitting in his comfortable cabin chair reading a good book when a big wave, one of those enormous waves which suddenly arrive for no reason at all, came swirling into his cabin, lifted him and his chair out through the door on to the deck. He found himself sitting there still reading his book up against a railing after the wave had gone.

He did not notice that he had said: "Still reading the book," so he full heartily laughed when I said to him: "It must have been a very interesting book indeed."

I was very sad the next day when the Captain told me he

had just heard that this old engineer's son had been lost on another ship. The Captain asked my advice as to whether he should tell him about it or not. It was very difficult .to say what to do. I thought of the happy old man whose heart would be broken when he got the news that his only son was dead, and it might easily have upset the others on the tanker very much. I thought, on the whole, it would be better to tell him when they were ashore for a spell. Standing on deck beneath the stars, watching a ship glide through the big soft sea, is always conducive to philosophical reflection. The first officer and I often used to talk about life in general. I said I was inclined to believe in some form of reincarnation whereby we came back after death to continue with our previous efforts on the road to perfection and understanding. He agreed it was a satisfying theory, but I do not think he needed it, for he was not afraid of death. His main thought was for his wife and daughter in Norway. He told me that he and many others had ordered woollen clothing in South America for their families and paid for it so that it would be delivered to their families by the first boat which went home after the war. The officers had told me how radiant and beautiful the sea outside Karachi looked in the moonlight. We were due to pass by there during the night, so I went up on the bridge at about four o'clock in the morning, for I was determined to see if they had exaggerated their description. I could not believe my eyes. The water had changed into a sea of fire. We sailed in light. The other ships in convoy pushed fire out to both sides as they moved along.

I remarked to the first officer: "Surely this light must be very dangerous, for a submarine can see us from far away." But he answered: "On the contrary, it is the other way round, for airplanes can see a submarine much deeper down in the water when it has phosphorescence all around it. So I think it tends to keep them away in these waters. Sometimes, of course, they mistake a big fish for a submarine because the movements of the fish also stir up phosphorescence."

How often, I thought, had I discredited sailors' yarns, but now I would be more inclined to believe in their truth, especially when they related to natural phenomena. I often used to stand on the bridge looking anxiously out to sea to spot a periscope. I would go over in my mind what I would do if I -saw that periscope. Suddenly a great black mass came right up out of the water between our ship and the next one. I got so frightened that I shrieked a bit, but the officer standing next to me, an old whaler, laughed and said it was only a fine big whale. It spouted and then seemed rather confused to find itself surrounded by boats and dived immediately. We saw it several times after that. The boys on board were excited at having a whale alongside. I could see how anxious they were to catch it, but there was no hope of this as we were in convoy and had no equipment in any case.

Well, that had given me some little experience of being frightened. By now, an airplane kept flying over our heads all the time. I stood watching it, and when I saw it dropping down flares, I guessed it to be an indication of a submarine in the vicinity. My guess appeared to be correct, for we started changing course very rapidly several times. I went to bed that night wearing my life jacket and repeated all Wildenvey poems right through before falling off to sleep.

It is a strange experience to walk about on a ship which is liable to be torpedoed any minute. In the end, one gets used to it to a certain extent so that one does not really think about it. But the fear, ever-present in one's subconscious mind, always makes one add the conditional sentence: "If we ever reach harbor this time." When the harbor arrived, I could easily understand why sailors came ashore saying: "Let us drink and enjoy ourselves. Let us feel life for once, for we never know what will happen next voyage."

One night the Captain asked me if I would accept a souvenir he had bought in Java. It was a lovely salad set made of horn and inlaid with beautiful silver work, "I really meant to take it home," he said, "But I doubt if I shall ever get home." I thanked him very much, but there was a mutual understanding that if I got home to Norway, I would give it to his wife.

My own fervent hope is that I shall be able to do so and also be able to tell her how her husband was respected and loved for his fair dealing.

He liked to talk about the danger we were in and how he would act in certain situations. "I know," he said, "The enemy pays most attention to the Captain in order to try and extract secret information from him." He said he had heard of one officer who was captured by the Japanese and, in order to save the Captain who always carries the code book with him, said that he did not know where the Captain was. The Japanese then said that they would shoot everyone in the lifeboat if the officer did not tell them.

Another story was of the Japanese taking the Captain of a torpedoed ship on board their submarine. They tied him to the conning tower, and when he refused to answer any questions, they just dived, taking the Captain with them. I think our Captain tested his own strength by picturing himself in similar positions. I could tell when he had come to a conclusion, for the change in his face was very marked, and his expression grew more determined.

We arrived in Bombay harbor after many days' delay. We saw Canary Island on the right, Trombay to the left and Elephanta Island straight ahead. All these hills were well-known and dear to us. I felt and knew it was our journey's end, home to safety and comfort, while our sailors had to go on and out again in a few days' time. Nevertheless, my conscience told me I ought to go on and risk my life as they did.

It was difficult to say goodbye because I could not tell them they were safe to go out again. However, in my heart, I was thankful that I had been able to meet such fearless men, and I was proud that they were my countrymen. The only thing was to welcome them to Bombay again and say we hoped to see them all safe and well.

EPILOGUE

One day, afterward a few days later, I went to my husband's office in Bombay, and he said: "I have very sad news for you today. The tanker you sailed in has been torpedoed; the survivors are in India and they will be coming to Bombay in a few days' time."

I was most anxious to meet them, and I asked the sailors' home to let me know as soon as they arrived. When I went to see them, I was so excited about who had survived that I hardly dared put that question to them. We sat down, and they started to tell me the story. I picked up courage and, looking around, said: "Are all the survivors here," for they were very few. "Oh no," they replied, "Some have got out already on another trip; others have gone to London." "We did not have much chance," they said. "The torpedo went straight into the engine room." I interrupted them and said: "How is it that so many of you have escaped? I remember you told me that we would have no chance whatsoever in these circumstances?"

One of them answered: "It is a curious thing, but it was the first time in the career of the ship that we carried oil and not gasoline. It took the japs more than two hours to pump sufficient torpedoes into the ship to make her sink. After that, all of us went into the lifeboats. We only had three lifeboats in working order, for one had been smashed."

"Kristiansen, our wireless operator, sent out an S.O.S. signal as soon as the ship was hit and repeated it until he got an answer. The enemy shelled the wireless cabin and put the transmitter out of action. But by that time, Kristiansen had done his job. His efforts were not in vain. He managed to leave the ship when a plane came over later in answer to his own S.O.S. they saw him lying on a door. The plane dropped a rubber boat for him. They saw him swim towards the rubber boat, but he was too exhausted to reach it, so he swam back again to the door.

Unfortunately, when a ship came round to pick up the survivors the following day, he was nowhere to be found. "No man could have done his duty better." A young engineer told me how, as they hung around the submarine in the lifeboats, covered all the time by a machine gun, the Captain was ordered to go on board with the submarine. The crew of the Captain's lifeboat started rowing toward the submarine so that the Captain could step on board with the dignity due to his position. Still, the japs ordered them to stay clear, possibly for fear the crew might rush the submarine. The Captain had to swim for it, and when he reached the side of the submarine, the Japs lowered a long pole with a large fishhook on the end of it. He was meant to grasp this and be hauled on board, but the Japs saw an opportunity for sadistic enjoyment and tried to hook the Captain. After several attempts, during which the hook must have pierced his ribs, they succeeded in placing the hook under the Captain's arm and then hauled him up the side of the submarine. They did not haul him right on board but left him hanging halfway.

In the meantime, the other two lifeboats had succeeded in rowing pretty far away from the submarine. But the Captain's boat was still near the submarine, and the Japs proceeded to machine-gun the boat.

The young engineer went on to tell me that he was the only survivor from the Captain's lifeboat. Soon after the machine-gunning, he remembered hearing a terrible shriek coming from the submarine. It was the shriek of a man in awful agony, and the engineer felt sure it was the Captain being tortured for refusing to divulge information.

Physical strength and moral courage in Norwegian sailors seem to go hand in hand. This Captain was more than six feet tall, very broadly built, with a boyish face and a blue-eyed smile. Still, his expression could change into one of the firmest determination whenever his duty demanded serious thought or action.

FROM HIMALAYA TO SOUTH PACIFIC

The young engineer, who told me the story about the Captain, was a typical young Norwegian. He was fair, tall, clean, limbed, and looked you straight in the eye. I remembered how he always brought his life jacket with him and placed it carefully beside him. All his papers were sewn into his belt. You could tell from his well-groomed appearance that he was a boy of ambition and would be thorough in his work. In his spare time, he always seemed to be doing something of value. He would read a good book, play classical music on his gramophone, or sunbathe for his health.

This boy caught my interest, and I talked to him to try and find out what he wanted out of life. He told me he wanted to become an air pilot, and in his spare time before the war, he had studied and experimented with glider flying. He said that the greatest hour in his life was when he was flown over Oslo on a plane as a boy. He went on: "I took a job in this ship before the war so that I could see some more part of the world before I started on my real interest in life. Then the invasion caught me, and here I am wasting my time. I would have been bombing Germany long ago."

I was not surprised when I heard about his clever escape from the Japanese. As soon as the Captain had been hauled halfway up the submarine, he realized that the Japs intended to shoot them all, so he jumped out of the lifeboat, swam right under it, and continued swimming until he came up on the far side of the submarine, where he hung on to the side of the submarine. From here, he watched the Japs turn and machine-gun his friends on the lifeboats. He heard the gunner making sure the man standing beside him was ready with his camera before he fired.

All in the lifeboat were killed outright, except a little fox terrier which had been a pet on board the tanker. When the Japanese had completed their filthy task, the boy dropped off from the side of the submarine and escaped unseen. He then swam back to the lifeboat containing all his dead friends. Strangely enough, it was still floating, for though it was full of holes, none of the air tanks had been punctured. He and the dog were picked up a day later. I asked them where the first officer was, and I could tell by the expression on everyone's face that he, too, had died. My thoughts went back to the Captain's cozy cabin where we used to sit and talk. He and I had once discussed the best way to die if a convoy were attacked. I had said I would hate to be left lying on a raft in the sun, perhaps to die of thirst.

Being wounded, too, would make it worse. He had replied that if you were wounded, it was better to remain in the water because you did not see or feel the bleeding. You would just fade away. It was strange that he should have said that, for one of the boys told me he wanted to pull him out of the water into the lifeboat, but the first officer had just said: "Never mind. I am wounded, and I think I am finished." So he just stayed in the water and had the death he had planned.

The charming old first engineer was found lying dead on a raft. One boy had heard him call for help. The Japs answered him with machine-gun bullets. He was still clutching an attached case containing all his important papers and a present for his wife. I wonder if he ever got to know of the death of his only son, who had been torpedoed in another ship. The Captain, I knew, had hesitated to tell him about it. His wife at home in Norway had lost a husband and a son in less than a month.

So there we sat, all the boys telling me everyone else's story. They very seldom told me their own story, for I think they were too reticent to do that. I was so absorbed by what they were telling me that I did not notice that another sailor was sitting next to me who did not belong in the same boat. He seemed a bit drunk by this time and in a rather excited state. Suddenly he turned to me and asked: "Why do you listen to those boys?" I replied: "I am very interested because I sailed on their ship." "Interested?" he flung at me. "The story they are telling you now is as old as the sea itself." "Over there," he said, pointing to a sailor, "Is a sailor who has been torpedoed five times, and tomorrow he sails again. He does not talk about it. Here is another sailor who was on board one of the last ships to leave during the evacuation of Crete."

"For myself," he went on, "I feel rather ashamed, for somehow the torpedoes always seem to miss my ship by inches. That has happened on at least six occasions. I have come to the conclusion that I am too bad a subject to die. Even the torpedoes change their mind when I am on board. I drink hard," he said, "and I can see that you blame me for it."

I hastened to contradict him. "On the contrary," I said, "I do not blame you, so as long as drinking does not interfere with your duty or upset the lives of those who are near and dear to you. I think that all of you here and others like you, by the courage and devotion you bring to bear in your perilous sailing of the sea, have earned the right to drink as much as you like, for who knows, tomorrow you may die."

FROM HIMALAYA TO SOUTH PACIFIC

Traveling the Annapurna Circuit

FROM HIMALAYA TO SOUTH PACIFIC

Traveling the Annapurna Circuit: 1998

One cannot imagine how wonderful the Himalayas are without being there, among these highest mountains in the world. The mountain range stretches over 2,000 kilometers from eastern Pakistan to western China. It is truly an impenetrable castle separating the Indian subcontinent from its Asian cousins, Tibet and China. A 20-day trip around Annapurna began in Kathmandu in the Nepalese kingdom. The city is a blend of middle age and modern architecture, Hindu temples, holy places, holy cows, and confined children's princesses. It's a fascinating portrait of an old-life dynasty while being overloaded with vibrant urban life and smog. Kathmandu is located in the warm, fertile valleys of the Nepalese Himalayas; geographic, Nepal is part of India, but politically very different and with strong independence. Humans are predominantly Hindu and worship the ancient Hindu gods Braman, Shiva, and Vishnu, their holy trinity.

Roy Smith, an old friend from England, was with me on this trip. He has led expeditions sponsored by National Geographic to Africa and Arctic waters. We had just finished a five-day ski trip from Crested Butte to Vail in

Colorado to be in shape for this trip.

Small and trim, the Nepalese live on a simple yet life-giving diet of rice and vegetables, all growing on small terraces that dominate the landscape with scattered farms and villages. Slowly, the water buffalo and bull hand-held wood plows over small irregular lands. Rural Nepal has changed little for 500 years, and here lies the beauty of the country, a way to live which has almost disappeared from our planet.

We arrived in Kathmandu in early March morning from Norway. After our stay, we received our trekking visa for Annapurna at the immigration office. We received a 6-hour rollercoaster jeep transport through winding roads to the outskirts of Bessisahar, where our trekking began. When we got out of the jeep, we were met by two very young men from southern Nepal near the Indian border, who asked if we would hire them as carriers. We had heard rumors that the year before, a group of carers had refused to leave when they were overtaken by a snowstorm in one of the highest passes. This group then had to carry their own and the carrier's backpacks to come across the passport. Many carriers insisted that our 30-kilo backpacks would not bother them with any issues and that they knew the route well and had walked it many times before.

FROM HIMALAYA TO SOUTH PACIFIC

It settled the matter, and we sat down and agreed on a month and conditions with our new carriers and guides, Cuba and Toya. We agreed to 500 rupees per day ($ 6.65), which included food and accommodation.

A trip from Bessisahar began through the local meat market, where stripped portions of buffalo were stacked in small hills. Then we left the small town and began the journey into a world that has changed a little over the centuries. Every day, a rollercoaster was up a thousand feet and descended again and again on the same day. During the entire trip, we went up and down over 30,000 meters and covered a distance of about 250 kilometers. As we got up, the landscape became more wild, dramatic, drier, and less fruitful. Risåkre was exchanged with eel mashed potatoes and oats, the most important food in these high mountain ranges.

Even higher up the long-haired yaks and goats on the bare, windy blades. Their praised milk is used for yogurt, butter, and cheese. They are used as replacements for wheat and rice grown at lower levels. The winter over 3,000 meters is long and cold, and snowstorms and snowdrops make many of the higher passes connecting one valley to another too dangerous to cross many streets.

Perhaps the most dangerous aspect of drawing in the

Himalayas is the many cruises on hanging bridges over sizzling rivers. They give a scary feeling of *"will this be holding you over to the other side?"* It was always an encouragement to see a fully loaded ass or a carrier who walked in front of us, albeit hesitantly, while the bridge was swinging back and forth. In the village of Ogre, I was astonished to see a carrier wearing a white man on his back in a netting basket. I asked Toya. "What was the purpose of this theater?" He explained that this was the ambulance and that the man was taken to the hospital. "But it's three days from here," I exclaimed.

"Yes, but the man's family hired me. I'll look for him along the way and cook his food. 3 days to the hospital! We will send a letter to the newspaper if the ambulance does not arrive within the hour." He said. While thinking about this, it was easy to forget the wearer who would carry the patient, about the same weight as himself, for 3 days, probably 10 hours a day. The battle for speed is possibly based on survival. The carrier will not be paid if the patient dies on the road. I wonder how it worked. He had no insurance that included ambulance assistance. I assume probably not.

Nepalese is a unique nation. They are sparse in growth but have a strong constitution and good lighting. Their sherpas from the Everest region are the world's best-climbing climbers. A sherpa (Rita) has climbed Everest 10 times, several times without oxygen. The carriers can take up to 100 kilograms of weight on their shoulders and go for up to five days from the bottom of the valley in the Kathmandu Valley up to the snow in the top mountain range, an increase of over 3,000 meters; and the Ghurkas coming from west Nepal in the Annapurna area are the world's best warriors. They are feared by all opponents for their strength and confidence. There are still 6 divisions of turkeys in India and 2 in England, which are rented to Hong Kong and Brunei.

We lived in many tea houses that were owned and operated by older Gurkas, now grandfathers in their 70's who often sat and cradled their grandchildren.

In the village of Manang, approx. 3,500 meters, we stopped to rest for two days and got acclimatized. Four days later, we had to cross Thorung La Passet at 5,200 meters, one of the highest passes in the Himalayas. In Manang, the giant mountains were the peaks of Annapurna and Gangapurna, 4,500 meters above us. The absolute magnificence of these mighty mountains lacks a description. We bathed in the green, clear water and enjoyed the beauty of the lake. We took 4/5 baths in the rivers and under the waterfalls.

On the second day of rest, we climbed 300 meters to the little Tsamkhang temple in a cave beneath a cliff. Between ancient artifacts and Buddha statues, some could have been from one of Marco Polo's accounts, an elderly lama was dressed in holy clothes and led a short *puja* - a short prayer - to make the coming trek over the pass be successful. We were told that a group who had visited the temple before had failed to accept the blessing and had not managed to come over the passport. The blessing looked like a good assurance in the back.

We found out that many people who lived in Manang and in the high mountains of Nepal had emigrated from Tibet. The whole community had traveled over the tall, clear passes to Nepal during the brutal invasion of the Chinese in the 1950s. They brought flocks of yaks and goats, which have tragically caused serious erosion problems in the high mountains. Closer to the Tibetan border, in Mustang province, Buddhist bean flags became more common over the beautiful stone houses. Bean wheels at the entrance of the village made travelers improve their familiar state or karma by spinning the wheel. People in the mountains greeted us with their traditional '*namaste*'. It is a great acknowledgment of the kindness that lies in all of a hit.

The day before we came to the primitive, snowy settlement of Thorung Phedi, about 4.300 meters, we began to feel the effect of the height. This was the last village before Thorung La Pass. The terrain had changed from meadows to hill cuttings and terraces with potatoes and oats to a rugged, spartan, fearful, alpine landscape with steep mountainsides and dark, bare stone façades that rose steeply from the bottom of the valley up to the clouds. The day was grand and a little promising. Alone on the trail, we followed a narrow trail that crossed a steep slope with a great danger of rock cliffs. Underneath the trail, the valley bottom was full of deep as it had fallen from the mountains above the clouds, many thousand feet above us. Two kilometers before we arrived at Thorung Phedi, we were astonished to find more chunks with yak hairs on the track. We stopped to investigate it further. About 100 meters below us, we saw the carcass of a dead yak lying in the snow. Something had eaten the body, but it was still almost untouched. Scarier than the dead yak were the big footprints of another animal we had seen earlier, further down the valley. It looked like this animal had followed the yak for many miles before it attacked and killed it. This was a threatening, cold, and hassle-free place. Low clouds drove down the valley and shouted us into a world of mist and silence. When we arrived at Thorung Phedi, a lonely collection of low-stone buildings half hidden in snow, we knew that the yak had been killed by a snow leopard. The big tracks we had seen were way too big for a leopard, but we said nothing.

Many mountain people in the Himalayas are trying to conceive of any discussion about the jet. We thought it was a jeti's deed or perhaps a mythical, eremitic animal's, as some legend says, roams in these mountains? Although it resembles a bear with human characteristics, it is said to avoid contact with humans. Don Williams, a famous mountain climber, is not far from Thorung Phedi, a member of a British expedition who climbed Annapurna in 1972. He called the jeti when they set up base camp. He would have followed this weird beast, but the expedition's sheep, which came from the Everest region of Nepal, fought him to follow him. Since then, he told Roy, who was a friend of his, that the carriers would not even discuss the possibility of the jeti's existence.

With these thoughts, we went to bed early in the primitive retreat. We played chess against two young students from Oslo and an older hippie from San Francisco. He, together with other foreign teams from Germany and

FROM HIMALAYA TO SOUTH PACIFIC

Denmark, had gathered in Thorung Pehdi in today's race. As all were prepared for an early start the next morning, the 5.500-meter high pass. All the other teams had decided to start at 4:30, one hour before dawn, but we had departed at 6:00. It had been raining all night, and the outbreak of today was bad, but we set off. The blinking headlights from the trekkers in front of us slowly melted together with the faint morning dawn.

Daily weather updates of the last week forced many pullers to go back down and give up the trip over the passport. With this in mind and not set for any retreat, we went upward into the clear shining light of the dawn, and we gradually took the others. The clouds were still low and threatened to hide the route through the mountains. Other tractors like us were fully prepared for the weather with warm, fiber-filled jackets and strong boots. In contrast, the carriers of the French traits were dressed in a dress. The female carriers carrying 30/35 kilo children were dressed in lightweight cotton skirts, indeterminate sweaters, and worn-out shoes. The men were not better dressed.

The weather was getting worse. Low clouds driven by a wind of increasing strength from the east gave us a violent snowstorm and reduced sight. The situation was possibly dangerous due to the nuisance of the French, who had many slow pullers who did not look like they had acclimatized properly. Just a few days after we came across the pass, two Englishmen died in a snow race sweeping down from a mountaintop over the pass. We stopped for a moment to look at the cairn, which marked another Englishman who had been taken by a storm no sooner and was buried under the cliffs. His parents had asked that trackers remember him when they passed by; that was the least we could do. We stopped for a moment at the top with our backs to the wind to see if there was no need for help. People came to the pass, but the weather got worse, and we found it wise to start the downhill ride to the village of Muktinath, 1800 meters below us in the west. A woman porter we had seen earlier came by, bowed by the weight of her heavy bask. She tried to walk as fast as she could down the steep slope. Suddenly she lost her balance and slid down the mountain wide, and she could not get back into her worn-out old flip-flop shoes. We tried to lift her basket so she could catch her head over her forehead, but it was too heavy. We suggested that she lay down at the bottom of the basket and slowly rise.

She managed this but had difficulty with the balance. This was the last we saw of her. With the diminishing visibility, Roy and I increased the descent by sitting on our tails and sliding down off and on the path. This way, we made a high-speed fast descent and came down 1500 meters to the end of the snow. We continued down through a surreal landscape of mountains surrounded by swamped and insulated farms, all partly hidden by the snow that fell low and swirling.

The village of Muktinath appeared as a medieval revelation, a sight of bare hills with clusters of stone houses. On the walkway to Muktinath, we passed a decorated Innemurt temple complex that had attracted pilgrims of bore Hindu and Buddhist religions for hundreds of years. But, unfortunately, it broke down as we walked by, and we felt for the special clothes, pilgrims sitting and pushing together to keep the heat.

Muktinath, which is only 100 kilometers from Tibet, is the second holiest Hindu place in Nepal and attracts thousands of pilgrims consisting of entire families, and whole villages, through the deeply squared Gandaki River Valley that flows north/south between the great mountains Annapurna and Dhaulagiri.

We were pleased to have come across the passport in good shape but wondered how it had been with the French. We later learned that their carriers had lost their children on their way down and that an organized action was organized the next day. So we continued down the dramatic Dhaulagiri valley and southward. We walked through the famous rhododendron forests, where the trees grew up to 15 meters tall and were in full bloom when we arrived in April.

We had previously often walked over distant distances. Still, here we went together because there was a famous assassination of robbers who could sneak into the woods, so you should not travel alone. Just where the forest was the darkest and most frightening, we arrived at the Tadapani village, which had been well suited to the rhododendron forest in the great early 19th century Annapurna South. After a good night and with untouched energy and our bodies 5 kilos more than once, we started we were on our way to Chomrong, sitting at the mouth of Modhi Khola, a magnificent road leading to the Annapurna Sanctuary and the sacred peak of Machhupuchhre, a crooked, undisputed spire of rocks and ice guarding the entrance to the reserve.

Ascent and descent are an inevitable reality of trekking in the Himalayas. I always remember the otherwise beautiful village of Chomrung for its stone stairs with 2300 steps that we used to go up and down when we came through the city. Fortunately, at this time of our trip, 2300 steps were more an interesting point than anything that was physically challenging. We had to come down the same vertical height in the next few kilometers and start over to Ghandruk.

Many times we stopped, full of awe for the skies that looked beyond the simplicity, the stone houses of the mountains, each with their own Buddhist bean flag as flagged in the wind. The landscape has an indescribable spiritual quality that invites one's imagination to wander and wonder. With the origin of Hinduism, Buddhism has fewer divinities and keeps all living life in touch. The Buddhists believe that our destiny is coming back in a wide range of reincarnations until we achieve spiritual freedom when we do not need to be born again unless we choose to come back to help others on their way to Nirvana. They believe that all events in their lives count on the final judgment day. Your spiritual bank account is known as *karma*.

An unexpected and unwelcomed weight loss started somewhere in Mod Khola K1 when Roy and I both began to feel weak with stomach problems. Roy became so weak that he had to return to Chomrung for a two-day convalescence. At the same time, I continued to the base camp in Annapurna Sanctuary alone with Tonya. We met again a few days later in Ghandrok. During the last two days, we had gradually lost height as we pulled South through Ghandruk; the city was high on the western side of Modi Khola and through Birethani. At last, we had put the mountains behind us. As the last dusty miles to the trail ended, we felt sad at the thought that we had to leave this incredibly special place in a remote part of the world.

At this time, our trip was over!

FROM HIMALAYA TO SOUTH PACIFIC

To Kashmir

Retired brigadier General Baig was my agent in Pakistan. We first met as I flew into Karachi to discuss the possibilities of expanding our trade with our ships to Pakistan from The Far East, Australia, and New Zealand.

He was a small man, wiry, thin small, and dark, with heavy eyebrows covering the upper half of his dark eyes. General Baig was the captain of the Pakistani national polo team. Sitting at the prestigious Karachi Club by the court, breathing heavily after beating me 6-2 in the afternoon heat, he told me about his recent game again this the British polo team.

I played against Prince Philip last year – he was a good polo player, but our team is the best in the world. Our love for our horses is in our DNA. If you travel through the Himalayas and Tibet, you will find that there is a love for horses and polo, like ball games in the mountains. His opinion of the Chinese was formed during his military service in the Kashmirian mountains and was expressed once during a World Wildlife Fund meeting that "If it has got four legs and it is not a chair, if it has got two wings and flies but is not an airplane and if it swims, and it is not a submarine, the Cantonese will eat it."

Baig's father was a minister in waiting for the Nizam of Hyderabad. The Nizams were closely linked with the Moghul rulers of Delhi, and the state was one of the largest and wealthiest in India.

Nazim owned the famous 162-carat diamond Jacob and was reputed to be the richest man in the world from about 1900 to mid 1960'ies. In the 1930s, the Nizam had some 100 million British pounds (GBP) worth of gold and silver and a further 500 million GBP worth of jewels. Despite this immense wealth, the Nizam did not flaunt his wealth, and he wore inexpensive clothes. On the formation of the Indian Union, Nizam chose to remain independent. Eventually, his land was invaded by Indian forces, and the state of Hyderabad was annexed by the Union.

His castle was sitting on top of a diamond and a gold mine.

Barbara Hutton – the world's richest heiress - visited him in the 30s and requested an interview with the Nizam. Although, she had to wait for more than a week. Meanwhile, she was permitted to look at some of his possessions in the Palace. It included a huge room of emeralds, another of diamonds, and another large vault of gold.

When she finally met the Nizam, she asked whether he

was insured. After she left, he asked my father what insurance was.

They then invited the courtiers of Tiffany and Cartier to the palace to assess the value of his holdings. After a few days, they informed the Nizam that his possessions were so large that they were incapable of arriving at a conclusive evaluation. Like many rulers before him, the Nizam had a harem of wives. Sometimes he would have his sweeping stairway upstairs to his bedroom lined with his naked-breasted women on each side of each step, and he would grab one breast at a time on each side as he climbed upstairs to his chambers.

Baig and I traveled to the Persian Gulf and visited several merchants and shipping people there. Hesky Baig was from an aristocratic family of Hyderabad Deccan and had married Nawabzadi Salima Begum from the family of Nawab of Surat. We later met in our flat in London, and my wife and I took him to the theatre to see "live" James Stewart in the rabbit story "Harvey". Our friendship ended when my wife made two rabbit ear holes in his new bowler hat. It is an amazing rabbit story about a 6" invincible rabbit where sometimes one only sees the rabbit ears. Hesky's son-in-law Shah Rafi had an affair with Ava Gardner. In 1955, when MGM studio embarked on a big movie project named

FROM HIMALAYA TO SOUTH PACIFIC

Bhawani Junction in Lahore. The Pakistan government supported the venture with film stars Ava Gardner, Stewart Granger, and other crew members spending several months in Pakistan. A 13 Frontier Force Rifles battalion provided some of its officers and soldiers for the film. Shah Rafi was a member of the Lahore Polo Club, and some of the cast members visited the club. He and Stewart Granger had a fight over Ava Gardner.

"Hesky" (#4 from the right) with Polo Player Prince Philip and Queen Elizabeth.

We are now going back 40 years in time to the mid-thirties.

We came with our 14 climbing horses and followed the Sonnemarg 7,200 foot meadow below the 5 glaciers in Kashmir. The river bends through the long valley, surrounded by high mountains on both sides. Here we set up our tents. We intended to stay for 2 weeks. The next day we heard that this was the place where Aila missionaries from all over India vacationed. So we went for long day cruises and came home for a good dinner made by the Kashmir chef and a big festive fire in front of the tents.

One evening we were sitting in front of the tent when came the tax collector came for a few payments for the tent sites. He was very talkative and told me that Kashmir once had one big lake. Then it was one of the old song gods who had opened the mountain wall at Barambella, so the water ran out, and the bottom became the fertile Kashmir Valley.

About 300 years after Kr. was Kashmir an important philosophical center, he said where scholars came from China, South India, and all the countries around the Eastern Mediterranean and from the Near Orient. One of the most famous was a female philosopher.

Great dictators also had arrived. One who came to South India and his long-standing Viking kingdom when the birds flew north to Kashmir was read by ale.

He sat in the fire and dreamed and talked warmly. His eyes shone when he told of Sri Sankaracharya, who wrote many reflections on the Upanishads. The Upanishads were a total of 150 fonts, but there are only 20 original writings left. They were many thousands of years old, but the first orientalists who were still bound by the ruling misunderstanding of biblical chronology (timesheet) had their theories about the Upanishad's age and, of course, made it too low. Because they say that it only occurs from 600 years b.kr.

The scriptures contain the beginning and the end of all human knowledge. The Hindus say, "The scripture destroys all ignorance and generates spiritual freedom through the pure doctrine of the hidden truth."

Unfortunately, these writings are hidden away in the monasteries and unavailable to the Hindus today. Only the Smartane Brahmins in South India know them, and these Brahmans sit in secret knowledge and are highly respected.

"And then we had the great Nazarene here in Kashmir," he said. "Who?" I said. "Yes, Jesus from Nazareth was also here in our philosophical circle. They probably remember that there was nothing written about him in their teachings from he was 12 until he was about 30 years old, and at that time, he was here too. Godly Arier, or Hindu at that time, sent his son to a teacher (Guru) when he was big enough to make him live as an eremite until he was 20 or 30 years before he married and settled. Later, they left their family after a while and went over to seek loneliness and meditation.

Later, I also learned Hindus and Muhammadans have said the same about Jesus.

"It was spiritual greatness in India at that time," he said, and "Idealism was great." When they got married, of course, the parents did the selection, and they carefully watched that the bride and groom had horoscopes that matched. Otherwise, the marriage would not be happy. Then they went to astrologers and found out what stars they belonged to.

"I think so," he said, "that one can get a woman whose temperament fits into one's own way. But it happened that a rich man could try a bribe astrologer or cardboard if it was an extra beautiful woman he wanted."

Then he asked me if I had seen the grave in Kashmir as they thought it was the grave of Jesus. I also asked them about it because I was very interested in seeing it when I heard about it.

It was a Kashmir pandit that took me in a tonga (horses and Giggs). It is located outside the city of Srinigar, an ancient city built around a bay in the Jhelum River. The houses look like real Setesdal living rooms in several places, with gables and railings.

FROM HIMALAYA TO SOUTH PACIFIC

The temple around the grave was built in the same style with grass on the roof, while the building rested on a solid stone floor. In the middle of the big room was a large stone block of the same shape as Muhammad's tomb. Around this one, it was set up as a tree kit to keep people away. Next to the stone was a small block where there was a print of the dead's feet. This is often found at the graves of the Osten. I noticed that my feet were particularly big and that all the toes were as long.

On the staky, there was a chalkboard that was in Persian by a prophet who would have lived in Jesus' time. I got a scholar from Kashmir to translate it for me, but I can not guarantee it's correct. It was written:

Ziarat Uas-asaf, Khanayari Khåwaja Mohamad Azam Dedamari in his history "Waqåt-i-Kashmir" Nasir-out-your Khanyari

Translation freely given:

"There is a nearby gravestone known as the grave of the Holy Prophet, who was in Kashmir in ancient times; his name was Us-sef us-asof."

I asked him what he meant about it. He replied, "Tired of that sort of thing destroying all philosophy and harmony. It belongs to materialism."

Later, I heard some Hindus say it could possibly be a tram from the Muhammadan's side against Christianity. I met a Muhammadan in Afghanistan who said, "We do not think God would allow such a great prophet as Jesus to be a crucifixist. We believe that Jesus brought his mother through Persian and Afghanistan across the mountains to Kashmir. Mary died on the road, and the place has been named after her - the current mountain town of Mary in Turkmenistan." However, Jesus said he had reached Kashmir, where he lived until he was 72.

"It was for spiritual greatness in India at that time," he said, "and idealism was great." When they got married, of course, the parents did the selection, and they carefully watched that the bride and groom had horoscopes that matched. Otherwise, the marriage would not be happy. Then they went to astrologers and found out which star they belonged to.

I think so, he said, that one can get a woman whose temperament fits into one's own. But it happened that a rich man could try a bribe astrologer or cardboard if it was an extra beautiful woman he wanted.

"The time of birth had a lot of say to us," he continued. "For example, when a prince died and did not have any thorns, they went around looking for the child born at the same moment as the Prince died, and he was then chosen as king."

Then the flames died, the servants had rested in their tents, and the horses rested under the big prawns. The mosses are large and clear of the glaciers in the west. "Salåm," said the Hindu. He put his two hands up against the forehead and walked.

The day derpå counted it. Hindus came again. I knew you would be home today, he said. By the way, I was sitting alone and talking to him. He said I always carry a book with me, which I can read a bit. Bhagavad Gita, Hindu holy writings from the Upanishads.

"Here it is." He said. He read that the secret of happiness here in this world is to make other people happy. He read, and it seemed as if he was reading the Bible. "I fight a struggle with myself," he said, whether I should leave my family as I love them and all the world's goodies and pleasures. It is the fight that Sry Krishna urges Arjuna to lead. He really looked like he was fighting with his inner self. "Why do not you go away and talk to the missionaries over here," I said. There were five tents full of missionaries from several nations. "Ah no," he said, "They never talk to us about our philosophy. They cannot discuss; they just get upset. Ask them a question, and they cannot answer, so they only say that God's ways are unbearable and it's better for us people not to ask why. We believe in Jesus as the master he was, but the missionaries will never listen to us when it comes to philosophy."

Then he read on from the book about the soul and the dangers that he met on his pilgrimage. He finally asked me what to do since he was at such an important turning point in his life. Then I said, "Well if you've reached as far as you say, you probably know what you should do."

The next day we were with the missionaries for coffee. Someone had just been downstairs and taken a bath in the river that came straight from the glacier. We had to do the same thing the same day since the missionaries were bathing in ice water every day. They brewed delicious cakes and waffles. Then they sang for us, and one of them played so funnily on a case. Later they invited us into the tent. Here they suddenly fell down on their knees and prayed for us poor sinners that God had to take care of us on the long journey we were about to make through the passport to the Baltistan and Little Tibet and Gilgit. I understood there was hope for the other two, but it was quite hopeless for me, that had a somewhat different attitude. For the young girl who was going out in the world alone, they prayed for God to help her guide her on the right path. "She was searching," they said, "So they would probably do that." Now, the man, they could not get it right, but they probably believed that he was of the easy convertible. But the lady, God, you're gonna take care of herself because she's totally out of bed. It needs a stronger hand to guide her on the right path.

We stood there in the tent and looked down on the two who prayed for us in a kind of ecstasy, and we walked away with mixed feelings.

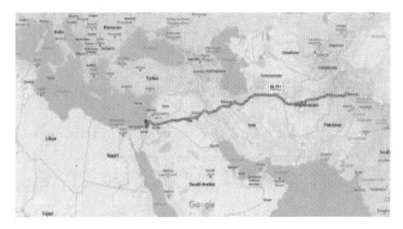

The purported route by Jesus, Mary, and Thomas from Jerusalem to Kashmir.

FROM HIMALAYA TO SOUTH PACIFIC

A Norwegian Tale

KJEAASEN, HARDANGER

KJEAASEN

FROM HIMALAYA TO SOUTH PACIFIC

Kjeaasen = a mountain with goat kids

CONTENT: PRE-HISTORY

- ➢ THE 14TH - CENTURY BERGEN
- ➢ THE 17TH - CENTURY DENMARK
- ➢ THE 20TH - CENTURY KJEAASEN

FROM HIMALAYA TO SOUTH PACIFIC

PRE-HISTORY

Evidence of human activity can be traced back over 30,000 years ago in Scandinavia. However, serious settlements only began some 5/8000 BC. The early settlers must have been unusual men, leaving Central Europe in search of the betterment of living conditions, leaving the center stage by will and by centrifugal force to settle at the periphery of civilization. They were here to build an existence where none was meant to be, with the main constituents of snow, mountains, and the cold sea, which gave little grounds for cheer. They were following the birds of passage, some of which travel up to 17,000 kilometers from the Southern to the Northern latitudes every spring, and the salmon, which returns to the extensive, cool rivers every 2 to 4 years to its spawning grounds.

These men were the ombudsmen of a fresh current; they were questing for a life outside the orthodoxy, away from the civilization of middle earth as it was known only then. Little by little, they would chisel out their lives by subsistence hunting by traps which would be steadily improved. They were to develop fishing methods that would give harvests of salmons in such a plenty amount that it eventually became less desirable so that workers' employment contracts would contain a clause requiring salmon only to be served three times a week. Fish is still flourishing in these waters; below the icecap in the Barents Sea, the ocean is teeming, feeding off the rich fauna of algae and plankton that is nourishment for the smaller and larger dwellers of the deep. Fishing early became an important industry of the Northern monarchies, with herring, cod, and flatfish accounting for most of the catch.

The men became rugged and tenacious by their burdensome existence in the physically abusive environment with brief summers, raw and damp seasons, and harsh, cold winters. They set upon the land in the north, from the 60th to the 80th latitude. Further north and closer to the poles than any man anywhere else on the planet. In later centuries, the same spirit moved their progeny to explore the outer limits of the earth by ship through the Northern Arctic and to ski across the North Pole, ship to Greenland and cross it on skis, through the North-West Passage to the Bering Strait, and eventually the South Pole. The Vikings issued from Vika (the huge bay) in Skagerrak, an eastward extension of the North Sea – located between Northern Denmark (Jutland), Western Sweden, and Southern Norway. Here the elements inauspiciously assail men and ships when the northwesterly seasonally is gusting from the Atlantic and bounce off the receding coastline of Denmark and the granite crust of Norway and Sweden.

The Vikings were explorers and, in due time, evolved into astute builders of ocean-going ships and traveled over great distances, navigating by bearings on heavenly bodies and landmarks; they settled in Greenland, Iceland, and Vineland in the Western hemisphere and voyaged down the Volga to Constantinople in the East. However, the Vikings also were feared for their brutal, innumerable plundering over 200/300 years. As they would discontinue their raging and instead exact tribute against peace.

Erik the Red's father (Thorvald Asvaldsson) was banished from Norway for the crime of manslaughter when Erik was about 10 years old. He sailed west from Norway with his family and settled in Hornstrandir in northwestern Iceland. After marrying Thjodhild (Þjóðhildr), Erik moved to Haukadal (Hawksdale), where he built a farm called Eiríksstaðir. The initial confrontation occurred when his thralls (slaves) started a landslide on the neighboring farm belonging to Valthjof (Valþjófr). Valthjof's friend, Eyiolf the Foul (Eyjólfrsaurr), killed the thralls. In retaliation, Erik killed Eyjiolf and Holmgang-Hrafn (Hólmgöngu-Hrafn). As a result, Eyiolf's kinsmen demanded his banishment from Haukadal. The Icelanders later sentenced Erik to exile for three years for killing Eyiolf the Foul around the year 982.

Erik then moved to the island of Öxney. He asked Thorgest (Þórgestr) to keep his setstokkr – inherited ornamented beams of significant mystical value, which his father had brought from Norway. When he finished his new house, he went back to get them, but they "could not be obtained". Erik then went to Breidabolstad and took them. These are likely to have been Thorgest's setstokkr, although the sagas are unclear at this point. Thorgest gave chase, and in the ensuing fight, Erik slew both Thorgest's sons and "a few other men".

After this, each of them retained a considerable body of men with him at his home. Styr gave Erik his support, as also did Eyiolf of Sviney, Thorbjiorn, Vifil's son, and the sons of Thorbrand of Alptafirth; while Thorgest was backed by the sons of Thord the Yeller, and Thorgeir of Hitardal, Aslak of Langadal and his son Illugi. Finally, the dispute was resolved at an assembly, the Thorsnes Thing, with the result that Erik was outlawed for three years.

Even though popular history credits Erik as the first person to discover Greenland, the Icelandic sagas suggest that earlier Norsemen discovered and tried to settle it before him. Tradition credits GunnbjörnUlfsson (also known as Gunnbjörn Ulf-Krakuson) with the first sighting of the land mass. Nearly a century before Erik, strong winds had driven Gunnbjörn towards the land he called "Gunnbjarnarsker" ("Gunnbjörn's skerries"). But the accidental nature of Gunnbjörn's discovery has led to his neglect of the history of Greenland. After Gunnbjörn, SnæbjörnGalti also visited Greenland. According to records from the time, Galti headed the first Norse attempt to colonize Greenland, which ended in disaster. Erik the Red was the first permanent European settler.

In this context, in about 982, Erik sailed to a somewhat mysterious and little-known land. He rounded the southern tip of the island (later known as Cape Farewell) and sailed up the western coast. He eventually reached a part of the coast that, for the most part, seemed ice-free and consequently had conditions—similar to those of Iceland—that promised growth and future prosperity. According to the Saga of Erik the Red, he spent his three years of exile exploring this land. The first winter he spent on the island of Eiriksey, and the second winter he passed in Eiriksholmar (close to Hvarfsgnipa). In the final summer, he explored as far north as Snaefell and into Hrafnsfjord.

When Erik returned to Iceland after his exile had expired, he is said to have brought with him stories of "Greenland". Erik deliberately gave the land a more appealing name than

"Iceland" in order to lure potential settlers. He explained, "People would be attracted to go there if it had a favorable name". He knew that the success of any settlement in Greenland would need the support of as many people as possible. His salesmanship proved successful, as many people (especially those Vikings living on poor land in Iceland and those that had suffered a recent famine) became convinced that Greenland held great opportunity.

After spending the winter in Iceland, Erik returned to Greenland in 985 with a large number of colonists. Out of 25 ships that left for Greenland, only 14 arrived, and 11 were lost at sea. The Icelanders established two colonies on the southwest coast, the Eastern Settlement or Eystribyggð, in modern-day Qaqortoq, and the Western Settlement or Vestribyggð, close to present-day Nuuk. Eventually, a Middle Settlement grew, but many people suggest it formed part of the Western Settlement. The Eastern and Western Settlements, established on the southwest coast, proved to be the only two areas suitable for farming. During the summers, when the weather favored travel more, each settlement would send an army of men to hunt in Disko Bay above the Arctic Circle for food and other valuable commodities such as seals (used for rope), ivory from walrus tusks, and beached whales.

Medieval Icelandic tradition relates that Erik the Red and his wife Þjóðhildr (Thjodhildr) had four children: a daughter, Freydís, and three sons, the explorer Leif Eiríksson, Þorvaldr (Thorvald) and Þorsteinn (Thorstein). Erik himself remained a follower of Norse paganism, unlike his son Leif and Leif's wife, who became Christians. After being baptized by King Olaf Tryggvason, Leif brought the message of Christianity to Greenland, becoming something of an evangelist. While his wife took heartily to the religion, even commissioning Greenland's first church, Erik greatly disliked the faith and stuck to his Norse Gods – which, the sagas relate, led Thjodhild to withhold intercourse from her husband. Thjothhild was the daughter of Jørundur Ulfsson and Thorbjørg Gilsdottir (from whom Gilsfjørd is named). Jørund's mother, Bjørg, was the granddaughter of Irish king Cerball Mac Dúnlainge (Kjarval) through his daughter Rafarta. While not the first to sight the North American continent, Leif Erikson became the first Viking to explore the land of Vinland (part of North America, probably near modern-day Newfoundland). Leif invited his father on the voyage, but according to legend, Erik fell off his horse on his way to the ship and took this as a bad sign, leaving his son to continue without his company. Erik died the winter after his son's departure. There is no evidence that Leif was aware of his father's death until he returned to Greenland.

Christopher Columbus did not discover America. The Vikings did. The Vikings made it all the way to Istanbul down the Dnieper River. They were eventually hired and became the Byzantine emperor's favored warriors to protect his kingdom.

Bergen was founded in the year 1070 by King Olav Kyrre. It was a natural nexus on the western coast of Norway and soon became the largest port in Norway, built around the fish export trade. North Norway had one of the world's most prodigious fishing grounds with a basis in the enormous amount of cod. The cod follows the spawning herring – the 3rd largest fish stock in the world - from the coastal waters of the West Ford and north-west around Spitsbergen at 81 degrees north and then returning. The catch was sun and wind dried for 3-4 months in the near arctic type prevailing weather. The cod trade started during the Viking period and has been going on for more than 1000 years and created one of the world's longest-lasting trades between Norway and Italy, Spain and Portugal, where the dried cod is served as the main ingredient in their wonderful bacalao which also contains potato, onion, tomato, paprika, and pimiento.

In the 11th century, the Vikings conquered all of England

and brought permanent settlements to Normandy. At the beginning of the 12th century, the Vikings' period was over, and normal trading patterns evolved with the export of fish and timber. The Vikings' period ended about the same time as religion arrived. King Olav was buried in Trondheim where Norway's largest cathedral – Nidaros Dome - was later erected over his grave. Olav became Holy Olav as many odd "holy" things happened before and after his death after it was found that his beard and hair were still growing after he was exhumed sometime after the funeral.

FROM HIMALAYA TO SOUTH PACIFIC

Norwegian Literature

Snorri Sturluson was an Icelandic historian, poet, and politician. The Heimkringla is his compendium of a huge collection of sagas (stories), such as the Egil Saga and The Younger Edda, including the formation of the kingdom of Norway and the descendant kings following this. He was elected twice as a law speaker at the Icelandic parliament, the Althing. As a historian and mythographer, Snorri is remarkable for proposing the hypothesis (in the Prose Edda) that mythological gods began as human war leaders and kings whose funeral sites developed into cults. As people called upon their dead war leader as they went into battle, or their dead king as they faced tribal hardship, they began to venerate the figure. Eventually, the king or warrior was remembered only as a god. He also proposed that as tribes defeated each other, they explained their victory by proposing that their own gods were in battle with their rivals. He postulated a synthesis between the Christian faith and the old heathen tradition. He wrote dissertations on grammar, astronomy, and geography and translated medical writings from Latin.

One Saga story is about an Icelandic gang of farmers who had come to Gunnar's house to kill him. One person climbed the roof to see if he was home. Through the skylight, Gunnar threw his atgeir (a type of spear-axe) into the invader's stomach, and he fell down. His members asked him if Gunnar was home, and he replied, "The only thing I can say is that his atgeir was home," Then he fell dead on the ground.

There was a strong sense of honor embedded in the behavior of the old Vikings. Once, a farmer was killed by his neighbors, and the wife asked her family to avenge his death, but they refused. The wife then took the task upon herself, went to the neighbor's home, and killed him with her sword. The brothers of the dead neighbor respected the woman for having carried out the honorable deed and left her in peace.

Most sagas may start with a prophecy for something that may be happening in the future. Queen Ragnhild, who was a wise and highly respected woman, had a dream of a large tree that covered the whole country and beyond. The interpretation of the dream was that Halfdan Svarte's family would be given the right to be kings, and so it turned out. Eventually, the monasteries took over Saga's writings and merged them with the religion.

Knut Hamsun is considered to be "one of the most influential and innovative literary stylists of the past hundred years" (ca.1890–1990). He pioneered psychological literature with techniques of stream of consciousness and interior monologue. He influenced authors such as Thomas Mann, Franz Kafka, Maxim Gorky, Stefan Zweig, Henry Miller, Hermann Hesse, and Ernest Hemingway. His most famous book was *'Growth Of The Soil,'* for which he was awarded the Nobel Prize.

Sigrid Undset - her best-known work is Kristin Lavransdatter, a trilogy about life in Scandinavia in the Middle Ages, portrayed through the experiences of a woman from birth until death. Its three volumes were published between 1920 and 1922. She was a Norwegian novelist who was awarded the Nobel Prize for Literature in 1928.

FROM HIMALAYA TO SOUTH PACIFIC

The Norwegian Women

It is important to get across the incredible strength, independence, and beauty of the women of Norway in many ways. The Nordic countries and Norway are very radical when it comes to gender equality. In the days of the old, women always had a strong say in their family lives, and they would always carry the keys to the home in their belt, indicating that she was running the household. They also were involved in maintaining peace or war. In Norway, there are more women who complete higher education at universities and colleges than men. In 2011, 24,743 women completed higher education, while the number of men was 15,825. In addition, there are more female doctors, priests, and academics than men.

The fight for Women's Rights in Norway began in the 1970s. Their slogans were: *'Equal pay for equal work'*, *'Fight Prostitution'* and *'Women – take control over your own body'*.

In 1961, the first female Norwegian priest, Ingrid Bjerkås, was ordained. In 1981, Norway's first female Prime Minister, Mrs. Gro Harlem Brundtland, was elected. In her 1986 government, she appointed eight women ministers out of a total of 18 – the largest percentage of women in any

Western government ever. This event attracted considerable international attention.

Today we can see the results of the women's fights for equality. Norwegian women decide what careers they want, how they organize their lives, and who they want to share their lives with. Women in Norway are crane operators, carpenters, nurses, police, and doctors – anything they want to be.

This does not mean that Norwegian men have become weaker or that the gender roles are blurring. On the contrary, Norwegian men love their women. The strength of women has made many men happier. Who would not want a partner who knows what she wants and what is equal when it comes to financial matters, sexuality, and decision-making? It is still true that muscles, physiology, and interest are important factors when it comes to gender roles. Norwegian men shovel snow, chop wood, mow the lawn, paint houses, do carpentry and go hunting – but he knows that the matriarch is waiting at home.

As in many other countries, urban areas are the head of development. Boys do not move from home to rural communities where farming and fishing are the primary industries. At the same time, the girls travel to urban areas for education and job seeking. The sex ratio is skewed between urban and rural areas: There is a surplus of women in the cities and a deficit in rural areas.

Another 'problem' is that women know what they want and what requirements they impose on a man. He must be handsome, smart, warm, educated, funny, well-dressed, interesting, loving, good at managing kids, caring... He must be everything at once, which, of course, can be challenging.

Men, however, still have relatively simple requirements for a woman: She should be sociable, beautiful, caring, and contribute to the family economy from time to time. But she can also be highly demanding and annoying.

The development of equality has, for many men, gone so fast that they do not 'stick in the turns'. This is partly due to the upbringing they have received from their parent's generation. So, how does a Norwegian man regard the Norwegian woman of today?

Many Norwegian men look upon Norwegian women as independent, strong, and well-educated. She is beautiful, well-kept, and feminine – with many masculine qualities. But is she really tall, blonde, and busty? Mostly not. Believe it or not, she can be chubby, lower than 5.4ft, and she can be a huge monster taller than 6.2ft. Norwegian women can be thick, thin, blonde, or dark – but they are always strong and independent. And do not forget, you can also find Norwegian women in saris, Bunads, hijabs, burkas, miniskirts, trousers, and with or without sneakers.

Coquetry is not a typical Norwegian woman quality! You can hear when a Norwegian woman walks along the sidewalk – both her feet are firmly planted on the ground.

The Norwegian woman's strong position in society has earned one party: The Norwegian man! What has not equality and equity meant for the Norwegian man's position and sexual liberation?

Today, the Norwegian government is ruled by three parties, each of which has a woman leader.

FROM HIMALAYA TO SOUTH PACIFIC

The 14th Century - Bergen

In the 1340s, a rat pest called the Black Death killed some 50 million people in Europe. It remains one of the most devastating pandemics in human history. To Norway, it came by ship from London to Bergen. In February 1349, a British merchant ship docked in the Hanseatic City of Bergen. It carried a deadly stowaway, The Black Death. Two years later, about two-thirds of the population was killed. Perhaps if it were now, the disaster would have been averted, but it spread so quickly before barely anything could be done. And the ignorance? It was another which contributed to the spread and death tolls.

When the deaths began to hit, confusion set in. Blames were cast on the lepers, the Jews, the poor, and the foreigners. They, of all people, had to be responsible for this unknown disease. Many believed it was the end of the world, and they surely were right. It was the end of millions of lives and an end to an era. Many blamed it on God; it had to be punishment for their sins. Perhaps they should turn back to God, but as they discovered, it was surely too late. Death was knocking on their doors.

The streets were often filled with waste from both humans and animals, and people often went without shoes.

FROM HIMALAYA TO SOUTH PACIFIC

This meant that people easily got infected, spreading the disease through food, clothing, and body contact. It was later established that the bacterium Yersinia originated in oriental rat fleas living on black rats and came from the dry plains of Central Asia – some came by boat and some along the silk road, possibly with the Mongol armies, and arrived in Crimea about 1343.

Olaf was a fisherman in Bergen selling his fish in the local market. A man of humble beginnings, Olaf was hardworking and made good use of his hands as his source of income. He was married to Maria, a woman whom he loved and admired; just like him, she was hardworking and a formidable pillar by his side. Bergen was filled with panic as Black Death came knocking. It was no surprise that it swarmed through the streets; Bergen was, after all, a populous city with a running port well frequented by neighboring towns. It started with the coughs, and then the spots began to appear, and soon, from house to house, there were wails as darkness descended upon them.

With the disaster looming over them, Olaf and Maria decided that soon they would leave Bergen with their three kids, Torfinn (14), Ragnhild (9), and Astrid (5), for Hardanger, the fruit capital of Norway, where the climate was drier and hopefully no trace of the pest. So they sat around the fire in their home in Bergen, and Olaf had just opened a letter that had arrived in the morning, delivered by the old letterman.

"Maria, I just received a letter from my uncle Bjorn," Olaf said as he tore open the seal. There was not much to the envelope. It was brown stained and had seen better days. It had been exchanged by several hands and gone through several routes to reach its final destination. How long had it been on the road? A fortnight? Or more? Olaf removed the letter, которая was scrawled with black inked handwriting.

Dear Olaf,

A merchant ship arrived at the city of Haugesund two weeks ago. The crew started dying the day they commenced discharging the cargo. The ship brought black rats and, with it, the fleas and the Black Death. Although what was left of the crew was quarantined, it was too late; the plague had escaped. It started with the butcher and moved on to the baker, who stayed by the dock. In no time, it had spread like wildfire through the city. Our city searched in despair after a cure for the plague. But this was something we had never seen before. How quick it ravages the body still scares me. Never have the doctors seen something like this. We had heard of the plague, but nothing prepared us for the damage it would cause to us. I watched as mothers wept for their children who were lowered into small graves; following days later. Father and mother started to feel bad after a short time. They had nausea, fever, headache, bloody headache, and were mentally confused. We tried to make them feel better with a hot disinfected bath, hot soups, and the tonic, but nothing we did could make them come to their senses. Filled with fear, we hoped for the best. A few days later, mother died and then father a few days after. Oh! How unfortunate it is to lose both parents in a matter of days. We could not even organize a befitting funeral for them, as a mass funeral was performed for all of them by the already ailing priest. Haugesund had become desolate with the sick. We saddled a horse and cart and took the course down in order not to be hit. We had a lot of misery and hardship on the journey as we set the course toward our home, Stavanger. The plague had not been left behind in Haugesund; it had gone ahead of us, and whatever town we stopped by was filled with the ravaging plague. To avoid being infected, we had to camp outside the cities. Some of the cities were empty except for the looming graveyards. The large flocks of pestilence had caused the people to flee. We had to manage our food and cater for our animals because of fear of getting infected lest we purchase from infected towns. The illness had spread from place to place, and dead bodies lay along roads and streets. Oh, Olaf! Words cannot express the sadness we felt. There were ailing children, graves the size of little boxes, the cities stank of death, and there was nothing we could do but make our way through in haste, lest we get infected as well. As we approached Rogaland county, most of the towns had become desolate and haunted. Farms and houses were abandoned, and our hope began to wobble. We arrived Stavanger after 6 days. Stavanger is no better; our worst fear was confirmed as our horses pulled into the city; the plague had arrived ahead of us. We have lost a great deal, and we have no idea what else to do to stop this plague. As we tried to cater to those around us while trying to protect ourselves from the plague, we got a letter from our uncle. Remember him? Uncle Frank? He writes about a terrible plague that has hit Trondheim, 'Are you still alive, and the terrible plague has it hit Stavanger?' 'What about your parents? And especially your mother, who was so sick and bad when I was there this summer. Here in Trondheim, the terrible plague has hit the skin of inhabitants, and the city already feels completely empty.' It is the same plague that has affected Stavanger, just as it has done to Trondheim. Uncle writes of how far the plague has spread; we heard it has spread over the seas, even to parts unknown. It makes us worry even more. Something of this magnitude, how then will it come to an end? Do you have any idea of where this plague comes from or what it can be at all? How are you faring, and how has life been for you and your family? I have no good news to give you, but I pray that you find yourself in a good state. Hope to hear from you.

Uncle Bjorn.

Silence shrouded the room when Olaf was done reading the letter aloud. He wondered about the fate of his Uncle Bjorn, had he survived the plague, and if he had, for how long he would survive before the disease struck him?

"God in heaven! Those poor people," Maria said with a pensive look, her hand to her chest.

"Yes, but the same has just happened in Bergen. A ship arrived from England fully loaded with grain and ran aground at Askoy – just outside the harbor. After they towed it in and started to discharge the cargo, it was found that the Black Death was on board and brought ashore by the crew. They quarantined the ship, but it was too late," Olaf said. The plague was still a newborn in the city, but from what he had heard, it would take no time for it to spread around. There was a disaster looming, and he had his family to worry about.

"Our children, what can we do?"

"As we have discussed this eventuality, we must escape the town as soon as possible. Now that the plague is in Bergen, it won't take long for it to spread. We have no idea who is infected now; it could be the butcher, it could be the baker, it could be anyone. We need to run from it. I am working on a solution."

"What about our home and our things?" They had birthed their three children in Bergen and considered it home. Their house was little, but it was comfortable with personal belongings which had accumulated over the years. Surely, there had to be a way out? Would they just leave it all behind?

Olaf shook his head incredulously. "The house and things have little consequence if we are dead. As long as we're alive, as long as we have our senses intact, then we can start afresh."

That night, Olaf did not sleep; all he could think of was how to protect his family from the plague. He sat in the dark, thinking of how to get his family to safety. There was no time to muse or panic; time was a luxury that no one, not even the rich, could afford in this circumstance.

"I have found that we may be able to find a safe harbor

and protection in Hardanger," Olaf said the next morning to his wife.

"How are we going to get that far?" Maria asked, perplexed.

"It is 250 miles by boat, and we can all load up into our fishing boat and row there; I may rig up a mast with a sail. And I reckon that Torfinn can assist with some of the rowing. It should take us a few weeks to get there."

With their minds made up, Olaf began to make preparations. There was no time to spare; they needed to leave as soon as possible. From the bottom of his heart, he hoped they were making the right decision and not headed into a further disaster.

During the next few days, many friends and relatives were infected, it would start with dark spots, which caused skin and flesh with freckle-like spots and rash, and swollen glands in the armpit and groin that became as large as apples, and it propagated quickly all through the body with death coming within 3-7 days.

Then Maria and Astrid started to cough and show signs of the disease. There was no time to lose.

They filled up their rowboat with all their belongings and quickly began the long voyage down the coast past the beautiful skerries around the coast of Bergen, past the Folgefonn glacier, and continuing up the long Hardanger fjord into the arm Eidfjord and finally arriving at the town of Eidfjord at the very north-eastern point of the passage.

The total distance was some 130 miles turning south from Bergen some 50 miles until they entered the Hardanger fjord and continued northeast for the balance of the voyage. Their boat was a rowboat with 3 pairs of oars, and everyone aboard could take their time rowing, although Olaf and then Torfinn did most of the work. Olaf had estimated some 15 miles per day, keeping a pace of some 2.5 miles per hour with no wind and calm seas, and some days nothing with bad weather. However, it took them a good month in view of much rain and bad weather, so they had to seek shelter en route. They finally reached the Eidfjord exhausted, wet and sick and were fortunate to find a home.

FROM HIMALAYA TO SOUTH PACIFIC

The Hardanger fjord with the Folgefonnen glacier in the background

After moving in with a local farmer in his boat house, they contacted the local doctor who was familiar with the pest and started a strong, hygienic regimen, including cleaning with rosemary and vinegar. After a while, it started to work, and Maria and Astrid were in time gathering their normal strength. This family was favored, having just escaped the world's worst pest ever. They had been lucky to survive the ravenous disease whose death toll would amount to millions, including the lives of their relatives.

One day Olaf spotted a seemingly inaccessible green shelf 600 meters above the Simafjord. It looked beautiful up there.

"What if we were able to move up there to live? I have noticed that when we have rain or foggy days down here in the fjord, the sun is shining up there," Olaf asked his wife.

"Yes, but how do we get there? It does not look possible to climb that mountain; we are not mountain climbers – are we?"

"I have investigated and found that many years ago, a man actually was up there and had in mind to build a home, but then his health failed, and he had to give it up. I will investigate it further."

Olaf continued establishing a reputation as a good fisherman. He and his family also tended to the farm's animals, cutting grass, collecting firewood, etc. Olaf would every day look wistfully up in the clouds wishing they were there.

The Simafjord was a short extension of the Hardanger fjord into the river gushes down from the huge glacier some 3-4000 feet. On each side of the fjord, steep, dark mountains fell down as vertical walls, and Kjeeasen was on top of the western wall. This place was known as Kjeaasen (the Kjeaasen), a several hours climb up an almost impossible path, crossing the very steep mountainside, with rocks and plain rock faces where you had to look for a crack or rock to hold on to.

The first man at the Kjeaasen may have been escaping

the law. He must have been a very strong and persistent man for the incredible efforts needed to get up to what looked like a small heavenly green spot from below. However, the access seemed nothing but a massive black unapproachable mountain mass, ending perpendicularly right into the cold, dark, blue fjord.

Olaf realized he would have to be armed with an axe, chisel, bolts, rope, and knives to make a viable path and erect wooden ladders. They would need considerable time to make a path up the mountain sides which were interrupted by torrents of river falls that had to be traversed. He would need for Torfinn to help with the construction work. He soon earned the help of the other men and their families, who like him were interested in relocating up the plateau.

The altitude was some 600 meters with a 45% slope; the actual path traveled would probably be some 1500 meters. This path had to be secured all the way with ropes, bolts, chisels, mallets, and hammers. But first, they started to build a stone building down by the fjord where they could live whilst the building was going on, and also as a sleep-over hut in the future when they would come to town to sell their farm products.

FROM HIMALAYA TO SOUTH PACIFIC

The boat house on the shore

They spent a good year building their little house on the fjord. It was a stone hut with a stone upon stone being laid after chiseling most rocks to be contoured and molded to fit into each other. In addition, they used sand, lime mortar, and water as binders. The wall was a good 1.80 meters tall, and on top of this, they used timbers angled to the pitched roof and crisscrossed with timber beams that would double up for drying fish and meat. It was a tightly built cottage that had to withstand the strong South Westerly winds and rain that besieged the fjord constantly during the six winter months. They covered the roof with several layers of peeled birch bark from trees up the Sima valley, and on top of this again, they laid fresh soil on which they planted sod and grass. A perfect roof structure is achieved this way.

After two years of strenuous labor, they had built the boat house, made the pathway, and built their farmhouse on Goat Hill. They could now finally settle in peacefully at their farm.

In the summer, as soon as the grass started to grow up high, they migrated the animals up to an altitude of some 8-10,000 feet, where they built their stone house dairy farm. The children loved the summer, and from the age of about 10 years old, they would spend all their summer with the animals. These were long days of gathering the goats and milking them and, at night, bringing the milk back to Kjeaasen. Here the women would churn the milk into butter and cheese, which was stored away for the winter, and also brought down to the village to be sold or bartered into other goods.

At the end of the summer, some of the older goats and half of the young kids were killed for the meat whilst the children cried during the process as they always developed a strong fondness for each animal and also gave most of them names; it was often a very sad time. The elders would also participate in the summer and shear the sheep and dry the wool, some were used and spun in their home, and some were sold in the village. They would fish in the long lake near their mountain hut, catching trout, which was a welcome addition to their monotonous diet. They grew some vegetables and potatoes by their house and hung meat to dry in the sun and wind during the summer.

Bows and arrows were made from boxwood or yew for hunting, and they were strung with hemp or silk if they had it. Arrows were three feet long and double-edged. A hunter stalking for the game always had his bow ready and partly drawn in order to avoid a quick motion. The arrow was to pierce the animal's breast.

Olaf was a great hunter, and he traveled for several days across the mountains up toward the huge glacier above Sima valley. He would often return empty-handed, but he would often catch a reindeer after days of staking the animal across rivers, up mountain ridges, and swampy land. He would be armed with a bow and arrows and a javelin spear. In his best year, he caught seven reindeer. After the kill came to the labor of cutting up the animal. He would use his knife to cut off the valuable fur, rid it of its inside other than the heart and liver, and then cut it into several large slabs. He would then drag the largest sections for several days back home and return for the rest for several more round trips. At home, the meat was dried and salted.

As the autumn fell upon them, they went out to bring in wood for their ovens, and trees were cut, chopped, and carried or pulled for long distances. This was for hearth and heating on bitterly cold days. Flour had been bartered in the village for the winter and was stacked high away from rodents and other animals. The timber was debarked, and the bark was made into flour and mixed with the wheat flour to get by when food was scarce at the end of the long winter period.

They brought hay from the highest mountain down to the water's edge. They later brought it back to the farm to have enough fodder for the animals during the cold period. The hay was rolled down in bundles. They would cut the grass with a scythe, but sometimes it was too rocky, and they needed to use a knife. Sometimes it was so steep that the men tied ropes around themselves when they cut so as not to fall off the rock face. It happened that the haymakers stretched out too far and then lost their footing and fell off the mountain. Many ended up lifeless down below.

During the winter, the men practiced wood cutting of their precious tree roots and large timber into bowls, chairs, and even skis which they often would barter with flour or other needed detail; such work could be in great demand at times.

They often brought fresh soil from above or below to enlarge their pastures. But the growth was good as the sun heated the rock face, and water made the grass and bushes grow well. There were large wooded and grassy areas for their livestock. They did not go hungry but worked hard.

Felling pine trees was another task for strong-willed men who were used to building houses or repairing old ones. Gradually, they had several houses, the main house, a barn, the storehouse, and a furnace. And at least one house was placed up on the higher mountain as their living quarter was built of stone. Timbers would be felled around the farm, either higher up the steep mountainsides or far below. They sawed planks and beams on the spot. They saved on materials whenever they could. Many of the outhouses had inside walls covered with birch branches rather than planks.

One late fall day, they learned that the tax collector was in the village and intended to come on a visit. Very few, if any, ever came their way. The taxes would be in kind – and the only kind they had was firewood or dairy products. Olaf knew the answer. He pulled the ladder up from one of the very steep walls in the middle of their pathway, and they never heard or saw the collector then or later.

As the years went by, they became regulars in the village for bartering and sometimes for social visits. They had no railings to hold onto and sometimes no paths to follow after heavy rain or snow. How could man, woman, and child climb up and down these slopes in deep snow and ice without so much as a foothold for an old shoe? Imagine winter days with snow blizzards crashing down on their houses. Only hermits would choose to live there.

The children were tethered in the yard up on the mountain ledges. The tiny ones moved around quickly and were a close run from the doorstep to the mountain's edge. Sometimes a goat would be stuck on a ledge. They would bind a rope around a child who would be lowered down to the ledge and untie himself and tie the animal which then was hoisted. The child again roped himself and was brought back to safety.

The people had no fear of heights and no fear of work. They loved their outdoor way of life and learned that through work and toil, people become righteous.

One Christmas day finds one woman on the way up the mountain. A birth was on the way at any moment with no midwife available, so this old experienced woman set off to help. She was seventy-five years old, and how she managed to make her way through the worst icy parts is still a mystery to locals. One place which she had to pass was difficult enough for a strong, experienced man on a summer day. And here she was, the old woman, in the middle of winter, balancing on small, icy edges over staggering precipices;

please send a thought to this old woman who put her life at risk in order to help a neighboring wife in labor as you sail past. But as old Lajla stepped into the cottage, she heard the newborn baby crying. The fear of getting ill without being able to get help was something to live with. It had to be a serious matter before the doctor was sent for. They lacked the money to pay and did not wish to take up the doctor's time needlessly. So one bore the pain and the hardship and kept quiet about it.

One woman who bore eleven children went to the doctor for the first time when she was seventy years old. Another woman had her first meeting with the doctor after she reached the age of ninety. But both had probably felt sickness and pain more than once throughout their lives.

A woman once had an eye infection that the doctor could not help with. The only possibility was a specialist in Bergen. But Bergen was a boat journey over 400 kilometers away, and the woman had neither money for the journey nor the treatment. But her husband knew what to do. He tied a rope around their ox and set off with both his wife and the beast. Upon arrival in Bergen, the beast was sold, and they were able to pay for the doctor and the tickets back home. Four weeks later, they arrived home, cured of the sickness, but without the ox. Finally, they were able to find the means for most things.

One morning as they woke up at Kjeåsen, Maria felt a sense of ominous danger, and as she ran out the front door, she saw Astrid walk down the last stone step in the garden and disappear around the edge. "Astrid! Astrid!!" Maria shouted, running as fast as she could, now with Olaf following. Turning the bend, they saw Astrid bouncing down the vertical wall crying, "Mama! Mama!!" and then silence. They ran down the precipitous steps, crossing the log over the deep chasm and down the ladders, through the woods across the river. They searched for hours, but there was no trace of Astrid; she was gone out of their lives.

Maria was hysterical. It was unfathomable. Incomprehensible, outlandish. Terrible, horrible. "Oh, where have you gone, our dear, dear child?" She continued to ask. The following Sunday, a funeral was held at the Saint Johannes church. The whole town was mourning in silence. Only the priest's words still hung in the air. "From dust hath thou come, unto dust we thee return." Olaf, Maria, Torfinn, and Rika Ragnar received hugs and quiet sorrow. Everyone had loved the quick-legged bright little child. For the next year, Maria was silent. She did not utter a word. She carried out her normal chores, tending to and milking the goats, weeding, and harvesting the vegetable garden. Kitchen work trips to high mountains to the goats in the summer and returning the milk to the farm, a trip that could take 3 to 5 hours each way, carrying 10 to 15 liters of milk and churning the milk to butter and cheese.

Maria decided they had to leave Kjeaasen; she could no longer live there. Every day she heard Astrid's cries. Maria would wake up every morning and glance down the turn of the vegetable patch and see Astrid falling. She could hear her cries again and again as she was falling, forever falling. She could hear her thumping as she hit the rocks. If she stayed, she and Olaf felt that she would follow Astrid to neverland in a final fall down the rock face.

So one-day early spring, Olaf started to log all their belonging down the steep path. Their time at the Kjeaasen had come to an end.

Eidsfjord

In Eidsfjord – below Kjeaasen – Rika-Ragna (means the Rich Ragna) was born to wealth and riches. Her father owned large parts of the land, rivers, and even mountains where large numbers of goats, sheep, and cattle grazed. Their holdings were slowly acquired through generations of hard work, sweat, and tears in the hard climate of the north, where clouds, rain, wetness, and snow were the prevailing inclement weather and where a single sunny day was received with celebration and gratitude. Before the arrival of Rika Ragna, her father and mother had been wrought with childlessness. It had been a thing of sorrow for the noble and hospitable couple to have no child to hold in their arms and rock to sleep. Rachel had drunk local brews, but her stomach never elevated. Finally, in her fifth year of marriage, she began to notice the soreness in her breasts. She remembered with a leaping heart that it had been twice a fortnight since she had last seen her flow. The months following were bliss for the couple who had received the very thing they had prayed for. It was in the mid of the night a cry ran through the endowments; alas, a child had been born. The midwife held in her arm a wailing little girl who was handed to her tired mother for suckling.

Rika Ragna grew up to be a strong child. Growing up, she frequented the high valleys and often crossed the Jokul glacier to find lost goats at the end of the summer. She climbed the trees and called out to the birds to which she had given names. As an only child, she never had any lack of company. She was surrounded by the villager's children, who held her family high esteem. Her days were always eventful, and when she fell asleep, her window open to the moon, she was filled with adventurous dreams. She was god-fearing and had a strong sense of commitment to her family and friends. Whoever she considered a friend, she heard dearly to her.

Rika Ragna did have a short temper which could, at times, be fierce. She had been known several times to flare up at the quickest provocation. Once, her favorite lamb had been pushed into a well by her cousin. Her cousin Greta still had the scar which rose across her thigh when Rika Ragna pushed her down from the hill. In her fit of rage, one noon, she had set free her father's horses, trampling some of the crops. But then, every human has a flaw. For kindhearted and independent Rika Ragna, it was her temper that she tried to rein most times, knowing how huge the wrath it could be when unleashed.

Rika Ragna grew up into a beautiful woman. At 5'9, she

was the epitome of strength. Filled with curves and contours, she was feminine and consumed by softness; her long wavy hair always freed like the wind as she sat off. Her hands were not coarse, but she had worked hard in the farms milking the cows, she had herded the goats back home, she had squeezed the dripping water off the clothes, and she had spat fire into the woods. Yes, indeed, Rika Ragna was a hardworking lady.

Many men eyed her as their wife-to-be, but none measured up. Most of the men who came calling were men she had grown up with, men she had sat on and twisted their fingers when they were mere children. These were men who believed they could rein her, but Rika Ragna could not be by any man. They took her out to the rivers, they took her out dancing, and they even offered to help her father with the cutting of the wood. But for every man that wanted to be her husband, she turned them down. It wasn't that she was spoilt. No. But Rika Ragna knew it would be a terrible mistake if she married any of the men who had come her way. She had not felt any form of attraction for any one of them. What was it she sought in a husband? Protectiveness? Counsel? Company? Rika Ragna was not sure, but what she knew was that the man she would marry had not been found. She needed a man who could challenge her, a man who could go on adventures with her into the valley, and not the overfed babies who were called men and surrounded her. So she waited, continuing to turn the suitors down.

Then one day, a young man arrived from the East, a man of apparent breeding who was strong with a sanguine grasp of outdoor sports and hunting and always felt at home in the upper valleys by the tall mountains. Rika Ragna heard this man from the ladies as they talked shyly about him in laughter. He was a quiet man who had been blessed with good looks. A stranger to these parts, they all wanted to get to know him. Not fazed by the bickering over him, Rika Ragna wasn't concerned. She had the opportunity to meet him a week later when he came to pay a visit to her father. From across the room, their eyes met. For the first time, Rika Ragna was shy, averting her eyes. She realized at that moment that, perhaps, this was what she had waited for so long.

He was awed by her, and as he talked to her father, his eyes were placed firmly on her face. When he sought her hand out for a trip to the river, Rika Ragna was excited and spent hours preparing herself to look good for him.

From there began a relationship that overwhelmed Rika Ragna. For the first time, she was beginning to care for someone in a romantic way. He was all she had ever asked for. He was a caring man, slow to anger, and adventurous with a kind heart. No one was surprised when they were soon betrothed and moved upstream into one of her father's farmhouses.

Her husband was a man who looked for other aspersions in the manner of company. As Rika Ragna came to find, perhaps her husband had hidden from her a lot about his life, but this did no wrong to her as long as he respected and treated her right. Although he had his faults, he still remained a caring husband, and Rika Ragna could cope with the burden of being his wife.

Her mother was the first to go. This happened in the second year of Rika Ragna's marriage. A loud cry erupted, and she knew that her ailing mother had gone to the other side. Years after, her father, who she considered one of the greatest men to walk the earth, joined the afterlife. As his surviving heir, everything he possessed was passed down to Rika Ragna, who had already managed them for a long time. No longer was she a rich child; she was now a rich woman.

One day as they rowed into town across the fjord, Ragnhild queried her husband about his whereabouts the previous night. Rika Ragna was beginning to get tired of his ways. She would have let it go in the past, but his whereabouts were becoming more unquestionable.

He laughed, his face twisted into a smile, making him even more dashing. "You have no need to know where I was or where I will be. You're, after all, just my wife."

His answer gave her reason to jump up with a thunderous cry, and somehow she pushed him over the transom, and he ended up in the water. As he swam in the cold fjord, she saw him pull up on a small island a few hundred feet away.

Ever since she got married, Rika Ragna had only been angry a few times, and for those moments, she had only flung her shoe or an unfortunate object which had been beside her. At the moment, she was greatly overwhelmed with anger. Furious, she rowed away; she intended to return to pick him up after she had carried out her errands in town and was at peace to reconcile with her husband.

The "island" he crawled to was caught by the ebbing tide. As he waited and passed out on the shore, hoping for his wife to return, the island was soon submerged by the cold water. He raised his hands, waving, trying to call to her as her boat moved away, but his throat was already filled with water and seaweed. When Ragnhild was out of sight – he drowned.

As Rika Ragna went about her doings in the town, she forboded that something had gone amiss. She abandoned her chores and searched for her husband, but it was too late. All that remained in the wreck was a lifeless body. In her anger, she had lost her husband, who she loved dearly, and who, in his way, had loved and admired her. She was in deep remorse after this.

"If only I could," Rika Ragna repeated over and over to herself. Indeed, if only she could, she would have done things differently on that windy noon. However, it was too late; the fates had made the decision. Rika Ragna would break down the nights that followed, filled with guilt about what had happened.

Not long later, merely a few days after the death of Rika Ragna's husband, a strong flood came through her valley. It came in the dead of night and continued into the morning. It was unexpected, but then what would they have done? Move on to higher grounds with the little possession they could gather? Perhaps so. The flood, which lasted for days, destroyed many of the farmhouses and most of their livestock. Unfortunately, a few lives were lost, but the damage done was enough to make some wish that their lives had been taken along with the flood. With no house, with not even a lamb, where would they start their lives from? Farms that had been ready for harvest had been completely ruined, with nothing left but waterlogged soil. This was the first time they would ever experience such a misfortune, and it filled their hearts with sadness as they looked around their homes and source of livelihood, which had been destroyed.

Rika Ragna was a pillar of support to the people during this trying time. Her lands which had been on higher ground, had been left unscathed by the disaster which had come knocking. In the past few days, she had come to realize that even if she had it all, nothing would make up for the loss of her husband. Perhaps, helping the people just as she always did would give her some sort of peace. She went down to the farms and helped them with the cleaning of the ruined farms. She provided the services of her farmhands to help the devastated farmers. Rika Ragna also took further steps in helping the ruined. She gave them her farm animals and portions of her land to cultivate. It was an act of kindness that the affected would never forget. She had turned a mood of sadness into jubilation. A feast of appreciation was held to honor her good deeds, but Rika Ragna still felt empty in the midst of it.

In a further act of redemption, Rika Ragna gave most of her belongings to have a church built in memory of her dead husband. On the wall was a stone edging of Rika Ragna kneeling before Saint Johannes with an outstretched open palm on which sat a model of the church. It can still be seen to this date.

Rika-Ragna's endowment built the church

Rika Ragna had a son who had been adopted at a very young age from the Kjeaasen family. It seemed that just like her mother, Rika Ragna had difficulties bearing a child. The fifth-year into her marriage, she decided to take the bull by the horn. She made up her mind that she would not go through the travails her mother had gone through to bear a child. On one of the days when the Kjeaasen family came into town to sell their wares, Rika Ragna sat in the middle of the market, her eyes on those trooping in as the scheme formed in her head. It was noon when she spotted the little boy who would be her child. He was a little boy of about three years. The Kjeaasen people were called poor, but Ragnhild did not think this of them. She saw the hard work in them, she saw the satisfaction, and to be sincere, only a few of them were truly poor. The little boy she saw was one of such. He had on a shirt filled with patchwork. He was not malnourished, but in her eyes, he looked underfed. Love whelmed in her heart as she watched the little boy play with sticks. She knew at that moment that she wanted him as her son.

After an hour of waiting, a tired-looking woman turned out to be his mother. Straddled on her back was a wailing baby, and by her side was another child who looked not a year older than the little boy. Rika Ragna approached the woman who had wary eyes.

"I greet you," Rika Ragna said with a wide smile.

"My lady," the woman greeted. Even to the Kjeaasen people, Rika Ragna was well known.

A lanky, bearded man who the children had taken after in looks joined them. It was the perfect opportunity for her to tell the little boy's parents her intention. The parents listened attentively and told her to give them a fortnight to think about it. It was not an unusual request for a child to be adopted; young boys were given to masters to learn to be apprentices, and young ladies were given to Ladies of the manor to work their way to the top of the house. Rika Ragna was filled with anticipation as she waited for the decision of the little boy's parents. Surely they would not disappoint her; they had a litter of kids already, would giving one up to a needy woman be a loss to them?

Rika Ragna was called to the door one morning by the maid.

Standing outside was the little boy and his parents.

"Times are indeed hard, and we're all leaving our homes. We pray you to treat him right," the lad's mother said.

"I promise to," Rika Ragna swore.

Rika Ragna had never known there was a void in her life until Verald arrived. She showered him with love from the day he stepped into her threshold. Not for a day did he lack whatever he wanted. Spoilt, he wasn't, but raised in a home of love and responsibility. Verald was very close to his mother; as a little boy, he followed her around, his thumb in his mouth. When she went to the market, he followed behind her with several questions. Even as he turned into a man, he stood by his mother's side, loyal to her love. Although he loved his father, his relationship was cordial with him. But when his father died, and his mother gave her life to the church and became a nun, he decided to list in the Royal Guard in Copenhagen. He was 16 and ready to leave his broken home and place of birth. He loved his mother dearly, but he knew in his heart that she would only find fulfillment in the church and her good deeds.

Verald's upbringing had been one of excitement, adventure, and frequent challenges at sea, in the mountains, and farming sheep and goats in the summer. At school, he had been a tenacious, fast learning student who found all subjects equally fascinating, stimulating further investigation. He was excited to leave his hometown and explore the world, which he had heard went on without stopping. He had heard of so many tales of huge cities with tall buildings whose end could never be seen. He had heard of people too many to count in towns. He wanted to be a part of the adventures in the huge world out there.

A few days prior to his departure Verald went on an

investigative trip climbing up the mountain at the end of the fjord. He had for many years been wondering about the trees and bushes and grass that seemed to grow out of the mountainside way above the fjord; the mountainside was perpendicularly precipitous and naked with no apparent place to put a hand or a foot. He had always wanted to go exploring the fjord but had never done so. Perhaps it was the thought of being away from home for a long time, or he had gained a sudden new strength. Verald walked along the fjord until he saw a fast stream coming out of the rocks and started to climb up. He had to watch every step as it was slippery by the water streaming under his feet. After about 300 feet, he encountered a huge rock; he had to hang on with his hands and walk in the stream to get across the rock. As he continued, it became even steeper. Still, he was prepared for the trip and had brought a rope that he tied around his waist and threw the other end around a tree with a small rock tied at the other hand. After a long time, he was able to get it to slip around the tree and could pull down the other end of the rope. He could now walk up the mountainside whilst pulling himself up the rope until he reached the tree. He did the same maneuver several times over the next few hours, stopping on the way for a breath of air. At one time, he fell, but his shoe was caught between two rocks and stopped him from sliding down 1000 feet into the ocean below.

He passed a huge flat stone that formed the roof of a sheltered space that could keep out rain and bad weather. He came to 10-12 steps that were hewn into the black massif ridge where he could walk. There was a huge oak tree that barred his way, and he had to use the rope again, then a rock ladder of some 25 steep steps. At the top, he could view the entire fjord some 500 feet below – the water had a green turquoise color, and the mountains rose up all around the fjord up to 4-5,000 feet. Finally, he arrived at the open "shelf" that he had seen from below. What a place to have a home, away from everyone and with rivers, trees, and bushes as far as the eye could see. He absolutely loved the wildness, incredible views, strength, and wonders of this mountainous hideaway. He deeply regretted not coming here sooner; he would have spent most of his childhood here. Surrounding him was a magnificent beauty. It was at peace, devoid of mankind which had abandoned it years ago, and it pleased his heart. For the first time in his life, he felt truly awed.

Verald made himself a promise that if he ever returned, he would come here and build his home and have his family where his ancestors had lived. It was indeed a true paradise on earth.

As it turned out, his promise would be carried out one day, not by him, but by one of his descendants running away from the law. Verald returned to Eidfjord and started his voyage to his new life in the service of the Danish king.

FROM HIMALAYA TO SOUTH PACIFIC

The 17th Century- Denmark

The country was Christianized in the 12th Century and Lutheranized in the 15th. This story opens late in the 16th century in Aalborg, a small town on the east side of the Jutland peninsula. Aalborg existed as a small hamlet since about 1000 and was chartered as a town in 1342. It grew into a commercial center in the 17th century. Its landmarks are the Holy Ghost Monastery, The Castle, the Viking ship burial ground and the cathedral.

It was a cold, misty afternoon in December. The light was starting to fade, and the air was heavy. Mixed with the human throng and sounds of the town, shutters were being closed, and articles were stored on shelves and in basements and lofts. Dogs, men, women, horses, and carts in plenty were moving in a frenzy, making the work come to an end and start the journey home.

She was not in the habit of straying off her path home. The school was in the village behind the stone church next to the vicar's house. After school, she would hurry home to the safety of the homestead and the daffodils and green hedges, the chicken farm and the three horses, the barn and the cows on the green pasture, her little room viewing the large oak trees and the small brook beyond. And her little bed in the corner with her few possessions stashed away under it. But this day, she had been alerted by the shouts and fretful noise coming from the harbor, and her curiosity took her there. It was not her first venture alone into the harbor. She had come to the conclusion that whenever there were shouts at the harbor, surely there was an adventure. The last time she had come to the harbor on such trips, she had seen the sailors drag stowaways who had hidden in the boiler room. The stowaways had been scary skinny men and handed to the constable; that had been the last she heard of the men.

The inestimable treasure of thrusting herself into this transitory, the excitement made her move with confidence and unshakable intent. She turned the street corner into the market where the traders and farmers, mechanics and laborers teamed with the populace in the movement and buying and selling of vegetables, meats, fresh flowers, pots, brazen vessels, cups and saucers, an endless calamity of handmade linen, cotton cloth for dresses, tables, bathrooms, children, and uniforms. She was always enthralled and absorbed by the rush and liveliness of the people bartering and haggling, the alacrity of the farmers weighing, the swiftness of the merchants measuring, the rapidity and punctuality, the sonatas of human symphony that prevailed.

But today, she was converging upon a gathering whence a cacophony of discordant noises arose. Several new arrivals were dockside, green and white fishing vessels with men off-loading from the holds to the dock. Here women and children sorted the catch in types and sizes into large boxes and wooden containers, and it was brought into the warehouse.

On the outside of one vessel was a large grey and blue substance being hauled slowly towards the beach, and this was the subject of all. As she came closer, she heard the prattle and chatter - "it's a whale" - "bounced into the ship" - "was almost dead". The whale had collided with Halvdan's. And while the boat was safe, the whale was not; it appeared Halvdan's crew was able to have a line around it and pulled the wounded whale to shore. It was soon grounded on the beach and killed by a spear behind the eye by Johnston, the butcher, familiar with animals and large targets. It was sliced up into pieces and taken to the icehouse. The beach was full of blood and slivers of meat, and everyone was given a large piece for their folks. There was so much excitement as it spread around the market. Maria, in her excitement, wished she had been around much earlier to see the whale. She had never seen a whale, but she had heard stories of how big they were.

FROM HIMALAYA TO SOUTH PACIFIC

There was a long line as they waited to have their share of the meat. There were several talks about the whale, and Maria strained her ears to listen. She knew she should be back home, but she couldn't move her feet to walk away from the excitement and conversation.

Maria, for such was her designation, had a piece of 5 kilos wrapped in her tissue, and walked elevated and content home. The boy who had given it to her was one of Halvdan's sons. He had noticed her at the marketplace with her maid, but neither had the temerity nor the intrepidity to speak. She was aloof, above his class, of another world, another planet. Not solely wealth and position in society; it was in the comportment, the carriage, and the regality of posture. In some ways, she was his antithesis, swan versus tadpole, perplexity versus simplicity. A Viking princess she was, a wondrous and striking beauty in her early teens with an elongated, graceful swan neck on the summit which was poised in perfect equilibrium, a wistful eloquence of exquisite joyfulness, a high forehead with an archetypal nose, large cheekbones, shining white teeth which, when her mouth opened - smiled and laughed and beckoned to the world with a shaft of warm light beams. Her hair was ash blond, long to her waist, and the ears were jeweled accouterments with small pearls extending her chins into symmetrical apexes. She was tall for her 15 years and slender and walked with a quick dispatch; her time was not in surplus.

No words were exchanged, but her hands rubbed as she received her meat. She noticed his vigor and strength; a salty ocean smell came with him, not offensive. His eyes were large, light blue, and his hair was blond, and she favored his disposition. There was an undercurrent as they eyed one another. Herald felt a pliable intensity in his chest; there was a lift of awareness as he trimmed off the meat, sectioning it in portions. He perceived her keen eyes watching him and felt his blood flow as he finished the wrappings. She thanked him and started to walk home, sensing him being in her heart. As she moved frivolously along the cobblestone streets, she observed the snow dropping off the canopy over the green café and the figures formed by the ice crystals on the small windows of the cottages.

Herald had joined his father at the age of 11 for fishing in the Skaw; and he became very fond of the ocean, the waves, the scent of the salty seas, the action of the swells on the ship, the movement, the mechanism of the boat as its bow dove into the sea, the howling winds, the ocean foaming. He loved the sound of seagulls as they joined in their catch, the expression of delight expressed by his father when they had a good day. He was also elated by his father's prudence and vigilance paid to every detail; in his keen observance of the distant bad weather clouds, the winds turning east, perchance a foretoken of more severe weather conditions, in their frail open boat foul weather could quickly mature into perilous conditions. He also became friends with the other fishermen, and they met in the bars on the dock for a beer or coffee in the afternoons. They were a mingled lot, friendly and always had a good word for Herald, who was keen to learn and a polite boy with a good heart. Herald was growing and gradually assumed more responsibilities; he would take the fish to market and often be able to obtain little higher prices through his humor and good looks than the competing fishermen. The maidens and wives who came to buy from him took a liking to this tanned, blond boy, and he was finding his own amongst women as well as men.

The first kiss was at 13 as he accompanied a young maiden to her home. As he left her, he became aware of a hitherto unknown desire which made his organ feel like stone, and his testes were giving bombastic pains so he could hardly walk and had to stop time and again to bend over to ease the spasms. His sexual urge was now manifested in his approach, and at the age of 14, he made a nocturnal visit to an unsightly damsel, where he felt the least prone to rejection. When it was over, he was embarrassed and ashamed and cleansed his parts and made the girl swear not to reveal the lustful act, but the desire only grew with the experience, and conquests continued. One night as he walked around there was a woman crossing his concourse. It was too dark for him to see her face, but from the way she moved as she walked through the dusk, it was enough to fire his passion. He followed her up the dark road through the forest at a sufficient distance that he would not be seen. She walked quickly and eventually came to a house in the better part of town where she walked in and locked the door behind her in what he judged to be the servant part of the house. He saw the light go out and another on, assuming that this was her bedroom. He walked up into the hills whilst reasoning over this possible subjugation and, in conclusion, could not disobey his craving. As he came back to the house, the light was out; he approached her bedroom and found the window open. He crawled in the window and eased himself into the bed, where he found her sleeping. He touched her gently on her hips and breasts and then proceeded to make love to her. They kissed and fondly embraced each other's erotic regions and anything else two adolescent lovers could do, and he then left through the window and walked home. He never repeated the visit, and they never met again. She may have been the housemaid and had previous relationships with the master of the house and presumed it was him, or she may just have been a free-loving person open for a nocturnal guest.

So many things in his life happened without premonition and without any formula or plan, a dive into the deep end of the lake without knowing how to swim. As a four-year-old, he once fell into and then swam down the stream where his father found him as he crawled into the pebbled shore. The spontaneous sparks and fires erupted frequently and were dangerous and enjoyable, hurtful and healing. The interest in the news was so explosive and eruptive that nothing could stop the explorer from burnt hands and mental pain. Nothing could stop him from being what he was; no urging, pain, or thought process could change the program of what he did and where he went. There was no forward planning; it all happened at the spur of the moment. Friends were many, but only those who insisted his friendship would be with him - he did not go out of his way to make a friend or build a friendship, but he was kind to those who stood by him. He had a strong sense of fairness and loved animals; he could not accept the mistreatment of others.

That night, before Herald fell asleep, he saw Maria in her undiminished sufficiency. She was coming towards him;

her skin was like ivory, her breasts were full of spring, her hips were motherly, and her legs were strong. He had a great desire to conquer her - a tremendous drive to have her in his arms in the raw. He said her name, "Maria, Maria... love you... I love you..." He fell asleep and dreamed about her. They were walking naked on the beach, running, cavorting, and picking up rocks and pebbles. She gave him a round, white marble rock with two holes in it, he attached a straw to it and wore it around his neck, and she held him by the straw as they walked into the ocean. She kissed him as he held her in his arms, floating into the open sea, faded and dissolved.

He woke up the next morning, and the first word he uttered was Maria. He had not been in love before, nor did he now know he was now. His growing awareness of her had taken on a life of its own by virtue of his adoration of her composition, her flesh, the color of her nipples, the size and undulating pulsation of her hips, her breasts, her very divergence from his, and his outrageous desire to hold, touch, and feel her in all her predicaments. His desire was not for words; he did not want her for worship, only corporal conquest. But now, a new sun was rising in him. Maria had occasioned in him a novel aspiration, a yearning for the unification of body and spirit to something inviolable, chaste, pure and virginal.

A month went by before he saw her again, this time on the street where she lived. Since the last time he had seen her at the beach, he had looked out for her. So many times had he found himself looking at a blond girl, imagining her to be his Maria. Once, he had stopped a lady on the street, his hand on her shoulder. His Maria had turned out to be a wide gap-toothed old woman who had given him a knowing smile. He had caught himself daydreaming of Maria several times, hoping he would get the chance to see her again. He had seen Maria by luck, or perhaps it had been destiny. When his father sent him off to deliver a basket of fish to the quiet street, he had murmured in his heart, wishing he could remain at the beach where he felt more at ease. It was a quick transaction at the backdoor with the house cook. As he stepped back into the street, his feet were soon frozen on the sidewalks. Walking across the street was Maria. Perhaps, if she were alone, he would have walked up to her. No, he doubted it. In his state, he was too nervous about approaching her. He was relieved that she was with a friend. Yet, it hadn't stopped their eyes from the meeting. He had seen the recognition in her eyes at that moment. He knew without a doubt that, just like him, there sparkled interest in her. His encounter with her set in motion the things that followed. Asking questions here and there, Herald found the school she went to and sought her out.

Maria's eyes widened when she saw Herald standing outside the school. She needed no sign to be told that he was waiting for her. He fell into step beside her, and they walked comfortably in silence. She was not headed home, nor was he.

"I'm Herald."

"I know," Maria said shyly. It was the first time she would talk to him without the presence of others. It was actually the first time she would talk to a member of the opposite sex who was not in her family this way. She followed his lead as he led her into a café. She knew she would be scolded for getting home late, but she could not leave the sight of Herald, who she was curious about. By the time she headed back home, she was flushed and filled with excitement. Never had she ever had such a lovely time. Herald was interesting. He was amusing, and she had snorted out loud at his jokes. He was different from what she had expected. But then, what she believed him to be? To be crude? He had been charming to her and had stared at her as if she had been the only one in the world. Not a word of her meeting with him did she tell anyone, not even the maid, Regina, who she confided in most of the time.

They met over the next several months in clandestine gatherings where they would not be seen by anyone known to her family. Whenever they met, Herald would always tell her where they would meet the next time, and if there was a change of plans, he would let her know through a note, for it he would pay the little boy to deliver to her. They were both very aware of the distance between them socially and that her father would not approve of Herald. Maria's father had long planned for her to marry Gunnar, a son of the Rosencrantz, the nobles. They were in love, and yet they knew that their situation was irreconcilable in an antagonistic ocean with little to pin a future.

Their meetings always made Maria happy, at least for the moment. First, she made up excuses to stay out during the day, and when they could no longer meet in the day for fear of being spotted, they began to meet at night. For Maria, this was safer. Saying goodnight to her father and her brothers, she would go to her room, where she arranged her pillows, covering them up with her blanket. Locking her door with a simpleton key, she would climb out the window, her face covered. Herald was always waiting just around the corner of the house, leading her off to their destination. He would escort her back home as the dawn drew closer. Not a word would be said as he ushered her into her bedroom, but their eyes glistened with excitement. Maria had never had a secret of her own, at least of such nature. But the secret she had was more than a broken lamp; it was about her love for a man who would make her father go up in rage if he became aware.

The first time Maria had been aware of her betrothal to Gunnar, she cried all through the night. She had never liked the cocky young man who seemed to be the life of his group of noble friends. Good looks were an inheritance for Gunnar. He was stout, but he made up with his muscles and well-chiseled face. The ladies giggled and fluttered their lashes when he walked past; he made sure to fix his blue eyes on them and, if he was in a good mood, to ruffle his brown-blonde hair. He knew he was a prize, and he adored it. In addition to his looks was his name. He came from a long line of noble Vikings who had fought in the sea, conquering most of England before they finally retired home. Maria, however, fancied none of him. Ever since she was ten and told that she would someday marry Gunnar, she had been consumed with a dislike for him. You see, Gunnar's father and Maria's father had been friends when they were boys. This friendship became even more solidified after an incident. Maria could barely remember what had happened that afternoon, but her father told her the stories several times that it was stuck in her head. On a picnic by the river, she had slipped into the water, the waves shutting her cries. Only young Gunnar, who had had a crush on her, had noticed her absence and listened to her cries. Without care for the strong waves which could crush a full-blooded Viking man, he dived into the water. He pulled out of the water and almost drowned Maria, who quickly rushed to the infirmary, where the water was flushed from her lungs. Forever indebted to Gunnar, Maria's father had wrapped the boy in a hug, asking him what he wanted in return.

"Can I marry her?" Gunnar asked in a shy voice.

The adults laughed over it, but Maria's father rather took the request seriously. It was granted, and Maria was betrothed to the boy who had saved her life. However, Maria didn't know that her arranged marriage to Gunnar was just a business deal with Gunnar's father, to whom her father was indebted. The gambling debt would be paid off when the marriage took place.

Tried as she may, Maria had tried to come to terms with liking Gunnar. Of course, she was considered lucky to have Gunnar as a husband. Her friends in school were envious; she, of all ladies, would be by his side as his wife. Maria had never been enthralled by him. She found his smile cocky; she found him deceitful; he was a ticking clock, ready to explode. He wasn't kind, either to man or to animals, the test of humanity; how then could she be married to someone of such sort? The few moments spent with him left her with a throbbing head. She was convinced that her life would be cut short if she ever married Gunnar. His pride, too fierce to back down, his refusal to consider others, and his frequent visits to the whorehouse were just a few flaws that she could point out. Beneath his smile, a mask, she could feel his daunting eyes of his. However, nothing could she do to end her betrothal with him. A Viking man never broke his promise. Not only would his honor and name be ruined, there could also be consequences if the pledgee sought to take what was promised to him. Before Herald came into her life, she had made up her mind to marry Gunnar and be his wife. With Herald in her life, her buried dreams were coming to the surface. How would she break a promise made by her father without hurting anyone in the process? It seemed impossible. It was a burden she carried every day, knowing that she was betrothed to one while her heart belonged to another.

Then one night in June, after Herald had dined aboard, the police appeared shipside and asked for him. As soon as he put his foot on the dock, he was arrested and immediately taken to prison. The charge was aiding a woman with abortion.... a voice from his past was spoken for. Not a single day had passed since he had conspired to take human life that the thought did not prevail. Punishment for trespass was long due. This was his karma.

He had met Gretchen a Saturday night in town, and they had both been drinking. They laughed and drank with each other. What later happened-- who could be blamed? He took her with him to his loft room to make love to her was his design. In the insignificant room in the small building on the hillside, they discussed incomparable affairs; wine and smoking made them spontaneous. Soon they were both dishabille. They were hot, young and loved hard. They were quickly orgasmic, then fell asleep until the next morning, and then they loved again. They slayed the sorrow and anguish since they both knew their tryst would soon be a memory. He took her home to her shed, next to a bed of flowers, and it was over. But this was not the last he heard of it. Six weeks later, they met again on occasion in the market. She was sad and unhappy. She was no longer the woman full of life he had once been with till dawn. He asked her what was wrong; her reply went through him hot and cold; she was pregnant; it could not be by him, but it was.

Herald was left in a state of confusion as he went about the rest of his day. Pregnant? He was not ready to be a father. He did not have dreams, or did he? Oh yes. Of sailing the oceans. He was not within the means to care for a child and a woman. It was a horrible mistake he had made, but once a coin was cast into the well, it could not be taken back. Or could it? For the first time in his life, Herald had to make a devastating decision perhaps that would torment him for the rest of his life. After two more weeks, he found a doctor handler who proposed to help. He would knead and massage her lower abdomen through many visits, which would give a belated blood flow. It could take a week or more, so she moved into his loft at night - unseen - and went on a nocturnal visit - and quietly cried and wailed during the night. Ultimately the tiny impetus was dispatched; as it hung down from her - the little animated substance - he cut the umbilical cord with a sharp object. He - a child slayer. A child was no more. The sentence was three years. The room was small – twenty by twenty feet with a six-foot ceiling. There were no windows.

Sometimes she would try to find a reason for her existence in this world but failed to find comfort; she would grasp for a multitude of explanations, none of which were satisfactory. She would clasp and grasp and hold and let go and hope and lose hope: She believed in an afterlife; otherwise, God would not have placed her and everyone she knew here. She did not believe that death would be followed by a state of eternal bliss, nor did she believe in reincarnation so one could reach a higher level of human existence until, in the end, when we have passed the grade and will be permitted to cross the threshold of heavens and find our place in it. She found it impractical and conflicting with her beliefs that one must suffer for sinful misdeeds committed by previous generations.

In her maturing rational self, she felt rather that one had inherited to pass on a bequeathed ancestral order from the all-encompassing Omni-directional master of ceremony, who directs us to be prodigious and multiply so that the re-generations of the species can continue down through eternal times so that the race can improve up to the highest plane where the species and the code becomes inseparable and indistinguishable.

Life was sanctified, and one must live one's life every day. Every hour with a cognizant perception because of every action, every step one makes. Every word one pronounces will, in some way, determine the direction of the cosmos for all times.

One night, she dreamt that she was with Herald sitting on the boat together, with the moon rising in the east; it was yellow and large as a house. Then a sudden gasp of air seized the little ship, and they were soon moving at an enormous speed. The water was flowing with a blue vapor at the bow, the air was abundant with fish, and dolphins were sauntering across the boat in rapture. Suddenly, they were in the air, down the Milky Way at great speed, past Pluto, Saturn, and onwards far into the galactic universe. In another larger boat below them were their children, and their children, and their children's children, and they visited them every day, or week or month to join in their laughter and all their daily chores and pleasures which they enjoyed. But then they were away, but they could still observe; new generations were coming and going, but they could not be seen, and they sat in their boat in the moonlight, holding each other's hands in perpetuity.

With Herald in prison, Maria spent her days in a state of absentness. She caught herself staring at the walls in deep thought; she found herself refusing to sleep at night, hoping for a rap at the window pane.

"Perhaps you should pay a visit to the doctor; he must have a tonic to cure your paleness," her father would suggest.

There was, however, no cure for a broken heart. She had no one to share her pain with. Their love had been a secret, and now he was locked away. Oh, how she wanted to look upon his face and caress his lips. She wanted to be lost in his arms, but an appearance at the prison yard would cause wagging tongues. She heard the people talk; Halvdan's son was in prison for the crime of murdering the unborn. "He always seemed like a quiet lad," she heard them say. "The devil sure wears the color of the lamb," the others would respond. Maria knew her Herald; he was surely not the devil, and she cared not to be in hell with him even if he were.

In her moments of sadness, a hero arose. Gunnar, more than before, came calling. He brought with him gifts of flowers and freshly baked bread from the baker. Her maid, as a chaperone, sat by her side, telling her tales of his travels into the water and how he couldn't wait for her to start a family. His chatter still rang in her ears when he gave his goodbyes. All she felt for him was irritation. As she grew older, so did time draws near for her to be married Gunnar. She had no excuse to give. Would she be married to him while her heart pined for another who was beyond her reach? Her heart was in a state of turmoil with no remedy.

Maria had realized something was different in the last few weeks as her nipples started to harden a little, and then one day at school, she became so nauseous that she took a leave of absence for the day. On her way home, it suddenly dawned on her; she had not had her monthly cycle for two months. Was she in a prenatal state? Was a life advancing inside of her? She was stunned by this speculation; it could not be; it was not thinkable. What would her father say?

What about the school, friends, everyone? What about Gunnar, her betrothed? Even if she did not care for him, he would be disgraced by the shame he brought. It became so overwhelming that she burst into tears and went through the next days with feelings of total dejection, a sense of disqualification and inadequacy, and a sense of personal ruination and destruction. She had always been a perfect and immaculate child, in the way her parents perceived her, in school, in the home with her siblings, in the little assignments she was given, gardening, house cleaning, in her school, and in all her administration of herself in her presence and sociable overtures. She needed to have her suspicion validated by someone, that is, by someone she could confide in.

Cogitating on her circumstance for the next few days, she concluded with some certainty that she was, in fact, childbearing. She visited a woman in a neighboring township who confirmed her conviction. She then went to call on Herald in prison. He was the only one in the world she could share with. She still loved him and felt that he would vindicate her from her shameful situation, her fall from grace in her shielded cradle of humanity at home. At the same time, a part of her feared what would happen if he rejected her. Would she become all alone in a world gone bleak? With a veil over her head, slipping coins into the warden's dry and itchy hand, she entered the large compound; it was dark and heavy with a heavy oak door shackled with chains and lock. The air was raw, and there was hardly any daylight; she shivered and yanked her shoulders as if to rid herself of the morbid atmosphere.

Herald sat down behind bars, his eyes downcast. His months spent in prison had been the worst of his life. For the first time, he appreciated the freedom he had had. When he regained his freedom, he would forever cherish every moment of it. Sensing a presence, he looked up. He was frozen at the apparition in front of him. Herald was on his feet in an instant and grasped her hands through the bars, his eyes were moist, and his voice failed him.

Finally, he uttered, "Maria, what are you doing here in this dungeon? This is not a place I wished you to see me in."

She answered, "Herald, it is most difficult for me to be here, but the reason is so compelling that I saw no other way. I am pregnant with your child, and I have no one else to turn to; I cannot relate to my father, and my mother passed away not long ago."

Herald was startled and could not but hold her hands as she related what had happened to her during the last three months whilst he was in prison. At first, her suicidal thoughts, then gradually, her perception of the exalted nature of things as the little infant was taking hold of her, that she did not care what her family thought, of any consequence of any action she might now carry forth, except that which would lighten the burden for her so she could pave the road for the future of her unborn child. For Maria had made up her mind. She had come to love the child she carried in her womb, she had sworn to love her child, and no harm would befall her child. Be it a boy or girl, she would be there to protect her child.

Herald, who was watching her whilst she spoke, realized that he was probably the luckiest man alive to have had a love of this strong woman. A father-to-be, he realized at once that he would have to escape his bondage in some yet unplanned manner and take a flight to somewhere where he could look after and give nourishment and protection to this family in conception. He stood up and told her that he felt immensely favored by her visit and that he would now contrive a plan which would alleviate the pain she was in; he asked her to try to visit him again in one week, and in the meanwhile, he would work out all the details. They embraced, and she left.

In her departure, Herald was in deep thought. He

considered himself a fortunate man to have another opportunity of being a father. He may have feared being a father in the past, but there would be no better father than one to Maria's child. The past months in prison had been hell for him. First had been his family's disappointment. That of his father had been so great that he heard the man's bitter words in his head every day. He had brought shame to the family and would never be forgiven for this. He was not to return home if he made it through the years. He knew they still cared for him; his mother had cried as she was pulled away by the bulky frame of his father. His family though of low stature, considered a life of great importance, he had done the abominable, and while time could heal the wound, it would never be forgotten. He had been in despair after losing Maria. Initially, he had never set out to love her, but his love for her was so great that he felt himself withdrawing into a shell. Every day that ended, he wondered how she fared. Was she as heartbroken as he was? Had she moved on and forgotten all about him? Was she disappointed in him like his family? If there was anyone who he wished would ever forgive him, it was Maria.

Herald fell asleep and dreamt of his dog, which was a brown and black curly terrier, it was a good dog, and it liked to play and walk in the forest with him, exploring the wetness of the morning dew, and the paths through the rich fauna around his home. He leaned his head into its neck and wept. Later as he awoke, he felt how strong his love for Maria was, and he realized within him a force he not hitherto had known, that almost nothing would be impossible for him now, that there was a yoke between them which was of eternal substance. He realized again that before he had met Maria, his strong tug towards women was a magnetic burn towards the female countenance and all its wonder; but with Maria, there was a rising of a pact, a sprouting communion of body and spirit, souls were in symphonic relation, and a bud would attain full blossom in six months. He knew now that he had to do whatever was possible to reunite with Maria and their unborn child.

One day Herald had encountered Gunnar in one of the local pubs, not perchance; Gunnar had learned about the passion his as good as betrothed Maria had for Herald, and Gunnar was about to put an end to this social climber's futile rivalry attempts. You see, nothing can be hidden under the sun. Even during their tryst in the darkest of the night, the hidden smiles shared had been noticed by the owls who had whispered of this progress to   Gunnar. Of course, Gunnar had been furious, storming into a whorehouse to rent his anger before he decided on what to do. How could his fair and untouched Maria stoop so low as to be with a pauper? Surely it had to be a lie spread by the lazy mongers. But underneath the moonlight, he watched his precious lean on the bastard's shoulder. Meeting Harold at a pub the following night, he quietly stated that Herald must instantly abstain from meeting Maria again; she was engaged to becoming his wife. How furious Herald had been. Having had no dealings with the noble, he had always despised him for the hold he had over the woman he loved.

"I will do no such thing. Maria belongs to me," Herald said, full of conviction.

The first blow had been rendered by Gunnar, knocking Herald off his stool, but with enough time to retaliate. Their ensuing struggle led to a fight where Herald was the victor. Walking away with a bruised face and shame, Gunnar declared to his friends in a highly animated state that he would get revenge in due time. He would bring the pauper groveling to his feet.

Gunnar, who came from a stalwart family with adequate means, started an investigation of Herald's background to establish if there were any disreputable exploits in his past, for he was sure that even in the goodness of all men, there was an evil he wished not to be associated with. There were only stellar reports of Herald, but Gunnar kept digging. As time progressed, Gunnar met Gretchen. How pleased he was to hear Gretchen's tale, and by intimidation and venality, he induced her to make a charge against Herald for the abortion, and Herald was jailed.

But Gunnar was not finished with Herald. Be it by his sweet words or whatever spell, Herald had succeeded in putting a blind over Maria's eyes, and she was enamored by him. Gunnar loved Maria, but he was irritated with her laying to a man of such status. He had had her first, and he had her heart; for that, he would never forgive Herald. He would deal with Maria when they were wedded, but he was bent upon the extermination of his competition. When he heard of Maria's visit to the prison, he knew it was time to put his plans into action; thus, he continued his entrapment by placing a prisoner of the noble class in the same jail, a jackal, who befriended Herald and convinced him that he had a plan of escape from the prison that was virtually foolproof. As this coincided with Herald's own plans, he did not suspect foul play since there was an enduring idea amongst the upper classes that helping as well as educating the ordinary farmer would be good for the country in general, an idea which was now germinating in the governing class in every European country.

Gunnar anticipated him as he came over the wall and

dropped to the soil end on the other side. A smile was spread on Gunnar's face, filled with hatred for the man who had taken from him what he cherished the most. Shock replaced the victory as Herald stared at his contender; he knew at that moment that he had been tricked. Gunnar impaled him with his bayonet, and it went through his chest. Gunnar's intention was to slay Herald, as he was an escaped convict; on that account, Gunnar would have eschewed the legal process. But Herald was able to get up and pull out the bayonet, hit Gunnar in the head, and then crawled away and found shelter at a friend, where he would regain his health. After that, Herald escaped to Aalborg, a fishing village that was important for overseas trade, shipbuilding, fishing and related trades.

Maria knew that Herald was in trouble with the bells sounding loudly all around the city in the middle of the night. The news was confirmed the next day. The constable could not fit the pieces of a puzzle. He was confused as to how a prisoner had escaped, with a noble found dead in the prison yards. Labeled a wanted man, Herald had a bounty over his head. Her worry was replaced with fear, then relief when she received a message from his friend; Herald had survived. He had fled to safety and needed to meet with her. Maria met Herald in Aalborg, running into his arms at the sight of him.

They agreed that they would leave Denmark, and Herald would work on securing an escape route to Norway in the next months.

She found out about her pregnancy at the end of March when she was probably eight weeks on the way. Herald left Aalborg in the middle of June, and they agreed to Fredricton the first week of July at an arranged time and place. She would then be four months pregnant and start having difficulties concealing her state of being.

South of Aalborg in Randers, the tyrant Count Gerhard of Holstein was assassinated by Danish National hero Niels Ebberson in 1340, Herald was an offspring of this family on his father's side, and Count Gerhard of Holstein had a sister who married into the Rosencrantz family, Gunnar's ancestors, perhaps from this also flowed the apprehension between Herald and Gunnar. Between Randers and Aarhus on the Durand peninsula lies an area of castles and estates, including Rosenheim Castle, the home of the Rosencrantz nobles. Most of the county is fertile lowland forming a prosperous agricultural region.

Herald also knew the story of his Norwegian ancestors, Ragnhild's misfortune followed by her joining the monastery, and the little shelf of land above the fjord where perhaps a future home could be waiting for them. His forefathers had spoken of the tales of his ancestor, Verald, who had never made it back home but had a fondness for the untouched land. Herald was hopeful he would find solace there.

Herald had been able to acquire a small wrecked boat, sail and oar vessel of 18 feet; it was clinker-built with overlapped planks and carried a single sail. It needed the replacement of half a dozen planks, new oars and sails, but Herald hoped it should sustain the passage across to Norway for his growing family. Sisal dipped in tar was used in the abutments to caulk as a filler. These boats were exceptionally sturdy, with a high bow and stern, and the mast was supported by shrouds.

Saying goodbye to her family was an ordeal for Maria. She spent the days before her departure spending time with her father and brothers, rendering to them how much she loved them without raising any suspicions. The past months' events further diminished her hopes of them accepting Herald, who was a wanted man for the death of her betrothed and the family's friend. Her future would be safer, far away from them in the arms of Herald. She gathered a few belongings, and in the middle of the night, she went to the docks where a boat waited to take her to Herald. She had left behind a short letter telling her family not to worry about her;

hopefully, she would reconcile with them someday.

In Fredricton, Herald did the proper thing; he wedded Maria in front of a priest; witnesses were an old man and woman who had taken them into their home.

The day came when the boat was ready for the crossing of the Skaw to Norway. It was late July, a warm and quiet summer night, and they came with all their belongings, loaded the boat, and cast off.

Herald raised the sail and moved into the seas, and their spirits were high. They moved for the first few hours rapidly, then the wind died down, and Herald started to row. The boat was heavy but moved with an easy motion through the water, and most importantly, it glided between the strokes. Thus the forward motion of the boat never ceased; each stroke of the oar kept the boat underway, and a steady tempo could be kept up hour after hour. Herald was strong, and he estimated he would be able to keep rowing for six hours at a stretch, then with a few hours' rest and then another six. The crossing from Skagen to Lindesnes was about 130 miles, and with a steady wind, it, with an average speed of four knots, should take about thirty-six hours. Rowing across twelve hours a day at a speed of 2.5 knots would mean a crossing would take 4-1/2 days. The direction was about 300 NW, and the prevailing winds coming mostly from the southwest would mean the sailing would be mostly at close reach wit. The currents run northeast along the west coast of Denmark and westwards from Sweden towards Western Norway. A current from the east hits the northern coast of Denmark, and it continues northerly towards Norway.

The voyage ahead embraced three different segments, first to Lindesnes, then another 130 miles going north to Haugesund along the coast, and then finally 100 miles onwards in a north-easterly direction through the elongated Hardanger fjord passing the Folgefonnen glacier to the East and ending up in the off-arm of Eidsfjord. They would be stopping in Lindesnes and Haugesund on the way. The baby was expected in October/November, by which time they hoped to be safely ashore for the winter.

The first night the wind was mostly from the west, so their direction took a more easterly direction than desired, but within 24 hours, it turned to the southwest, and they kept a course right on to Lindesnes. The wind was steady, then it died down, and Herald started rowing. The current from the Baltic was giving them an extra knot. Maria was in her fourth month, and it was showing, but she was feeling well and was optimistic about their whereabouts and what was ahead.

On the third day, the wind picked up suddenly; Herald hoisted the sail that was reefed so that only one-third of the full sail was up. Then the waves were building – big and tall - as if they were coming from somewhere from far away – perhaps Greenland, and soon they were towering over five meters in height. This lasted for quite a while. In the middle of the night, there was a crashing sound, and the mast came down and almost struck Maria as she lay down in the bow, trying to avoid the spray from the waves. Herald proceeded immediately with cutting loose the metal, stayed holding the mast and the ropes and was able to throw the mast overboard. He tied down the rudder flat towards the side as it would do little in this weather to help the ship's direction either way.

He tied down the oars, laid down next to Maria, and tried to give her warmth and comfort. He had built a small little sheltered deck at the bow so they could curl up and stay under it away from the rain and the spraying waves. They were thrown back and forth and stayed like this for the next twenty-four hours when the wind finally died, and Herald took up the oars again. The current was somewhat neutralized by the reverse current coming from the western coast of Norway, meeting the Baltic current, so he could stay warm in the wet weather by rowing. During the night, they heard the sound of seagulls and took this as a token that land was ahead. And a few hours later, they could hear the surf hitting the coastline. Waiting for daylight, Herald found out by dead reckoning that they were right outside Lindesnes. Soon they saw the land, and they decided to go into port and wait until the weather cleared. One-third of the voyage was over - minus one mast, stays, and some of the rope, he had been able to cut loose and save the sails.

"I need to replace the mast – we are spineless without. I will search the shore," Herald said immediately after they got to land.

They needed spruce still in the ground. Straight and some thirty feet in length. They walked along the beach for a while, passing a duck family swimming by and diving for fish and fish eggs and plants, the offspring having little success. They came by a cluster of trees with a few spruce in their midst. Herald started off with his chopping axe and began making a V in the tree, listening for a cracking sound or a seating movement. It came down. He sliced off the branches and the bark. He painted the butt with tar and preserved the rest of the mast with pine tar.

Returning, he found his dear wife sunning herself on the beach in the nude – with a beautiful womb taking on the shape of a large egg; he was elated at this sight and felt bequeathed with the greatest gift mature could give us. They were alive, in love, having their first child, and headed for a fantastic future together. A few days later, they were off again, moving slowly towards their goal, and the wind gave them an extra push up past the shores of Western Norway. They were aghast at the beauty of the skerries, which were naked dark rock islands sometimes in the shape of huge whales and dolphins, and the shining black rock had a smoothness to it after thousands of years of waves crashing over it that gave it a sculptural effect. Sometimes they would anchor up and go ashore and find a shiny rock face with slides of up to 20 feet and nakedly slide into the warm, salty lovely ocean. They made love on the grassy heathers in the sun and sometimes slept during the warm and light summer nights. One day they caught 3 mackerel and 2 trout that tasted wonderful on the fire.

A week later, they arrived at Eidfjord, and as they turned into the fjord and caught the first glance of the Kjeaasen, they were exhilarated and found that the adventure had just begun.

They had come home.

In the next days, they would climb the mountain and find that the houses which had been evacuated a long time ago were still there; they were in disrepair, but they had all the time in the world to do the necessary. They were alone in abandoned land, tired and in great need of comfort, but they were free from prosecution and travails they would have suffered if the constables had caught up with them. For here, no one would find nor disturb them.

It was difficult as they settled into their new life in Kjeaasen. The mountain seemed to have been long abandoned, and they could barely ravage anything from the ruined homes. Herald had to go downhill to source for their needs. He returned with food and clothing. In the days that followed, he would bring back home goats and lamb, which would eventually grow into a herd. The climate was another hardship they had to deal with. It was so harsh; weather they were certainly not used to. Most of the time, the climate was at sub-zero temperature (Celsius) down to minus 25 Celsius.

The loneliness was also something they had to deal with, but they had each other. They were grateful for the opportunity they had to be in heaven on earth, away from everyone else. Here, there were no whispers; they were no judgments; it was just them with their unborn child.

In November, they were all installed, and the time had come for the new tenderfoot entrant. A midwife made her way up the difficult path, and one Sunday morning, Marta was born. A beautiful little girl with a load of blond hair curled around her head – they almost died of happiness; from where did this angel come to them – from heaven?

When they brought her to church the next month for her baptism, they thanked God for their good fortunes and the gift they had received from Providence.

Marta was an added source of joy to her young parents. She was a bubbly child who seemed to understand the situation her parents had found her in. She was a beautiful child who was barely crying and always satisfied from suckling her mother's bosom.

The difficulty yet still prevailed, but Herald and his wife Maria seemed to welcome it. Their peaceful environment seemed to make up for it. Leaving his family behind, Herald would go into the wilderness to hunt. On lucky days, he would return with a reindeer, and on dry spells, he would bring back home a rabbit that would cook over the fire. They relied on their goats and sheep for their diary needs.

Their little family would eventually grow, and with every day that went by, Herald and Maria would be grateful for their new home.

FROM HIMALAYA TO SOUTH PACIFIC

The 20th Century

When the kids at Kjeaasen had grown to the mature age of some 17- 22 years, they talked to each other that it would be nice to get out in the world and perhaps get to meet some boys of their own age.

At that time, there was nothing else but the dancehall in Eidfjord, but there the "pauper children" from Kjeaasen had been sternly advised that they were not wanted there and that they had to keep out.

Now and then, during the summer months, the grownup kids went down to Eidfjord on a Saturday afternoon and peeped into the dance hall to see how the young people were enjoying themselves and dancing. They were interested in the dance steps. Up in Kjeaasen, they started, when they had time to spare, to dance with each other, without music, only with rhythmic singing. As time went by, they were getting quite a hang of it.

None of the children from Kjeaasen could understand why they were not permitted to the dance floor. They had never hurt a soul, and they never had a quarrel with anyone. Maybe it was Sara's fault, they thought. During toil and hard work, Sara had already developed a body with large muscles in her very young years. She often had fought with the boys in town, and nobody had been able to outfight her. She only hit when someone made fun of her or her family. Then she had sparks in her eyes, and then it was all over. Sara only hit the one who hit her with a strong return, which normally settled it.

One day at the beginning of June, just after she had filled her 20 years, Sara decided that she would enter the dance hall in Eidfjord one of the coming Saturdays, come what may. She did not mention this to her family or her siblings, except that she was going to town to purchase a beautiful fabric to sew herself a summer dress. She found a flowery fabric that she liked and also purchased a new hat and a new pair of shoes. She felt she could afford this as she had been saving some money from the jobs she had had. After she came back to Kjeaasen, Sara immediately started to prepare to stitch and sew her costume. Her parents and siblings wondered what she was up to.

"Yes, I am going out to have some fun." More would she not divulge. She sewed all day into the night and continued the next day after she returned from the farm.

A week later, the garment was ready. On Saturday afternoon, after she had washed and set up her hair, she paraded in her new gown in front of everyone to show how nice she looked. Sara looked different from the woman they knew. Well, not different. She was still Sara, but she looked like a lady with a sense of confidence and power.

"What is the matter with you? Have you lost your mind? Where are you going?" Her father asked.

Sara replied, "Now I will tell you. In a little while, I will go down to Eidfjord and enter the dance floor and start dancing."

"But," said her father with a worried voice. "I understand that you want that, but you must know that none of you is permitted to enter the dance floor. And you also know that nobody will ask you to dance with them".

"We will see," said Sara. "When I get closer and hear them call that "this is the ladies" dance, then I will go and invite a boy, and if he refuses, he will get the choice of either dancing with me, or otherwise I will carry him off the dance floor. I just hope that they are so fair that they do not all jump at me at the same time, for I will not be able to handle it. As long as I can handle them one at a time, they will never forget what happened to them. I feel in me a fighting spirit as never before. We have now reached the age that it is time for us to come out and claim the right to enjoy ourselves just as much as others. I know we are not wanted at the dancehall, although we have never mistreated any people. And I also know that we are good enough when it comes to cheap labor as maids or other work. I am firmly set on changing the unjustness of this attitude. I am absolutely firm in my belief that no one shall stop me."

Sara had thought over this long and hard. Nothing anyone could say would stop her. She was going to the dance hall to experience dance for the first time in her life. Sara took off her new shoes and packed them, and put on an old pair for the walk down from the mountain. When she was ready to go, her family and siblings looked at her with considerable worry as to what might happen to her down there. When Sara came off the mountain, she started to walk around the bay of the Fjord and continued towards town. Just outside of Eidfjord was a dense tongue of a forest. Here she entered to change her old shoes into new ones. Then she walked slowly into town. She was quite anxious as to what would happen. Even though she radiated confidence, she was nervous on the inside.

Getting closer to the dance floor, she could hear music, laughter and talk. When she came to the ticket office, she bent her head down so the ticket man could not recognize her. But he appeared not to notice anything. She received her ticket and paid for it, it cost 25 cents, and she walked into the crowd, stopped and looked around.

Sara had just arrived as the music had an interlude, with the dance floor free. Suddenly there was a wildfire through the crowd when Sara from Kjeaasen entered the hall. It suddenly became completely quiet. People had spread out in small groups and were talking almost in whispers whilst they glanced over at Sara, who stood there as if nothing had happened.

Some thirty feet away from Sara, three youths in their twenties were talking to each other whilst they often threw glances at Sara. One of them was larger and taller than both of his friends. He was considered to be the strongest boy, not only in Eidfjord but also in the other neighboring towns. Sara had seen him once before when she had gone down to Eidfjord with her friends to the market. The girls had pointed him out to him amidst giggles and whispers. She had heard that he was an upright fellow like few of the other young boys. He had a good stand and was good-looking and very manly. He had often been in fights, but only for fun. He never wanted any trouble, but the boys from the towns often challenged him to a wrestling match in the hope of gaining the reputation of being stronger than him. But nobody had yet matched his skill.

Even Sara had heard the girls talk about his good ways. He was said to help the old and those in need. Once, he had helped pull a drowning dog out of a lake. He had not yet formed any relationship with any girl, as he first wanted to have his future set upon, so he could support his future family. Sara had also heard that he came to the Saturday night dance practically every week. If anyone made any noise or trouble, he would always be the one to cool down the tempers. He was a favorite among the young and the old, who called out to him whenever he walked through.

He did not come from Eidfjord but rather from one of the surrounding towns some 20-30 miles away, but he had heard tales about the people from Kjeaasen – the "Poor People", the "Pauper kids". This he had heard off and on from various people. Thus, he received wrong information and wrongly understood that they were all troublemakers whom one should rather not mix with. He did not like to have troublemakers in the dance hall.

None of the other boys in the dance hall dared to approach Sara. They knew how strong she was. Although she looked pretty, they were scared of wronging her and her beating them up. But the two boys who talked to the strong youth tried to convince him that he was the only one who could do anything. They were all too scared to stand up to Sara, the bully, so gradually, he was persuaded that he was the only one who could get Sara to leave the hall. He accepted their proposal but decided to do it as gently as possible. Even if she was a troublemaker, he had to be polite to her.

Sara could feel the gazes on her, but she had no regard for them. Her eyes looked around for the boy she would drag into the dance floor when the music began. Suddenly Sara noticed that the strong boy separated from the others and came walking straight towards her. Everyone on the floor was following curiously to what would happen. Her heart pounded. Was he going to ask her for a dance?

He stopped a few steps from Sara and looked at her, almost hoping for her to look the other way. He discovered that Sara was very attractive. Of the strength that his friends had said she was possessed, he did not become aware of. Instead, he was looking at an unusually soft woman, and he already regretted that he had taken on the task of asking Sara to leave, but he could not let his friends down. As they looked at each other, Sara was doing a great deal of thinking in these short moments. There she stood and admired him; she understood why all the girls were trying to gain his attention. He could certainly be the ideal man for any girl - yes, why not for herself, thought Sara suddenly, without knowing why.

She stopped her thoughts as he suddenly placed his

hands on his hips and said to her in his soft, comfortable voice, "You know that poor people's kids from Kjeaasen are not wanted here. If you would be so kind to leave without any trouble, I will accompany you to the exit."

When Sara heard what he called her – "poor people's kids" –a great fire lit in her eyes. The beautiful thoughts she had for him were immediately changed to an incredible hate. What then happened was so quick and unexpected. In a microsecond, Sara had hit a well-directed punch to his jaw that landed him on the floor. He had both hands on his jaw, suffering from pain.

Everyone present gathered in a circle around them. Sara took one step forward, bent over him and shouted with vehemence so that everyone in the dancehall could hear. "Did you say poor people's kids? I know that we are poor, but there is no shame in being poor if one lives an honorable life. But as poor of muscles as you are do not exist amongst us at Kjeaasen. That we have gained through suffering and hard work is how we train our muscles so we can defend us against anyone who comes out with such rude disrespect that you have so audaciously expressed! Pitiful!"

Everyone stood in silence and watched with great interest. It could not be helped; many of the boys looked at Sara with admiration. At the same time, they took joy from the fact that the boy every boy had wanted to defeat now had fallen by a punch from a woman.

Sara stretched out her arms and said to the bystanders, "Is there anyone else who has anything to say?"

But everyone was silent.

With a raised head, Sara turned around and left the dance hall.

She had had enough fun this Saturday night, but next Saturday, she intended to return and continue the fight for the people from Kjeaasen to be equal with everyone. When Sara came up to Kjeaasen that night, her parents were still up. They had waited for her arrival.

"Now, how did it go, Sara?"

"Yes, there was a bit of trouble, and I deeply regret it."

They did not get any more out of her, wherefore everyone went to bed.

Some of the following days, Sara was not herself. Her thoughts appeared to be far away. At the end of the week, as Sara was about to bind together the newly hewn hay, she saw a man coming up the mountain. From afar, he looked different from the men on Kjeaasen. He went straight up to Sara, and as he came closer, she recognized him to be the boy she had punched to the ground on the dance floor. How shocked she was so that she almost clutched her chest in surprise.

He stopped in front of Sara and greeted her, and said, "I have come up here only to ask for your forgiveness for the incredibly dumb things I said to you in the dance hall last Saturday. I have come to realize that the information I received from my friends was all wrong. I have even spoken with the store owner and a few other friends in Eidfjord, and they all agreed that you live an honest and honorable life. After you left the dance floor, I spoke with everyone, and we all agreed that you and all the others from Kjeaasen are welcome to the dance hall as often as you wish. What you gave me down there was well deserved, and I highly respect you for have defended your honor. Therefore, will you take my hand and excuse me for my bad behavior? I will be extremely happy!"

Sara willingly took his hand and gripped it strongly as they looked at each other whilst she said, "Even I must apologize for my behavior, but know that it was not you I was hitting, it was the word "poor people's kids" that I was hitting as hard as I could. I have heard that word spoken so much, and it fills me with rage for what it means. We're the Kjeaasen people, but we're not poor. We're happy people with content lives who are no different from others."

FROM HIMALAYA TO SOUTH PACIFIC

There they stood, still holding each other's hands, and then she could not keep back a few tears that suddenly started to gush down her cheeks. It seemed awkward, and he was indecisive about what to do to comfort her. She did not protest when he wrapped her in his arms. The squawk of a bird startled them, and they pulled away from each other. He bid her a short goodbye, turned around and walked toward the steep steps. Sara followed him until he disappeared out of sight. As she stood there leaning against the bushes, she burst into more tears and hurried behind a pile of rocks and sat down so no one could see that she was crying. Her whole body was shaking. She could not understand what was happening to her. Why was her heart pumping so rapidly? Why did it feel as if the blood was rushing around her body? Why did she feel like running to the steep to call him back, and throw both her arms around his neck and never let him go as long she lived?

Suddenly she remembered something she had read in a book she had borrowed, something called "love with first sight". Was it something like that that happened down there in the dance hall when she saw the boy? She felt something like that must have happened to her. It was so beautiful, yet it hurt her. There was something new that was about to happen, something she had never before experienced. This was the first time she had spoken seriously with any boy, the first time she had received genuine friendliness, and that from a boy she had heard was sterling, honorable and sincere.

Her thoughts inside crossed each other, back and forth, and unexpectedly she decided that she would never again go to the dancehall. She understood at once that whatever boy would ask her for a dance would never be comparable to the man she had just talked with.

Man, thought Sara, yes, the man was just what he was. He was no longer a boy; he was a mature man. And she didn't believe she would ever have the opportunity to dance with the man again. Thunder didn't strike at the same place twice.

Sara got up and continued with her work, silent and thoughtful. The following day was Saturday, but Sara stayed home at Kjeaasen, and her thoughts were still with him, whose name she did not yet know.

When her parents asked what boy it was that came up to speak with her, she told them everything that had happened on the dance floor, and also what he had said, and that everyone from Kjeaasen was welcome to the dance hall whenever they wished. Her siblings became very happy to hear this. She, however, left out the part about the new feeling she felt for the man. This was left for her to ponder.

The Sunday and following days, Sara worked in a dream. It was impossible for her to let go of the thoughts of what had happened on the dance floor and, since then, the meeting with him up at Kjeaasen. Then came the Saturday, fourteen days after the event, on the dance floor. As was the norm, they did not work at Kjeaasen on weekend evenings and Sundays. Sara took a walk up the mountain above to feel further what was going on inside of her. She sat there and thought back and forth, but she did not know in her wildest imagination that this Saturday afternoon and evening should be crucial for the rest of her life. She sat there for several hours until she decided to go back to the farm.

As she arrived, she saw, to her surprise, that her parents were talking to just the man whom she had thought of the last fortnight. The blood rose to her cheeks as she went over to greet him.

"How long have you been here?" Sara asked. "Just about one hour," he answered.

"What have you spoken about?" Sara could see something written on her parents' faces, but of nature, she had no idea. How queer it was for his man, who was a stranger, yet so familiar to her heart, to talk intensely with her parents. At least, that was what she had understood before she interrupted them.

"A little of everything," said her parents, "but it is best that you two go and talk to each other."

"Him", whose name Sara still did not know, stood up, looked at Sara and asked if she would like to take a walk, as he wanted to speak with her privately. Although confused and curious about his sudden appearance in her home, Sara had nothing against this. Therefore, they walked over to the water place and a little beyond that and sat down on a pair of rocks to talk undisturbed.

Then he said to her, "Last Saturday, I looked for you in the dance hall but could not catch a glimpse of you. I had no interest in dancing with any other girl. I only had one thought, if I could not dance with you, then I would not dance with anyone else. I have wondered why you did not come down after I explained to you that everyone from Kjeaasen is welcome there. But now I have decided that this evening you shall come down. I have never felt as strong as I am today, so if you refuse to follow me, then I will carry you down from the mountain."

Sara looked at him while he gave her a smile. For the

first time, she saw his agreeable laugh and how his white teeth lit up in the sunlight. She felt indescribable happiness inside herself, and suddenly she understood that she had become a mature, full-blown woman and that love had its waking inside her. Sara looked at him and said, "You have just said that you have never been as strong as today and that, if necessary, you would carry me down from the mountain. With me, it is the exact opposite. I know I am strong, but never before have I been as weak as I am today. Therefore it will not be very hard for you to get me down from the mountain."

He looked at her with a satisfied smile and said, "Whilst you go in and dress up, I will go outside and wait for you, and after that, I will go in and say goodbye to your parents, who, incidentally, I also like very much." Sara looked at him in anticipation. Her eyes looked like two large question marks. "As I also like very much," he said. What did he mean by that? Was it really that he thought much about her? Or perhaps she had heard wrong? With a happy and enjoyable laugh, she waved goodbye to him for a little while and hurried in to get dressed.

When they arrived at the dance hall, Ingvald said, "Now I will dance with you a few dances. After that, we walk down towards the Fjord and sit down on this beautiful summer night and talk. I have some very important matter I wish to talk to you about, so we must not be disturbed."

What could it be that was so important, Sara wondered. She wished he would tell her immediately what he needed to tell her. What was so important that he couldn't tell her now? But from the look on his face, he was firm in his decision to wait till after they had danced. They took each other's hands and started dancing. Sara felt something indescribable happening to her. It was the first time she had held a man in her arms. At the same time, she felt well and pressed herself as close to him as possible. So it was with the second and third dance.

"Now we have danced enough. Let us go and talk about more important matters."

They sat quietly for a long time, and she had no idea what was coming. Suddenly Ingvald said, "What I want to tell you is so important that I prefer that you do not interrupt me one moment before I am finished. Can you promise that?"

"Yes, I do."

"First, I want to tell you about myself. I live with my parents in the town nearby. We are not rich, nor are we poor. We are just regular people. But I have thought about becoming something more than a regular person, which means I wish to make a good living so that I can build a home and get married and look after my family. Many, many times, I have visited the dance hall, but I have not found a girl who interested me or that I wanted to be with. I have not seen a woman to be within my town either. My thought was to let the time pass until I found someone I really could get attached to and thereafter plan the future. The first time I met you and looked into your eyes, not only did you look good but there was a shine of incredible femininity in you. I already then regretted that I had been asked to have you leave the dance hall, but I did not know then that I had been wrongly informed. But as soon as I said poor people's kids, matters developed very quickly. And when I was lying on the ground and looked up at you, I realized that one could not measure people by whether they were rich or poor. At that moment, I gained an incredible respect for you, and I saw how your feminine charm was growing. It suddenly appeared to me that this was just the type of woman I had looked for, that I had never known, and that I had to use all my power to try to win you. As I came up to the Kjeaasen and asked for your forgiveness, I discovered not only tears in your eyes, but I also saw something else that gave me hope that I could get to know you better. When I left, it was with a heavy heart and with confusion as to what was happening to me. For the past fortnight, you have been in my thoughts, and after some deep thoughts, I realized with great happiness what I had to do. When I arrived, and you were not there, I spoke with your parents and told them of my future plans and dreams to try to earn a better living in a larger town and that I, even in this short time, have come to love you, and I asked for your hand, at the same time as I promised them that I would make you happy. They had no objections; therefore, they wished me good luck when I proposed to you. We also spoke about something else that I will bring up later. As you will understand, Sara – I am proposing to you."

Invgald kept quiet for a few minutes. Sara made a slight movement as if she was going to say something, but Ingvald made a wave with her hand and said, "No, Sara, please, you must not answer yes or no. I first have to tell you everything, something more that is very important."

Sara had the whole time he spoke been sitting quietly, listening to every word he said. She felt incredible happiness inside. Everything that had happened the last two weeks had arrived so suddenly and violently that she could not fathom it. She was squeezing her arm to see if she was awake or if it had just been a wonderful dream. But she was awake, and it was real, and she was the luckiest person alive. Everything he had said to her, every word, every letter, had formed in front of her as if written in golden letters. Why she thought, could she not talk now, and take him in her arm and cry out her "Yes!" so it echoed through the mountains.

Suddenly Sara felt Ingvald take her hand. She held his hand and pressed it hard; she leaned her head against his shoulder and started crying from happiness. She had always considered herself a happy girl, finding happiness in whatever way she could, but she had never been as happy as this moment.

Ingvald looked at her and continued with a mild voice, "With happiness, I can feel your answer already, but first, I must tell you why it is so important for me to meet you today. There are no possibilities for me to get any good work here, so I have applied for vacant jobs in other parts of the country. Just a few days ago, I was accepted to start working as a carpenter in Drammen, four miles from Oslo. Already this Thursday I will go there and cannot meet you until after 12 months. As you know, it is very far from here to Drammen, and the connections are very bad. One must take the postal diligence with many stops and horse changes and overnight stays. Roads are bad, in addition to which they are closed during the winter months. The only acceptable connection is by boat around all of Southern Norway to here. Therefore, I cannot meet you more often than once a year." Ingvald halted for a little while.

Sara listened to him with great interest. She thought of the long road and the long waiting time. But what harm would that do when Ingvald was doing everything for their future?

Ingvald continued, "I have not thought of staying in Drammen for a long time, perhaps only 2-3 years, to get better in the craft of the trade. My goal is to come to Oslo, where I will purchase a large property, plant fruit trees, and thereafter build a villa for us."

Suddenly they were in each other's arms, and their lips met in a warm, embracing kiss. They were two lucky people who seriously meant each word they said to each other. And Ingvald pulled out two rings from his pocket, "I bought this before I made the way up the mountain. It has been burning a hole in my pocket for so long. I dearly hope that it would be a perfect fit. One is for you, and I place it on your finger, I hope it fits, and the other I give to you so you can place it on my finger. If you do not mind, these rings are proof of our faith in each other for all years to come."

Sara continued to cry as the ring slid into her finger. It was just a simple band, but it felt like she had carats of diamond glimmering on her hand. It was a perfect fit, and she had never felt more comfortable. With a smile of happiness, she slid the other band into Ingvald's hand. Who would have known that today of all days, would be the happiest day of her life? It had started just a few weeks ago, but she had fallen in love with this man, and she could not wait to begin a family with him. They went back into the dancehall to the whispers of the crowd, who had not only seen them together but had also spotted the bands on their fingers?

"Has Ingvald asked Sara, the Kjeaasen girl, to be his wife?" "What a lucky girl she has to be!"

"I'm not surprised; I knew there was more to it!"

After the dance, Ingvald went back with her up the mountain back home, where her family awaited with smiles. Her mother wrapped her in a hug with teary eyes. How happy they were for Sara. She had never gone looking for love, but she had found it. It was just so like Sara.

A day later, Sara was married to Ingvald at a chapel in Eidfjord. In attendance were a lot of people. For the first time in a long while, the Kjeaasen people were in full attendance to give away one of theirs into marriage with a respectable boy. It was a glamorous event filled with laughter and happiness, not forgetting the flow of drink, food and humor as they celebrated in the darkest of nights, the happy couple unable to look away from each other.

A few days later, with a heavy heart, Sara saw her husband off as he went forth to plan a better life for them. "You will always be in my thoughts," Ingvald promised as he waved to her.

He ventured to Drammen, which was a small town outside of Oslo, the capital. And for twelve months, he worked steadfastly as a skilled carpenter. In this period, they exchanged letters which arrived late; in the absence of each other, they yearned more for each other. After a year, he paid a visit back home to his wife Sara, who lived with her parents in the Kjeaasen. Their time together was memorable, and he left back to Drammen with a promise that soon, they would be together. It took further eighteen months for Ingvald to be established and to move to Oslo.

Sara would never forget the day she said goodbye to Kjeaasen. She looked around her and tried to capture the beauty and strength around her. It was a place she had had countless memories, be they good, be they sad. It was her home, her first love, but she had to take a step into the future. She knew without a doubt that the future ahead of her was hopeful. She also knew that the future of Kjeaasen was hopeful and that she was leaving it in good hands. With satisfaction in her heart, she said her goodbyes and headed to Oslo, where she and Ingvald built their future home and had several children. Kjeaasen would always be in her heart, and she would never run out of stories to tell her generations.

A river fall in Hardanger

FROM HIMALAYA TO SOUTH PACIFIC

THE SOURCE OF THE GANGES

FROM HIMALAYA TO SOUTH PACIFIC

THE SOURCE OF THE GANGES

In 2001 Roy and I met in New Delhi - I was flying with Aeroflot via Moscow. Our plan had been to hike through the Nanda Devi National Park, a world heritage site, where trekking was banned in 1982 to protect its bio-diversity and then was partially opened again for a restricted number of trekkers. We found out on our arrival that it had been closed again, so we had to regroup to change our plans.

New Delhi was full of people everywhere; the throng was unbearable in its mass, smells, sounds and foul air and heat - even in October.

We could not wait to get out and North to the mountains. We were at the train station for the first departure and got seated by the window, and were happy to be moving. After a while, we were in conversation with one of the other travelers. He was a retired brigadier general of the Indian Army on his way back home to Hardiwar, which was our destination on the first day. A friendship developed, and he invited us to stay overnight in his large 3 story home on the outskirts of Hardiwar, surrounded by a large planted garden surrounded by tall walls and two large, wild german shepherd dogs guarding his compound to keep out thieves and robbers. He had spent most of his last years in the Army in Kashmir, where he recounted some horrible stories of their skirmishes with the Afghan/Pakistan Army. They would kill a whole family in retribution for the conduct of one member of the family. The Afghan would never be taken alive - typically, his Indian opponent would promise his prisoner that they would not kill him as he was having his Koran in his right hand and the left hand on the fuse of a hand grenade - and he pulled the fuse. The Pakistan Army typically would go into the villages in Kashmir and kidnap 25-30 young men and send them to a warrior training course of 6 weeks in the North Western provinces of Pakistan. This would constitute 1 or 2 platoons. Their mission was to kill Indian military men in Kashmir, and they would ravage the local villages. If they did not follow the order, they would be bound and towed behind a jeep and drive around with the purpose of scaring everyone, including themselves. When they caught Indians, they would gore their eyes or take out the liver and eat it. If they caught a war hero, they would take out his heart. The top echelons in the platoon would share it to inherit the sacrificed soldier's courage and might. . "What could we put up against this fanatic conduct? They were all brainwashed and ready to perform kamikaze any time".

We thanked him for his nice company, and the next morning, we took the bus from Hardiwar to Uttarkash for some 8-10 hours, where we stayed for 2 days to plan our 22 days trekking tour - purchased food and hired porters.

We were permitted to use the kitchen of the small hotel to make our own meals. We found the porters here. The Lonely Planet had listed a trekking fee of some Rupee 150/200 per day, but at this high altitude, they wanted Rs. 325 per day, and we hired 4 porters for 22 days at Rs. 28,600. And then we took a cab from Uttarkashi to Barkot - about 2 hours' drive. The trek started here.

In Barkot, the porters asked if they could have some of their family members join us for the trip - and we agreed. It ended up with another 6 males - cousins, brothers and/or uncles who came along for the fun of the trekking, which was evidently in their DNA. It became a great trip with some wonderful human beings whom we learned to know. We started on the 150 km trek ahead of us.

Our first stop was at Janki Chatti (2650m), where we set up our tents and had our dinner. Our food was fairly spartan with vegetables, powdered fish soups, tinned sardines, and some dried meat, and for breakfast, mostly oats and rye mixed with either dried milk or soya powder mixed with water. We brought a water filter and water purification tablets. We heated the water sometimes since the tablets gave the water a certain flavor that made drinking less pleasurable. We heard later that Katadyn Mircopur might be a good choice.

The next day we were up early and trekked for a short 2-3 hours to Yamunotri with its hot springs. We tried out the springs and altered with a dip in the cool river. The porters circumvented the call on the springs. At night the porters made a great campfire and sang native songs for several hours whilst having their dinner. We enjoyed it immensely.

The following day we moved up to a 4,150 m camp, and we could feel the altitude. We had a superb campsite with views of the immediate mountains and very special lights.

The next day we climbed steeply for about 1 hour, and I felt considerably reduced. After two aspirins, I felt much better. We made the Yamunotri pass - 4900m - in 3 hours by noon. It was actually a peak. And then down again to 3,800m, where we camped. On the way, we met a group of 8 Brits with 2 porters. Later the same day, we met 26 porters who had taken the British group on their expedition to the Black Peak for about 25 days without making the top. The top of the Black Peak (Kalanag) is located at 6,387 meters.

In the morning, we told the guide to send one of the porters home since he was too troublesome. He only wanted to lift 10 kilos, whereas the average lift was 20-30 kilos. So the guide told us he was to bring 3 porters back to Seema and pick up 2 or 2 more porters there. We advanced him Rp4,000. We bid goodbye to the two extraordinary porters who turned back to their homes in Seema and especially the tall, strong porter from Kazakstan wearing tight, narrow-knit, thick, woollen pants and kaftan made from the ibex - a wild goat, he had spun, woven and sewn the kaftan himself. We wished we would have had such a warm outfit. That evening we enjoyed a campfire with beef stew, tomato soup, chickpeas and fried vegetables.

We camped on a delta edge by a shepherd cave with fire. We spotted sheep tracks nearby. We did not eat much. The appetite was not high during the altitude changes, but we forced ourselves to take loads of liquid through tea, yogurt powder with water, and soups. Counting the calories, it seemed like we were having an intake of 1,000 calories per day whilst we probably burned 3,000.

We woke up the next am in the cold, crisp air, sunny and bright and started the descent down to the Ruinsara Lake at 3,300m.

We woke the next morning and did yoga and qigong by the lake in the morning sun and dove into the great river. By 1015 our guide came back from Seema after having walked the 24 km roundtrip.

FROM HIMALAYA TO SOUTH PACIFIC

We started upwards again towards Kiarkoti, where we arrived in the late afternoon.

The camp was just below the glacier, and we got into our tents just before the rain set in. We enjoyed fish soup, sliced salami and potatoes. A group of 5-6 *imexes* came close to the tent in the evening without any apprehensiveness.

The next morning we climbed up the left side of the glacier and camped on the glacier. We left again at 9am and arrived at the ABC camp at 2pm. It was in a bed of rocks next to ice falls. We moved very slowly as we had to acclimatize during the ascent. We had magnificent views of four different glaciers up the valley.

We awoke the next morning in a very cold tent, but the sun hit our site at 815am, and we continued up to the Phumdar Kandi Pass (5,798m) by 1230pm. We proceeded down on the Western side at the rights side of the Kalanag icefall over very hazardous rocks and iced scree and moraines that were very difficult and very steep. At one point, a rope was attached to a rock to assure safety, giving us a diagonal repelling system. We camped at Gaurator 5100m. 10 hours later, we were down in the valley where the guide set up the campfire and made *chapati* and *dal bhat*. It was most delightful in the sunset, and the sky was filled with stars.

FROM HIMALAYA TO SOUTH PACIFIC

We then advised our porters of our subsequent plan. The next day we would bid them goodbye at Jahal at the bus stop, and they would go back to Uttarkashi, and we would go on the Gangotri. We broke camp at 8am and walked from 5100 m to 4100m in 4-1/2 hours. The path was continuous drops through perilous terrain along gorges and deep fissures in the earth, arriving at Jahal at 1330, catching the bus at 1500 arriving at Gangotri at 3pm.

The next day we walked 13km to Ghogosa and stayed in an ashram of very dubious cleanliness, and left the next morning at 6am and walked 5km to Gambuk, which is located at the head of the Ganges. Here water sifts out of the glacier wall and starts the small stream that turns into the 2525 km holy Ganges river that empties into the Bay of Bengal. The Ganges is one of the most sacred rivers to Hindus. It is also a lifeline to millions of Indians who live along its course and depend on it for their daily needs. It is worshipped in Hinduism and personified as the goddess Ganges. The Ganges is highly polluted. Pollution threatens not only humans but also more than 265 fish species, 90 amphibian species and the endangered Ganges river dolphin. There were several Yogis sitting in lotus positions, dressed in loin clots and exercising pranayama for hours. On the way, we met several times people carried in litter on the shoulders of 4-6 people. This was normally reserved for the wealthy and often very heavy persons who were not able to get to the source of the Ganges in any other way. We returned to Gangotri the next morning and by bus to Uttarkashi.

Our trip was filled with many funny incidents, and Roy was an ideal travel mate. We had many laughs and chess games. He is articulate, thoughtful, and intelligent. He is quick-witted and charming. He is generally well-informed about nature, animals, and politics. He is in strong physical shape with persuasive opinions of the US versus the world, Afghanistan. He had great English diction and vocabulary. He could recite a great number of poets and often started the morning singing ballads. He does not keep the tune but has a strong tone. And he can have a temper when need is as one day a young boy had dropped a turd on his shoe - he lifted the shoeshine boy off the street and had him remove it there and then.

Roy arranged a 30 days trip down the Omo River in Ethiopia with a group of friends, and on the way, their lives were threatened by water buffaloes and crocodiles, and they became prisoners in an African village. He skied the Brooks Range in Alaska at -50 degrees Celcius. Climbed mountains in Mexico, Ecuador, Peru and Argentina. Canoed across the

FROM HIMALAYA TO SOUTH PACIFIC

Sea of Cortez in Mexico. Caught the MauMau leader in East Africa.

Smuggled tobacco in Algeria. And worked for the US Outward bound. As it turned out, this was our last trip together caused by age, deformities, desire and circumstance.

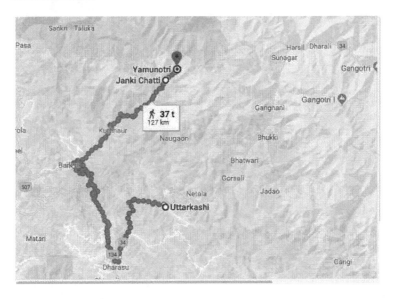

We trekked further East to Gangotri and to the source of the Ganges.

FROM HIMALAYA TO SOUTH PACIFIC

DOWN THE OMO RIVER, ETHIOPIA

Roy H. Smith

FROM HIMALAYA TO SOUTH PACIFIC

The Valley Where Man was Born

A 600-mile, two-month journey down the Omo River through one of the most inaccessible regions on the African Continent.

Support from National Geographic, World Wildlife Fund, and Yale University.

The Very First Man-Made Voyage of Its Kind

Early human fossils found by an ancient shoreline where the prehistoric Omo River emptied its silt-laden waters into Lake Turkana suggest that it was in the Omo Valley where the ancestors of Homo Sapiens made their first steps across the open savannah onto the pages of history. The river has retained its course for the past seven million years. It is conceivable that prehistoric migrations through this very ancient valley contributed to human settlements in the furthest corners of the earth.

The forty thousand square miles of the Omo River Valley lie in the shape of an oversized question mark across the rugged highlands of western Ethiopia. Its northern headwater, 120 miles southwest of Addis Ababa, lies only a stone's throw away from the immense watershed of the legendary Blue Nile, the "Mother of Egypt." For six hundred miles, the turgid brown waters of the Omo flow southward toward the equator through some of the wild and inaccessible terrains in Africa. The landscape of fortress-like mountains guarded by steep cliff faces and gorges is utterly different from anything else in Africa. It is a landscape created by the violent collisions of the vast Eurasian and African tectonic plates around thirty million years ago when titanic forces caused a two-thousand-mile section of the land to fault and sink, creating what we know today as the Great Rift Valley of Africa.

Much of the present geography is a result of catastrophic

volcanic activity that accompanied the creation of the Rift Valley. Such vast quantities of molten magma spewed across the land that even today, the mountains are still capped by as much as three thousand feet of black weather-worn lava. The Omo River has carved an impressive gorge of Grand Canyon proportions through this contorted mountain landscape, unlike any other on the continent. The abrasion of this timeless river has sculptured and polished the low lava cliffs that form its banks, creating abstract shapes that glint and glare in the tropical sun.

The river emerging from the mountains spills southward for another three hundred miles into the great Turkana depression. Here it meanders through a trackless sun-scorched savannah and desert thornbush until finally coming to rest in the jade-colored waters of Lake Turkana, the world's largest alkaline lake.

If the Omo Valley is where the man was born, it is also the place where time stood still. The upper two hundred miles of the river are uninhabited because of tsetse flies and mosquitoes, purveyors of the continent's most pervasive and virulent diseases, sleeping sickness, and malaria.

The Omotic-speaking tribes of this region live several thousand feet above the river in remote mountain villages, which, because of their extreme isolation, have changed little over the centuries. The boys and women ran away in terror in some of the villages we visited. We were the first white people they had ever seen. Beyond the mountains is a tall, nomadic, Nilotic-speaking people who hold sway and dominate the expansive plains with their large herds of zebu cattle.

It is a harsh and heartless land, far from the care and help of the outside world, where the vagaries of the climate can drive people to starvation and turn their land into deserts.

To learn the Omo Valley's secrets and gain access to its inner sanctuaries, one must travel by river. Beginning as early as 1885 with Count Teleiki's expedition, explorers have made brief and brutally difficult overland incursions into the lower reaches of the Omo Valley. Still, few came to understand the complexity of the land or its people. In the last twenty years, with the advent of new raft construction technology, western travelers and scientists have begun to explore this secluded valley. The river, while providing a pathway into the great gorge of the Omo, requires skilled boatmen to navigate the rafts down scores of hazardous rapids that plunge over house-sized boulders and squeeze through narrow canyon walls. Along its banks are great concentrations of wildlife that have virtually disappeared from much of Africa. It is the home for thousands of hippos and crocodiles that bask and lurks in its warm, still waters and eddies. Lions, hyenas, and leopards stalk its shores to prey on the waterbuck and gazelle that come daily to drink at the edge of the water. It is the "old Africa" preserved by its remoteness and inaccessibility.

FROM HIMALAYA TO SOUTH PACIFIC

Our Journey Down the Omo River

"Hippo!" I yelled and began to pull on the alloy steel oars in an effort to put some distance between our five-meter inflatable nylon raft and 2000 kilos of charging flesh and a gaping mouth. It was the enormous head and mouth that riveted my attention. A mouthful of fist sized molars adapted for the grinding of course grasses looked equally adept at crushing the life out of any unfortunate body that inadvertently came between its jaws.

Moments earlier, going through a small rapid, I had noticed what looked like a large lava boulder in an eddy by the east shore. The current had drawn the raft into the eddy, where it became immediately apparent that the rock was the badly scarred back of a large hippo. Half its torso, legs, and head were submerged. With no perceptible movement other than the gentle lapping of water along its bulbous battle-torn flank, I decided to move in for a closer look at what I was fairly sure was a dead hippo. It seemed strange that there were no natives on hand attempting to drag the two-ton carcass ashore or that the crocodiles were not already cleaning up the bones. Something was strange. I was beginning to feel a little nervous and slapped my oar down on the water to see if the noise would bring the carcass to life. It did, and with alarming speed, the hippo performed an underwater pirouette on its hind legs, wheeled, and charged directly for the raft. It was the largest hippo I had ever seen and the meanest. I instinctively pulled on the oars to get into deeper water, where it would have more trouble climbing on board and biting the crew. We had been on the river for ten days and had traveled over 100 kilometers.

Hippo attacks were nothing new, but we had seen nothing so large and battle-scarred earlier. There was no way I could outrun it. "Stand by to repel boarders!" I shouted and instinctively grabbed an oar as a weapon. Keith clutched his cameras and prepared to do battle with them. Tesfaye, our Ethiopian guide, and Addison, one of our expedition benefactors, grabbed an armful of rocks from the arsenal we kept on board in the event of such attacks. We were ready for anything! With the benefit of negative buoyancy, the hippo was narrowing the gap in a series of underwater sprints and spectacular surface lunges.

At twenty feet, I could smell his breath and looked directly down his pink throat as he blasted out a mouthful of water and a lungful of air. Tesfaye looked scared.

It was our last chance to slow his charge. Together we hurled fist-sized rocks at the gaping head and jaws. One of the rocks was a direct hit and disappeared down its throat. He must have known by now that we meant business, but he kept coming closer. A trail of bubbles and a surface wake created by his large bulk traveling fast underwater made it clear he was coming in our direction and meant to attack. His final lunge was directly alongside the raft. His reception was the orchestrated screams of a very scared crew, along with a battery of rocks directed at his head. At the last second, when disaster seemed imminent, he lost his nerve, dived under our raft, and headed directly for the second raft, which had been following us about 100 meters behind.

At that time, Terry Goodhue, our zoologist. A good-humored professional beekeeper from Maine captained this raft, including our botanist Emile Dusty our ornithologist, who was asleep on the rear of the boat. Sarah, our land use specialist at the time, was deeply engrossed in the novel *Tom Jones* by Fielding.

I gave several warning shouts, which seemed to evoke little response other than a nonchalantly turned head, which suggested an unusual complacency because of the impending attack. Perhaps they thought I was joking. Meantime the hippo was making good upstream underwater speed, zeroing in on its new prize. He was obviously disgruntled at his poor showing, and like a big bully, he seemed eager to make amends for a badly damaged ego. There was little we could do to help.

A loud roar, along with the emergence of two tons of hippo evoked a corresponding eruption of Dusty's prostrate body creating screams and general chaos. The hippo had timed its surfacing perfectly. As it lunged to the surface, Terry could ram one of his oars between the closing jaws. His quick action saved the raft, but the oar suffered two deep gouges in the alloy steel shaft. Once again, the hippo fled, thwarted in its attack.

We were on an eight-person expedition from the Yale School of Forestry and Environmental Studies that included three benefactors, Leon Farley, Terry Goodhue, and Addison Bell, who helped to finance the expedition. Robert Waggoner, an M.D. who captained a raft, and a botanist, Emile Gereau, from the Missouri Botanical Gardens. The Yale team included Sarah Brichford, land use specialist; Dusty Gardener, ornithologist; Louise Wilcox, land use planner and Roy Smith, who was making his second journey into the Omo Valley. My project was to initiate a biological mapping of the Omo Valley and to explore previously unvisited areas in the mountains high above the river. My larger agenda was to stimulate international interest in creating a Biosphere Reserve in the Omo Valley's mid-section and investigating the area's potential for Ethiopia's developing tourist industry. The expedition received financial support from the Yale School of Forestry, National Geographic, and the World Wildlife Fund.

In the early dawn, the night noises were finally overwhelmed by the first raucous scream of an Adada Ibis and the shriek of a fish eagle. A fine mist sometimes hangs over the Omo River, creating an atmosphere of timelessness and mystery. The bellowing of a bull hippopotamus echoes quietly across the valley. The noise is lost in the emptiness of the tall Hyparrenia grass-covered hillside and cloudless sky. It enters the river with caution and measured steps until enveloped by its warm brown waters. Only its large protruding bloodshot eyes set in a massive bony skull, its pig-like ears and nose remain above the water. It will spend most of the day like this, safe from the predations of both lions and hyenas.

The thin strip of dark green vegetation clung to the river's edge and appeared sinister and dangerous in the early morning without the revealing light of the sun. A crocodile swam lazily towards the center of the river, slowly turned, and looked towards my tent through the transparent drifting mist. High in the branches of sycamore fig, a colobus monkey began the day with a defiant sounding call like that of a monstrous tree frog and answered from across the river by another colobus whom he would never meet. The message of the colobus, whatever it might be, is passed on by a succession of voices that finally recede around a distant bend in the river. Dawn was breaking in Africa.

It was 5:30 am, and I could hear the sound of low voices coming from the direction of our campfire. Unsure about the danger of wildlife, I had divided the night into two-hour watches. On the dawn shift, Dusty was preparing our oatmeal breakfast while sitting crouched by the fire with six Hayda natives who had appeared out of the forest behind our camp. Their spears were silhouetted against the river, just beginning to reflect the rising sun's first light. They were herdsmen whose permanent village was near the town of Hosana, four thousand feet above our camp and thirty miles to the east. They planned to cross the river to the Kafa shore at dawn and return with cattle they had been grazing from a temporary camp high above the west bank of the river.

Wolde, the 15-year-old wife of the chief, who was six months pregnant, was also to be brought across. We made them a large pot of tea which they finished with relish. Before we had finished breakfast, they started to cross the river using inflated goatskins. With little ceremony, they waded out into an eddy which slowly spun them into the main current and downstream. The goatskins kept them high in the water while they kicked vigorously for an eddy on the Kaffa shore. A trail of smoke from smoldering charcoal, held high above the water by one of the swimmers, followed their progress across the river.

They had selected a section of fast-moving water to avoid crocodiles, but the operation still seemed a risky proposition. They were met on the far shore by other Hayda tribesmen who had brought their cattle down to the river and compounded them inside the forest margin. Wolde, the fifteen-year-old wife, was shy and refused to step beyond the forest's edge while we were there. Her husband told me he was a poor man and that his wife, of whom he was very proud, had cost him a bride price of two cows. He doubted that, at that price, he could afford another wife. I commiserated with him on the hardships of life and the high price of matrimonial happiness. The practice of cattle bride prices in marriage transactions is common among most agrarian people of Ethiopia but particularly among the nomadic pastoralists whose wealth is measured in the number of cattle they own. While the practice has the beneficial social effect of constantly redistributing wealth within a tribe, it also places extraordinary pressure on the often marginal grasslands that may already suffer from overgrazing. A situation that has been compounded by the current drought afflicting the Sahel region of Africa.

"Why do you keep your cattle so high above the good grazing near the river?" I asked, "If we keep the cattle near the river," he explained, "they will go to the Omo River to drink, and the crocodiles will pull them in and eat them. Also, there are lions on both banks of the river." When the time came for the cattle to be taken across the river, the Hayda tribesmen cajoled each cow to the water, speaking to it in reassuring tones, and then swam across the river supporting the animal's neck with the aid of the inflated goatskin. A reluctant cow could only be persuaded to cross after her calf had been taken across first.

The Omo River, rather than being a corridor for commerce and travel between villages, is more of an obstacle to the tribes who live far above its banks in the mountain villages.

Between the Gibe Bridge, on the Addis Ababa to Jimma road, and Lake Turkana, a distance of 600 miles, there is only one bridge, and the road approaching this bridge is virtually impassable on both the Kafa and Gemu Gofa banks of the river. Each tribe, in their way, has devised a way of crossing the Omo, from swimming with inflated goatskins to dugout canoes. Skilled rivermen make a living by ferrying others across the murky crocodile-infested waters.

Whenever we met people by the river, we asked them scores of questions, but they rarely asked us anything. They didn't seem interested in where we had come from or where we were going. Perhaps they were reluctant to embarrass us with questions when it was obvious we were nothing more than poor drifting vagrants without weapons, wives, or a permanent home.

I wondered if they didn't feel sorry for us. Telling them we were from Addis Ababa and heading for Lake Turkana made no impression; they had heard of neither. The expedition was measured by encounters with seventeen different tribes, each with their distinctive language, who live in the great gorge of the Omo and the plains beyond, whose lives have changed little with the passing of centuries.

Tesfaya, our guide, like most Ethiopians, was quiet, with a gentle disposition, and a born diplomat. Interestingly, he had been seconded to the expedition because of a political crime he had evidently committed. The authorities presumably thought that joining us for three months on the Omo River was sufficient punishment. It was his first expedition on the Omo, and he was pleased with the opportunity to learn more about his country and earn an extra per diem on his salary, which guiding provided.

He knew very little about the wildlife in the region and was new to the intricacies of the river, but he proved invaluable as an interpreter when asking for directions or buying food. After one particularly grueling and nerve-wracking day, when our raft had almost been capsized by a hippo that unexpectedly surfaced underneath us and then badly knocked around in several big rapids, Tesfaye asked me in a very confidential manner, "Why do people like you Americans do things like this?" I could only smile. I really didn't have an answer.

The gorge becomes deep and narrow when the river has incised deeply into the black beds of lava. The constricted waters are squeezed between the sculptured canyon walls and accelerate with a new energy that throws the rafts around uncontrollably.

It is the Grand Canyon of Africa. Many rapids are big and potentially dangerous and cannot run without serious reconnaissance. It was usually possible to predict where most rapids would be by the appearance of tributaries. Large boulders are washed down these steep tributaries during heavy flooding and deposited in the main river, creating rapids that vary in difficulty from "straight shots". It is an easy path down the center of the river to navigate through a jumbled mass of boulders choking the entire river width. Boulders recently deposited retain their angular shapes and sharp edges. A collision could rip open the raft.

The reconnaissance itself could be hazardous. The thundering noise of the river as it plunged and squeezed through a succession of boulders made it difficult to hear the movements of any animals that might have been in the trees and undergrowth. The riverine undergrowth is excellent snake habitat harboring a range of species, from pythons and Spitting Cobras to the deadly Black Mamba. While scouting a rapid at latitude 7.20 N. just before the confluence of the Gojeb, I was surprised to find an 1780 Maria Theresa silver dollar jammed between two boulders. Under what circumstances had the coin come to lodge between these boulders deep in the inner gorge of the Omo? I named the rapid Maria Theresa to commemorate the discovery.

Between the rapids, there was time to relax and look around the spectacular country with a more appreciative eye. Small villages of thatched tukuls surrounded by a colorful patchwork of cultivated fields of teff, ensete, and sorghum spanned the entire length of the mountains virtually to the east of the river. These higher elevations receive a higher rainfall and are more favorable to agriculture and human settlement than the drier valley bottoms. More importantly, they are above the malarial areas and tsetse flies. The landscape is dominated by tall grasses extending beyond the narrow strip of riverine forest in the valley bottoms to the summits of most mountains.

FROM HIMALAYA TO SOUTH PACIFIC

Each mile down the river took us closer to the equator and reduced our altitude. To escape the searing heat of the midday sun, we looked for side creeks where we could retreat until the mid-afternoon when the temperatures became more tolerable.

At the mouth of a tributary flowing between the mountains of Maigudo and Azu, we encountered a large gathering of men and women of the Gurage tribe on both banks of the river. The women on the Shoa bank of the river retreated into the forest amid screams and nervous laughter. The men on the Kafa bank stood their ground, but until we waved and smiled, they looked too nervous and were reluctant to join us at the water's edge.

Once they realized we were not there in any official

capacity, they relaxed and gathered around the rafts. An older man who appeared to be in charge stepped forward and asked us if we would carry some of his men across the river to the Shoa bank, where all the women were. They had been using small floating platforms of reeds and wood in an attempt to cross the river. These precarious crafts had not been working too well, and several had broken apart in the unusually fast water they had chosen to cross. We welcomed the opportunity to help and beckoned the man on board.

Reassured by our friendliness, the head asked Tesfaye if we would help him to ferry some sacks of produce across the river. We agreed, and a group of men disappeared into the forest, returning 20-kilo sacks of coffee. We had stumbled across a coffee smuggling operation aimed at moving coffee along obscure unmarked trails from the area around Jimma, Ethiopia's principal coffee growing region, across the Omo to Hosana and Welkite. About forty men, women, and adolescent boys and girls were involved. The women had been hired as porters to carry the coffee for two days through the Sengiya Mountains to Hossana, which lay over 1200 meters above the river and 40 kilometers east.

From Hossana, it would be transported to Welkite and sold for six dollars a kilo or three times its purchase price in Jimma. The porters received a meager fifty cents a day for carrying the 20-kilo loads. The reason for this ingenious enterprise was in response to the government's control of coffee prices. Any coffee grown in Kafa province must be transported across the Gibe bridge government checkpoint to reach Addis Ababa. Only the government was allowed to buy coffee at a wholesale rate. It was purchased at around a dollar fifty cents a kilo and then placed a 300% tax on the purchase price. Coffee is an important source of foreign earnings, and the tax is presumably a mechanism to reduce its consumption domestically.

They were delighted by our arrival as they had already lost a sack of coffee in the river and were in the process of trying to devise a better raft. All the boys wanted a ride on our rafts and jostled with each other to climb aboard. The older man was happy with his stroke of good fortune and instructed the women to prepare steamed maize, which made a brief, welcome change to our diet of beans and rice. Before leaving, the women spontaneously broke into a dance and song of thanks for our help. We responded by singing a song of our own.

The river tugged at our boats, and the journey continued. Our only company now was the white-tailed Colobus monkeys and endless troupes of Anubis baboons which paused at our passing to stare at the incredible spectacle. The young ones were less afraid and dallied long after their parents had run for higher ground or a tree. The warning screams of mothers and scolding grunts from the sentries finally persuaded them to seek cover. The older males seemed disdainful of our presence and, in a symbolic gesture of contempt, turned their backs to us while keeping a watchful eye on the youngsters. We approached a herd of waterbuck on the left bank, which stood motionless as we silently approached. They caught our scent or saw us move and disappeared into the forest.

During our 60 days on the river, we camped in 35 different locations. Many were unavoidably on hippo trails. On several occasions, we awoke during the night to see their large black shapes moving through our camp, which lay between the river and grazing. Lion tracks were discovered several times on the perimeter of the camp. Hyena tracks and scat were common, and it wasn't unusual to find the deep grooves of crocodile tracks made during the night only a few yards from camp. The priority in making camp was to gather driftwood so we could keep a protective fire burning through the night. A fire would have kept most animals away, but it was doubtful if it would deter a hungry man-eating lion or a really angry territorial hippo on whose turf we had made camp. We avoided camping under the giant sycamore figs after a bad experience near the Gojeb. Dinner on that particular night was constantly interrupted by figs falling from the overhead branches and looking suspiciously like bird droppings. I grabbed a flashlight to see what was going on and discovered hundreds of fruit-eating bats feasting on the figs. In their eagerness to get at the figs, they knocked many of them to the ground, defecating simultaneously.

The Omo Valley is one of the most spectacular wildlife areas on the continent. The grandeur of its geography surpasses anything in East Africa. Wildlife rafting safaris on the Omo River could have tremendous potential for Ethiopia's developing tourist industry, but a plan needs to be devised to protect its still abundant wildlife and unique people.

The creation of an International Biosphere Reserve that would include the existing Mago and Omo National Parks may be the best management option. Unlike most National Parks in Africa that have excluded the local people who historically hunted and lived there, the biosphere reserve intends to include local people in the economic benefits that accrue from the conservation of wildlife. Grazing and hunting would be allowed in a Biosphere Reserve within specified and enforced limits. If it could be demonstrated to local people that economic benefits are accruing from the conservation of wildlife and its habitat, management would be easier and more effective.

A factor that makes the creation of a biosphere reserve even more pressing is the long-term plan of the Ethiopian government to resettle four million people in the Southwest Highlands. Much of this land lies adjacent to the Omo Valley. The need for a land use plan to provide for the long-term sustenance of this new population, wildlife, and indigenous cultures, is critically important. Without it, the land might soon resemble the sterile over-used lands of the Northern provinces.

After fourteen days on the river, we arrived at the Soddu to Zima Bridge constructed by the British during their rout of the Italian Army in 1941. Bob Waggoner, our M.D., who had rowed one of the rafts through the upper gorge, had to leave us and return to his practice in Wyoming. Terry, who had been showing great talent at the oars, was promoted to captain of the second raft.

The river banks bustled with life, and it was rare to travel more than a hundred meters without seeing a variety of birds and a succession of Columbus monkeys in groups of six to twenty and troupes of baboons forty or more in size. Columbus would sometimes follow us down the river making spectacular twenty-foot jumps from branch to branch. Sedate white-breasted fish eagles were stationed along the entire river length, perched where they had a commanding view of long stretches of water. We got to know them as notorious pilferers, practicing aerial combat in their attempts to steal fish caught by the more industrious herons.

The largest and most violent rapid in the lower half of the Omo is created by its confluence with the Denise River, which has deposited boulders, some thousand cubic meters in size, along a three hundred-yard section of the river. It is hard to imagine the volume and velocity of the flood waters that moved such immense boulders. We could hear the roar of the rapid, named Potamus Plunge, long before we could see the turbulent waters. The rapid was named after the first expedition to descend the upper section of the river in 1974. Following too close to their raft and just a little too curious, a hippopotamus had been sucked into the rapid and miraculously survived its turbulent descent. Through its folly, it had earned itself a niche in the place names of Africa.

Our 1:1,000,000 map showed a north-south trail passing through the village of Womba on the high eastern slopes of Mt. Koliobamba, crossing the river and then continuing to the village of Banja in Kaffa province. Womba, perched high in the mountains, looked like a village we should visit, and the trail, I suspected, might make access easier if we could find it. We passed the tributaries of the Cila and Loda rivers, both running clear, but there was no sign of the trail to Womba. Some local Wallato-speaking people from the region were equally vague on its whereabouts, and the question of the trail drew nothing but a blank stare. I decided to make a quick reconnaissance and attempt to unravel the mystery of Womba and the elusive trail. Emile, Dusty, and I grunted and panted for 300 meters up a nearby hill in the still hot late afternoon sun. The view was good, but we saw nothing that indicated a village or a road. A wide hippopotamus trail, however, led up a valley in the general direction of Womba. Perhaps it would be worth following.

The next morning, our twenty-fifth day on the river, we were on our way to Womba. Sarah remained behind to guard the camp. We reached the small village of Sada three thousand feet above the river. It was only a year old and comprised of young farmers and their families from the Kullo Kunto region in Northern Kaffa province. They had moved across the Omo tosettle on the slopes of Koliobamba because of the more predictable rainfall. Already 400,000 people from the drought-scarred Northern provinces have been resettled in the southwest, and it is anticipated that a total of four million people will eventually be resettled in this region of Ethiopia.

About Womba, we learned nothing but discovered there was another larger village higher in the mountains named Bessa. We recruited two local guides and reached Bessa in the late afternoon after a 4,000 feet climb from the river. Except for Terry, everyone looked exhausted and slumped down prostrate at every rest stop. Our arrival in the village created great consternation. The women ran to their huts shouting in terror. Only the men and boys ventured out to greet us. The chief was visiting another village, and arrangements were made for a roasted goat and injera meal to be prepared at a nearby hut, where we also spent the night. It was already dark when the chief arrived, and we were well into our meal while sitting on cattle hides on the hut's floor in front of a small fire. Two cows, a calf, six goats, twelve hens, and a rooster were part of the family that shared the hut with us. A procession of curious visitors from Bessa and neighboring villages came to see us throughout the evening. Many to see their first white people.

They sat and stared at us for long periods, only occasionally asking questions of our host, who had become an overnight celebrity. Finally, I asked the chief, "Where is Womba?" There was a long pause. "It is no longer there," he finally replied. A short discussion followed between all the men in the hut. "It was attacked by the Golda people," the chief explained. "They stole all the cattle and killed many of the people, and the survivors joined other villages." "Who are the Golda people," I asked, "And where do they come from?" "They live to the south in the low hot country where there are no villages like ours," the chief told us. The raid had occurred six years earlier. The authorities' reprisals had been unsuccessful because of the inaccessible, waterless, and roadless terrain. The only people I knew of the south were the semi-nomadic Bodi people, and I inquired about them. There was silence for several minutes. "The Bodi are bad people," said the chief, "And they eat people." That was all he said. We were soon to travel through Bodi country, and the news made us a little uneasy.

Perhaps as their perennial enemies, they had cast this slur on the Bodi to diminish them in our eyes. We would have to wait and see. Our journey down the river would take us through the heart of Bodi territory.

During dinner, it had been decided by a majority of the villagers that we should stay in the village for another three days while word of our presence was relayed to other villages. I didn't take the idea enthusiastically and thought of Sarah, all alone guarding our camp by the river. I decided we should rise early the following morning and leave the village. Before the first cock crow of dawn, while our hosts were still sleeping, we quietly left our hut and hurried back to the river.

We had been away for two full days, and Sarah was glad to see us. "Where have you been?" she exclaimed. "There were lions around camp all night; I was scared." While we had all slept together on the floor of the hut in Bessa, Sarah had been forced to keep a fire going throughout the night to keep several lions away from camp. "I was in my tent when they first roared... They were getting closer, and I realized I had to get the fire going to keep them away." We saw their paw prints in the sand only fifty feet away from camp.

Our next objective was to cross "Plain of Death", as described by an old British map, to the villages of the little-known Dimi tribe, who lived in their mountain stronghold on the edge of the forest that cloaks the cloud-shrouded eight thousand-foot summit of Mount Smith. I decided to raft south for another ten miles past the mouth of the Denchija River and then try to cross the "Plain of Death" to the base of Mount Smith, following the edge of a seasonal water course.

For the past month, the only people we had made contact with were the highlanders who lived in villages far above the river, away from the heat, tsetse flies, and mosquitoes. The only reason they ventured into the lower gorge was to hunt or cross the river.

We were now entering the northern edge of the vast East African plains, which sweep southward for almost a thousand miles through Kenya into the heart of Tanzania. It is the land of the semi-nomadic Nilotic pastoralists, whose ancestors, with their large herds of cattle, migrated from the Nile Valley and the Southern fringes of the Ethiopian Highlands over two thousand years ago. They are tall, hardy people whose diet for most of the year consists of milk supplemented by meat and blood from the veins of the living cattle. The Omo Valley region's pastoral diet is augmented by sorghum, maize, and beans. They are grown along the banks of the Omo River. Many have strongly aquiline facial features that perhaps suggest a historical caucasoid connection with people far to the north.

The first of these people we met was a family of the Bodi tribe, clearing the thick forest and bush from the river bank with primitive axes in preparation for planting. The women scurried for the cover of the forest. A solitary Bodi man approached and beckoned us to sit with him on cattle hides in the shade of a huge Tamarind tree, under which a temporary kitchen had been established. He was tall, well over six feet, slender, and wore nothing more than a modest piece of cloth made from a plant of the sisal family. The women returned shyly and offered us cold coffee in an earthenware pitcher. Suspicious of the water, we declined it.

The six women wore brief, attractive, and bead embroidered goatskin skirts tied around their waists and several kilos of heavy brass and iron bangles on their ankles. All had children, and two were pregnant. One of the boys, about ten years old, had a badly ripped cheek from a recent fall. Instead of cutting down the larger trees to allow light to penetrate their crops, they chop off the big branches with primitive hand axes. The boy had fallen from a high branch, and a protruding limb had torn his cheek, which he covered with a piece of goatskin to keep away the flies. The man carried a Mannlicher rifle of ancient vintage and a short bandoleer containing six cartridges. It became rare to meet any pastoralists who didn't carry a rifle. Only the young, pre-adult-age men and boys carried spears. The family belonged to a section of the Bodi tribe who occupy the land around the lower slopes of Mount Smith, where they graze their cattle safely away from the tsetse areas near the river.

Agricultural plots extend along almost the entire lower length of the lower Omo, from where it bursts out of the mountains to the west of Mount Smith to the alkaline waters of Lake Turkana. Crops of sorghum, maize, and beans thrive in the rich silt, washed annually from the fields of highland farms. A look at the geography of the Ethiopian highlands provides ample evidence of the massive erosion that has taken place there over the millennia, some natural but increasingly man-made. In the dry years, when grazing is poor and the cows give little milk, these small riverine agricultural plots provide the margin of safety for survival.

"Who are the Golda people," I asked. The reply was unexpected. "We are the Golda People! It is the name the people of the North call us." I didn't ask him about Womba. We had come to Ethiopia to look and learn, not to solve mysteries or pass judgment.

FROM HIMALAYA TO SOUTH PACIFIC

Towards evening, a group of naked Bodi men waded the river, shouting as they came to keep away a large crocodile that had been cruising the river opposite our camp. They stood around and looked at our possessions with awe and admiration. The ropes, buckets, and matches held the greatest fascination. An older man had scarification marks on his arm resembling a snake, indicating he had killed a man. The pictures from an illustrated wildlife book helped us identify Burchell's zebra, hartebeest, leopards, and other regional animals.

I chose a camp opposite a dry watercourse which I hoped would lead directly across the "Plain of Death" towards Mount Smith. A short hike above camp provided us with an excellent view of the mountain fifteen miles away to the east, rising abruptly for over 6000 feet above the plains to precipitous cloud-shrouded granite walls that guarded a long summit ridge. The following day, we hiked to the low rim of the gorge as the sun climbed over a bank of clouds that still clung to the southern summit of Mount Smith. The open Ethiopian savannah was new to me. There were no ridge trails to follow like those in the mountains. We headed directly for a barely visible village perched high on the saddle of a distant ridge that descended out of the clouds.

After five hours of pushing our way through eight-foot

tall grasses, we discovered a trail that led us north across the western mountain flank. An old Bodi man and his son came up behind us on the trail, confirming that Dimi lay higher up the trail and that we might reach the village by nightfall. After an hour on the trail, we approached a secluded Bodi village set among tall trees. A young woman stood by the trail as we were expected and beckoned us to follow her into the village. We were welcomed by a tall, slender man about forty years old, wearing a cloth over his shoulder and carrying what looked like a rod of office. His name was Coroda, the chief of the village, which comprised twenty or thirty huts and several structures where cattle and goats were compounded at night.

Skins were brought out for us to sit on under the shade of a large fig tree. Refreshments of water and freshly cooked sorghum porridge were served by several women who gathered around to watch us eat. The men were interested in our clothes and equipment, particularly the binoculars, and they passed them around with great excitement. I asked Coroda if he would guide us to the village of Dime. He appeared reluctant and puzzled at my request. "Why do you want to go to the Dimi people?" He asked. "We are curious," I responded. He thought about it for a while and then agreed, but not with enthusiasm. He asked for two *bir,* but we agreed that I should give him one *bir* to start with and the other *bir* when we arrived at Dime. He rolled up the *bir* note and inserted it in a hole in his ear lobe.

Coroda's people were becoming beginning to take a proprietary interest in our possessions, especially Emile's machete, which evoked considerable interest. It was time to leave for Dime. Coroda led the steep ascent, followed by his two sons, armed with a rifle and spear.

A mile above the Bodi villages, we passed through meticulously constructed but abandoned stone-wall terraced fields long overgrown with trees and vines. There was a sense of mystery in their abandonment. It seemed to be a no man's land between the Bodi and the Dimi. But why?

Our arrival in the Dimi village was sudden and unexpected for the villagers and us. The trail immediately transitioned from tall grasses to even taller fields of sorghum and maize, in well-tended and neat fields, in sharp contrast to the unkempt fields of the Bodi. The villagers had a look of panic on their faces when they saw Coroda and his sons emerge from the bush, armed with a rifle and spear, but smiled when they saw us emerge behind them. Their huts were a traditional circular shape with thatched roofs, but the walls were made of stone, as meticulously constructed as the terracing we had seen lower down the mountain. In addition to sorghum which was almost ready for harvesting, they grew maize, beans, barley, coffee, papaya, and squash.

The land looked fertile and well cared for.

The Dime is shorter and has more Negri features than the Bodi. We were told the village men were still working in the fields clearing new land higher up the mountain, and would return before sunset. Coroda and his sons were obviously not welcomed in the village, but nothing was said. While waiting for the men, the women roasted freshly picked coffee beans and showed us how to cook sorghum seeds over an open fire. Coroda needed no invitation to eat and enthusiastically helped himself to the food. There was an obvious animosity between the Bodi and the Dime, and it was clear who was afraid of whom.

Finally, the Dimi men arrived carrying axes and hoes. Their legs and arms were covered with mud and scratches from their work, clearing the forest for new fields. The reason for the abandoned terracing was becoming clear, but it wasn't until we heard the whole story from the Dime Chief, did the awful dilemma of his people become apparent. "Whenever the Bodi needs food or cattle, they come and steal from us," the chief told us.

"They have killed many of our people in the last twenty

years," he explained. "They are bad people." A week earlier, a group of Bodi warriors armed with rifles and spears had made their way unnoticed up the mountain and stolen six cattle from the Dime, killing two of the herdsmen. The situation looked desperate. "They have rifles, and we have only spears," the chief pleaded, "how can we defend ourselves?"

Before the introduction of firearms during King Menelik, the second consolidation of the Ethiopian Empire in the late 1890s, the Dimi numbering 8000 were able to contain the Bodi to whom they sold spears and tools. The past three decades have been particularly difficult. David Todd, an anthropologist from the University of Zambia, estimates that the Bodi between 1968 and 1971 killed 700 Dimi. The Dimi chief obviously wanted to tell us more and suggested that the Bodi should leave. But Coroda and his sons were enjoying the free food and coffee and showed no inclination to leave. I didn't feel I should ask Coroda to leave. He guided us to the village, which was not without danger considering the animosity between the tribes, and we still had to return to the river through Bodi territory.

The evening at 6,000 feet was much cooler than the river accustomed to us, and after a filling meal of injera and berbere sauce, we bedded down for the night on woven grass mats on the floor of a hut. We planned to climb to the summit of the mountain the following day.

The night was comfortable but chilly. Just before dawn, a tremendous storm broke until daylight, and torrential rain fell, accompanied by strong winds, lightning, and thunder. No one moved in the village until the rain had finally stopped. During papaya and sweet yams breakfast, we were joined by another Dimi chief and a number of his men. The two chiefs then addressed our group through two interpreters and presented a litany of crimes committed against them by the Bodi, who, for the sake of delicacy and Coroda, were referred to as "our neighbors". Coroda and his sons appeared unaffected by the Dime chiefs' assertions. They looked at me to see how I was responding. I tried to remain impassive but couldn't help wondering how long the Dime could withstand the encroachment of the Bodi. The Bodi had the advantage of owning rifles, which gave them a clear superiority when it came to combat. On the new government's request, the Dimi evidently had handed in their rifles, whereas the Bodi had refused.

The meeting terminated with an argument between the two Dimi chiefs about our departure. The neighboring village chief was emphatic that we should stay in the village and not be allowed to leave. Presumably, he saw us as some kind of guarantee against future Bodi predations. The other chief felt that it was in their best interest for us to leave so that we could inform the authorities in Addis Ababa of their predicament. The noise of the arguments became louder, and it was obvious there was little hope of reconciliation between the two factions.

Our main concern was to get out of the village and back to the river quickly. Tesfaye advised us that our strategy should be to look unconcerned with the shouting and arguing and that we should walk off in different directions and try to rendezvous on the trail leading back to the river. Dusty, Sarah, and I split up and dispersed among the fields of tall sorghum, which gave us excellent cover as we slowly and circuitously headed back toward the trail. The intensity of arguments between the two factions precluded any attention from being given to our supervision. Their voices became fainter. When I was sure no one was following, I broke into a run and arrived at the trail just as Sarah and Dusty came running by, with none other than Coroda. He was hidden on the outskirts of the village, realizing we would probably want to get out of Dime, and had waited for us by the trail. We gratefully renamed him, Coroda the Cunning. I had no idea where Keith, Tesfaye, or Emile was, but for the time being, I wasn't going to worry. Three of us were out, and the others would hopefully appear later.

The enemies of the Dime, cattle thieves and possibly murderers, were our new friends, our guides to the river, and they seemed pleased to help us. There was still no sign of the others, but I was anxious to get back to the river, from where we could at least go downstream for help if they failed to show up. Coroda directed a young woman who was about to take food to her family at the river to serve as our guide. I was initially suspicious, for the trail was different from the one we had arrived on, but I had to trust Coroda. An hour out of the Bodi village, we rested in the sparse shade of a small Commiphora tree and reflected on the past few days' events. Strangely enough, it all seemed so normal.

We were getting used to the unusual and unexpected. Just as we were settling down, we heard voices on the trail, followed by the appearance of Tesfaye and Keith. Their escape had been even more bizarre than ours. Followed by a Dimi tribesman, they had climbed an ever-increasingly steep ridge until they were literally pulling themselves up with the aid of roots and branches. The Dimi man had eventually turned back rather than following them up such treacherous terrain. As soon as the man turned back, they struck a course for the Bodi Village, traveling over extremely rugged terrain, lugging almost 20 kilos of camera equipment. Both looked exhausted and were covered with scratches and bruises. There was no sign of Emile.

Emile didn't arrive that night or the following morning. I was getting a little worried but decided to give him another day before deciding what to do. At 3 pm on the second day of waiting, there was a shout from the interior, and Emile strode out of the bush extremely bedraggled and loaded down with a press full of flora he had gathered from the forest above the village. He had spent the previous night huddled under a tent flysheet. Determined to make a botanical collection, he had succeeded against all odds. A sympathetic Dime native had found him the morning after our escape and secretly guided him to the trail that led through the Bodi territory to the river.

Five days later, we arrived at the confluence of the Mui River in Mursi territory. The Mursi are a tribe of approximately five thousand "cultivating pastoralists". Culturally, they are largely pastoral people but now rely on agriculture for three-quarters of their subsistence needs.

A series of droughts that began in the early 70s forced about one-fifth of the tribe to abandon pastoralism altogether and migrate to the region around Mount Mago, 1776 meters, which lies in the rain shadow of the eastern wall of the Omo Rift. The Mursi men are tall, of a larger frame than the Bodi, and wear no clothes. Like most semi-nomadic people who live between the mountains and Lake Turkana, they are "armed to the teeth". The women practice an unusual form of lip mutilation, which is believed to have origins as a response to Arab slave traders who penetrated the area in the mid-1850s. Apparently the slavers could find no market for women who were disfigured this way.

When they are young girls, a small incision is made in the lower lip, and the hole is stretched until a five-inch diameter disc can be inserted. Only about half of the women now perform the mutilation, but those that do, consider it an enhancement of their beauty.

Our arrival at the confluence of the Mui River coincided with a period of heavy rains, which destroyed any chance of our last resupply being flown in from Addis. The savannah airstrip twenty miles inland from the Omo was underwater. Belita, the director of the Mago National Park, who was supervising the construction of a World Wildlife-funded ferry across the Omo, allowed his driver to take us to the Park headquarters, so we could radio Addis Ababa to arrange for a different resupply rendezvous. A rutted dirt road with axle-deep water led through a dense, virtually impenetrable ten-mile-wide thicket of an acacia-thorn bush. Once productive grasslands, overgrazing by the Bodi and Mursi has led to the invasion of unpalatable acacia bushes. The thick bush harbors tsetse fly compounded the problem. It causes bovine trypanosomiasis and provides a fertile environment for rinderpest which breaks out periodically. The Omo National Park, like many in East Africa, offers a landscape of rolling savannah and low wooded hills. The Mui river drainage, which originates to the west of the park near Maji, provides excellent habitat for a herd of four hundred elephants, which are tracked by rangers on a daily basis to protect them from the predations of hunters from the six different tribes who live on the edge of the park.

Historically, these tribes have grazed and hunted in the area, and despite the park's protected status, they continue to hunt whenever they can, avoiding the sharp eyes of the rangers. The government has tried to disarm the tribes but without success. A concern of the tribesmen is that they may turn in their rifles to the government but that other tribes might not. Some of the rifles are antiquated, dating back to the days of King Menelik the Second's conquest of the Kaffa and Gemu Gofa provinces in the late 1890s. Others are more recent, acquired during the brief Italian occupation in the late 1930. The Italians armed tribes near Kenya to form a protective buffer zone against British interference. After the Italians were pushed out of Ethiopia by the British in 1941, ammunition was purchased primarily from the sale of ivory. Since the creation of the park and the ban on hunting, ammunition has been hard to obtain.

Gold could become the substitute for ivory. While waiting for news from Addis Ababa about our resupply, we were approached by a Dizi tribesman from the district near Maji, to the west of the park. He was tall and slender, with very prominent scarifications around his breasts. From a small goatskin pouch, he produced a small quantity of gold flakes that he had taken from a stream bed in the vicinity of Maji. The undetermined amount of gold was bought for 20 *bir* by Tesfaye, who planned to have it made into a bracelet for his wife. Elephant and rhino populations, once large in the region, have been seriously depleted. The rhino is gone, and only the dedicated vigilance of men like Belita and his game scouts ensures the long-term protection of the elephant and all wildlife in the park. We discovered that less than fifty visitors had traveled the overland route to the park in the past year.

Access is excruciatingly difficult, and there are no facilities for tourists when they arrive other than a place to pitch a tent by the side of the Mui River. The park is truly wild like Kenya was over fifty years ago. The present road from Addis is circuitous, taking over three full days of driving, but all that will change in the coming year when the World Wildlife-funded ferry across the Omo is completed. It will then be possible to drive directly from Addis to Omo Park on good roads.

After four days on the radio at the park H.Q., it was decided that our resupply for the last 200 miles to Lake Turkana would be brought overland to Karo. Our map didn't show Karo, but Tesfaye assured me it was only two days downstream on the east bank of the Omo in the Mago National Park. We had one day of food left when we pushed off again into the slowing current, heading for a place whose location we were in doubt.

With the slowing current, the crocodile population increased dramatically, and there were never less than two or three in view at any one time, sliding into the river or cruising the downstream waters, watching and waiting for a possible meal.

A hungry-looking family of Mursi people asked us for food two days below Mui. Sadly, we were unable to help. We were almost out of food ourselves. We bought ten pounds of honey from the Nilotic Nyangatom people, whose hives were common in the branches of the tallest trees.

It helped to supplement our fast-diminishing supply of food and gave us the strength we needed to row the rafts, which now moved like slugs in the slow water. We would have been an easy target for crocodiles. Three years earlier, it had been under similar circumstances when my raft had been attacked by a five-meter-long crocodile and almost sunk. Two days, three, and still no sign of Karo. Did Karo exist?

Four days after leaving Mui and one hundred and twenty miles of rowing, we stumbled on Karo by pure chance. A matter-of-fact inquiry of a woman weeding her sorghum field revealed that our Land Cruiser was waiting for us inside the margin of the forest, only 100 meters from the river.

For logistical reasons, half the team returned to Addis Ababa from Karo, while Keith, Sarah, Tesfaye, and I continued to Lake Turkana, still another 130 miles to the south.

FROM HIMALAYA TO SOUTH PACIFIC

The Karo men were expressionless and stern as if maintaining a dignity appropriate for contact with strangers. The women smiled, unabashedly curious at everything we owned. As a goodwill gesture, I made several gallons of tea in a large pot, which I hoped would benefit our relationship. I was not sure to what extent the gesture was appreciated, for the last man to drink made off the kettle was me.

Early explorers in the region discovered the Karo strangled their firstborn children and threw them in the river. We were unable to discover if the practice continued. Two hours after the land cruiser had left for Addis Ababa, we reloaded the remaining raft and pushed off once more for the final one hundred kilometers to Lake Turkana. We now used a small motor to push the raft through the slow-moving water. Time was running out, and we now had only six days to get to Lake Turkana and return upstream to Omo Rati, our preplanned rendezvous point with the vehicle which would take us on a four-day overland safari to Addis.

Several crocodiles charged the raft, and we ran over one just beneath the surface, but the motor seemed to inhibit serious charges. The landscape between the Mui River and the delta is very different from the mountainous country to the north. The sky, rather than the mountains, dominates the view from the river. The plains extend and then seemingly merge imperceptibly with the haze-shrouded distant horizons. Only the isolated, long-extinct arid volcanic mountains and low hills occasionally broke the skyline. The land is parched, overgrazed, and hot, verging on the desert. The tall grasses have gone. Acacia thorn shrubs, a few bleached patches of short grass, and 15-foot high ant hills are the dominant feature of the land. Sometimes there is nothing but bare sun-baked earth, without trees, shrubs, grass, or a living thing. These are the northern lands of the semi-nomadic Dasanetch and Nyangatom pastoralists, whose lives and fortunes are inextricably intertwined with the well-being of their sixty thousand head of cattle and three times that number of goats and sheep.

The Omo River is the basis of existence for all the tribes in the lower Omo Valley. None could exist by pastoralism alone. To varying degrees, they all depend on the Omo's annual flood waters to revitalize the banks with nutrients and water so they can grow their crops of sorghum, maize, and beans.

At latitude five degrees north, on an outside bend in the river, I was surprised to see nine-inch pipes dropping from the west bank into the river, like giant pythons drinking at the edge of the water. We had arrived at Kangeten, where eleven years ago, Gert Folstan of the Swedish Philadelphia

Church Mission had established an agricultural project, clinic, and school. Sixty families of formerly nomadic Nyangatom people, who live on the northern borders of the Dasanetch people, now work thirty acres of land irrigated by three fifteen horsepower diesel pumps. Four crops of sorghum and maize are raised each year with a yield of fifteen bushels of sorghum a hectare from each planting.

Initially, the Nyangatom could not be persuaded till the land, despite food shortages. Once they saw the results of irrigation and the crop yield, there was no holding them back. A family could become part of the project by cleaning and leveling the new ground with tools provided by the mission. The water was provided free. Diesel was difficult and expensive to bring in overland from Addis. They were experimenting with a one-kilowatt solar panel that pumped five liters of water a second.

The mud and wattle schoolhouse seemed a contradiction in such a primitive setting. The nomadic relatives of the working the mission fields stood outside the school, carrying spears and rifles, curious at the changing ways of their kin.

The raising of the Ethiopian flag each morning was a special event, accompanied by the singing of the national anthem. Before raising the flag, one of the boys had to shinny up the flag pole to place the rope through the pulley on top. Ropes are a precious commodity, and leaving it there overnight would have invited their disappearance. Sixty-five students, all boys from first through eighth grade, received a half kilo of sorghum grain a day for attending.

Competition to join the school was fierce, and if a boy had poor attendance or showed little inclination towards the curriculum, he was quickly replaced by a more eager and perhaps hungrier learner. Their teachers, Joseph Darasa and Getache Mekonnen told me that there would be no attendance without the inducement of grain.

The Dasanetch owes its dominance to some extent to its favorable geographical location. Perennial access to water in Lake Turkana, the Omo River, and wells dug in the Kolon channel to the west of the Omo are vital for the maintenance of their large herds. The excellent grazing and agricultural lands in the Delta region have to be abandoned for several months each year, beginning around May, on account of the rising waters of the Omo.

FROM HIMALAYA TO SOUTH PACIFIC

Approaching Omo Rati, there was an appreciable and pleasing decline in the number of crocodiles. Hunting and fishing are generally considered to be beneath the dignity of any self-respecting Dassanetch pastoralist, but during times of extreme food shortages, the poorer families will resort to both to supplement their diet of milk, meat, and sorghum. We stayed overnight at Omo Rati, a hot, dusty outpost in the compound of the Ethiopia Relief Commission. Established in 1979, the commission distributed food to the nomadic people in the area, principally Dasanetch, whose cattle and inland agricultural areas had been affected by several years of bad droughts. Funding had come from the European Economic Community and the Catholic and Christian Relief Commissions. The 1983 harvest had been good, and there was little need for help from the government. We met women from the United Nations who had driven for four days overland from Addis to spend two days starting a project showing the Dasanetch how to dry fish.

The World Vision project, a few kilometers from Omo Rati, was much larger than the one at Katengen, but the intention was the same. The approach was different. One thousand hectares of land had been cleared of trees and shrubs and leveled, not by hand but by bulldozers brought in from Addis Ababa at considerable expense. Twenty-one kilos of grain a month was distributed free to each member of those Dasanetch families who had shown interest in the project, but while the grain lasted and was distributed, they showed little inclination to work.

A reduction in the grain allowance was expected to stimulate more interest. An experimental fifteen-acre plot was producing healthy fields of sorghum and maize. In addition, yams, eggplants, peppers, beets, and onions were thriving, but the remaining nine hundred and eighty-five acres looked like something out of the Oklahoma dust bowl. All the land needed was water and the interest of the Dasanetch.

Fifteen miles from Lake Turkana, the Kuraz Mountains on the Sudan border picked up the first reddish-orange glow of dawn. The tall statuesque bodies of the Dasanetch women walking along the river banks were silhouetted against the morning sky. An upstream breeze brought the unfamiliar smell of brackish water and strange vegetation. We were getting closer to the lake.

At Nyemomari, Ethiopia's last official outpost on the Omo, we were required to take an armed Dasanetch police guard so that our presence could be explained to the Dasanetch people. No one had been to the lake since the 1976 revolution. Before leaving, our guard, Gnmommere, invited us to his village, one mile to the west of the police post, where an annual festival was being held. The semi-spherical-shaped huts of the Dasanetch were no more than five feet high and made from a framework of branches covered with tanned cattle hides. Scattered among the huts were elevated grain storage bins containing sorghum and maize from the previous year's harvest. We were led to a semi-circular, formal arrangement of huts. Men and women were dancing there in small, tightly packed groups. Outside each hut were ceremonial robes of cheetah and Columbus monkey skins belonging to the head of the family.

Twenty heads of well-fed cattle were contained within the perimeter of the huts. Older men of the tribe were ceremoniously butchering several. We had arrived in the middle of the annual "Dimi" ceremony, one of the most important events in a Dasanetch man's life.

The ceremony is held for all the men whose firstborn daughters have reached the age of eight to ten, the age at which all young women of the tribe are circumcised. Each man participating in the "Dimi" provides eight to ten head of cattle and about thirty sheep and goats, which are slaughtered and distributed to members within the clan. The Dimi is only one of eight major ceremonies that accompany a man's passage through life. Each ceremony is commemorated with the slaughter of large numbers of livestock. The decimation of livestock on ceremonial occasions may be a cultural response to the severe environmental consequences that result from over-grazing. Sarah and I were invited to dance, but we declined. The day was advancing, and we still had to get to the lake by nightfall.

The success and dominance of the Dasanaetch over neighboring tribes have been attributed to their acquisition of firearms which gave them superiority over the more numerous neighboring tribes of the Turkana, Rendille, and Samburu, and the lack of governmental control in the early 1900s.

Perhaps, the tribe's location is of more importance. It is around the fertile delta region, congregated in large settlements in close proximity to water and rich agricultural lands. Neighboring tribes have described the delta region "as the place where food and water are plentiful". For several months each year, the rising flood waters of the Omo River overflow the east bank of the delta. When the water recedes, crops are planted in the fertile silt deposits, and the cattle feed on the rich pastures. Early European travelers referred to this region as "The Land of Goshen" because of the vast areas of semi-arid and arid lands surrounding it, where no cultivation was possible.

FROM HIMALAYA TO SOUTH PACIFIC

The river became wider and divided into two channels just before midday. Our Landsat photographs showed the western channel as the best route through the sinuous delta.

We went ashore several times to determine if we were getting any closer to the lake. All we could see were expansive flat meadowlands of knee-high dense grass, grazed by small herds of sleek-looking Zebu cattle, attended by naked Dasanetch youths. A continuous strip of cultivation followed the river banks.

Lookout platforms were strategically located every one hundred meters along the bank, manned by youths who maintained a day and night vigil against the predations of wart hogs and birds and raiding Turkana.

Tall semi-aquatic Phragmites and cattails became the dominant riverine vegetation, a sure sign that we were nearing the lake. Lush Nile lettuce, water lilies, and sedges choked the edge of the water, below which catfish and giant Nile Perch congregated to feed. In dugouts carved from fig trees, fishermen moved silently along the margins of the channels, motionless with poised spears, peering into the depths.

FROM HIMALAYA TO SOUTH PACIFIC

A waxing moon, already well above the horizon, assured us of light after sunset. The sun was starting to sink to a more tolerable angle in the sky and the heat of the day began to pass. A flock of pelicans high in the southeastern sky wheeled to the west and descended like heavy gliders to where I presumed the lake to be. The cultivation ended, and there were no longer any signs of cattle or people. We had drifted into a "no man" land, a strip of geography where neither Dasanetch nor Turkana would travel alone.

As we passed through the delta region, the Dassanetch had just made a successful cattle raid against the Turkana in northern Kenya and stolen an estimated 2000 head of cattle. As we approached the lake, the less well-armed Turkana were making a retaliatory raid.

There was a great sense of emptiness and silence, amplified by the vastness of the sky and the distant flocks of wheeling birds. The river finally turned for the last time and, with barely a pause in its pace, was quietly absorbed by the vast, still, alkaline waters of Lake Turkana. The great brown river was finally stilled; it was a one-thousand-kilometer journey from the far-off mountains to the north that was over. A gentle refreshing breeze blew across the lake from the south. The water sparkled as the late afternoon sun sank slowly over the arid volcanic Lapurr Mountains in Northern Kenya. It was difficult not to speculate on times long past, two million years ago, when our early ancestors stalked by this same shoreline to begin an era in history whose saga is not yet told.

As we had been descending the Omo, Richard Leakey and others had been unearthing the complete skeleton of a Homo erectus male who had died by the shores of Lake Turkana 16,000 centuries ago. There can be few other places on earth with such a pervasive sense of the past.

Made in the USA
Monee, IL
29 July 2024